JACQUES OFFENBACH

By the same author
Saint-Saëns and his Circle
Sacha Guitry, the Last Boulevardier
The Duke of Wellington
Massenet
Rossini
The Astonishing Adventure of General Boulanger
The Ox on the Roof
Gounod
Lost Illusions: Paul Léautaud and his World
Erik Satie
Folies de Paris: The Rise and Fall of French Operetta
Anthology
Lord Chesterfield's Letters to his Son
Translation
Francis Poulenc: My Friends and Myself

THE OPERA LIBRARY

JACQUES OFFENBACH
A Biography

by

James Harding

JOHN CALDER · LONDON

RIVERRUN PRESS · NEW YORK

JACQUES OFFENBACH first published in Great Britain 1980
by John Calder (Publishers) Ltd.,
18 Brewer Street, London W1R 4AS

and in the United States of America 1980
by Riverrun Press Inc.,
175 Fifth Avenue, New York City 10010

British Library Cataloguing in Publication Data
Harding, James, *b.1929*
  Jacques Offenbach.—(The opera library).
  1. Offenbach, Jacques 2. Composers—France—
  Biography
  I.Series
  782.8'1'0924   ML410.041

  ISBN 0 7145 3835 3 cased
  ISBN 0 7145 3841 8 paper

Typeset in 11 on 12 point Plantin by Margaret Spooner
Printed by Whitstable Litho Ltd., Kent.
Bound by G & S Kitcat Ltd., London.

Music

CONTENTS

Preface

Illustrations

For Gill-Herminie,

encore une fois

ACKNOWLEDGEMENTS

As ever I am indebted to Madame Martine Kahane and her staff at the Bibliothèque de l'Opéra, that most agreeable of research libraries. Mrs Irene Wells kindly gave me the benefit of her scholarship on a number of important points. Mrs D. L. Mackay and Mrs Stella Mayes Reed both helped with their valuable skills, the one secretarial, the other photographic, to make this book possible. And a thoughtful grant by the Phoenix Trust went toward some of the research expenses.

You're a little Jew from the Ukraine with something of a gift for painting. You come to Paris. And you become Chagall. You're a quite clever pianist who tinkles at the keyboard in Poland. You arrive in Paris. And you become Chopin. Careful, though! If you haven't genius Paris can do nothing for you. You can live in Paris for generations and remain a gas-meter reader or a ticket collector. But it's only in Paris that you become Offenbach, Nijinsky, Picasso or Apollinaire.

Marcel Pagnol

Seriousness is only a small man's affectation of bigness.

Bernard Shaw

Preface

At the time of the first Napoleon there lived an excitable military man called Nicolas Chauvin who, like Dr Guillotin and Lord Sandwich, has been turned by history into a noun. Even regimental comrades were amused by the virulence of what they called his 'chauvinism'. He had many spiritual descendants. In the 1914–18 war zealous French patriots called for a ban on all German music. Another of their demands was that Eau de Cologne should be renamed 'Eau de Louvain'. Their attempt at purification did not extend to Offenbach. The German Jew from Cologne had long since been accepted as the incarnation of Gallic wit.

On his arrival in Paris he did not know a word of French. But Jakob soon became Jacques. Within a very short time he mastered the language so completely that the blatant puns for which he had a lifelong taste were a source of amused horror even to his most frivolous literary acquaintances. He assimilated French customs, literature and music with equal speed. Quickly he became the most Parisian of Parisians.

Offenbach grew up with the Second Empire and his music breathed the cynical, careless, pleasure-loving mood which has been identified with the rule of Napoleon III. One view suggests that the régime patronised him because his operettas helped to keep the public's mind off more serious questions. It is true that governments are always thankful for anything that will distract attention from their bungling and it is also true that Offenbach received official honours. Yet to imply that he was a government lackey is absurd. Despite the favours he received from the duc de Morny, himself a frustrated dramatist, Offenbach was his own man.

Politics, for him, were nothing more than a source of material. There he could find the topical gags and daring allusions that made people laugh. He did not wish to destroy a society that had given him wealth and fame. Even the Emperor came to his theatre and enjoyed the pert witticisms that mocked the Court. But after the defeat of 1870, when political satire went out of fashion, Offenbach trimmed his sails. The public now wanted romance and spectacle and that was what he gave them. He was not a politician, but an entertainer who depended for his living on pleasing audiences.

For a decade or so no one could rival him at this slippery art. After the dazzling triumph of *Orphée aux enfers* came an uninterrupted stream of operettas that confirmed his position as licensed jester, and with *La Belle Hélène, La Vie Parisienne, Barbe-Bleue, La Grande-Duchesse de Gérolstein* and *La Périchole*, all written among others within four years, he reached the peak of favour. His capacity for work was inexhaustible. He could write, orchestrate and produce a one-act piece in a week. At home he composed amid the cheerful din of a noisy family; without the sound of their laughter and chat, he claimed, he was unable to work. To save time he had a little desk rigged up in his coach, so that he could write while travelling from theatre to theatre. By the end of his career he had written over a hundred works for the stage beside a quantity of miscellaneous pieces.

The greater part of his music, so gay, so brimming over with high spirit, was composed while he was suffering the torments of gout and rheumatism, a disease that must have been hereditary. He ate and drank little: at no time in his life did he weigh much over six stones; a few pecks at a boiled egg, a strawberry or two, and he was ready for the thick, strong Havana cigar that he preferred to any food. That, with gambling, women, and amateur dramatics, accounted for his recreations. All else was work. The agonies of rheumatic pain often immobilised his body except for the cramped fingers which held the eternal pen. It was an enemy he fought with courage until it paralysed his heart and brought him, exhausted, to an early death at the age of sixty-one.

At rehearsals, carried away by the exhilaration of his own music, he could forget the ache and discomfort. He drove his actors and chorus with unrelenting zest, always the complete man of the theatre. Every bar of the music had been calculated for effect. If, in performance, a scene did not work, he cut it instantly and replaced it, usually on the spot, with something else. He was the despair of his librettists. Although he had the priceless help of such experienced writers as Meilhac and Halévy, his contribution to the structure and words of the operettas was almost as valuable as theirs.

The world of Offenbach has an irresistible rhythm. It is impertinent and raffish. The men are either fools or knaves, the women are unsophisticated girls or ambitious harpies. There is room for sentiment, not too deep but poignant enough to acknowledge the existence of better things. This is the world of the boulevardier, amused, tolerant, shrewd, and on occasion slightly surprised to meet with honesty or goodness. The whole is accompanied by melody that flows with a spontaneous lilt, that recalls the airiness and simplicity of those earlier composers Monsigny and Grétry whom Offenbach admired. The current is free and lucid. The vitality of his music has preserved it over the years and ensured freshness when many more 'serious' works, the operas of Meyerbeer for example, have nearly vanished.

Yet beneath the carefree surface there lurks a tinge of pessimism. However unbridled the waltz, however joyous the polka, the revels must end some time or another. No one can evade the morning after. A shade of disenchantment colours pleasure, because pleasure by its nature is doomed to fade. Offenbach is not a conscious moralist. But, he seems to ask, when the final bill is presented, what then?

PART I

THE LISZT OF THE 'CELLO

1

The Man from Offenbach-on-Main

In the beginning was Solomon Rindskopf who begat Moses. And Moses begat Joseph Moses who begat Marianne Rindskopf and died. And all the days that Marianne lived were some fifty-five years. Also in the beginning was Isaac Juda Eberst.

Juda earned his living as a music teacher in Offenbach-on-Main. Among his pupils, it is thought, were members of the Frankfurt branch of the Rothschild family. He had a son called Isaac Juda who loved music far more than the bookbinding he had been taught as his trade. Isaac was a restless young man and curious to see what went on outside his home town. His passport, issued at Offenbach on 30 October 1799, records that 'the Jewish youth from this town, Isaac Juda Eberst, nineteen years old, of medium height and slight stature, brown-haired and wearing a grey beaver overcoat with covered buttons, wishes to travel from here to Karlsruhe and beyond in order to make music in synagogues. Hence all military and civil servants of every rank are hereby respectfully requested to allow the aforesaid Isaac Juda Eberst to pass to and fro through all towns safely and without hindrance.'

The slight, brown-haired youth in the beaver coat turned into a wandering minstrel. He went from town to town playing the violin at taverns and acting as cantor in synagogues. One day in 1802 he arrived at Deutz, a suburb of Cologne. There were many opportunities for him here. The place abounded in entertainment centres where music was played and, with its large Jewish community, in synagogues where cantors were needed. Here Isaac decided to settle. Since he was always referred to as *der Offenbacher*, the man from Offenbach, he thought it simpler to use the name from then on.

Some time later he wedded Marianne Rindskopf, the daughter of a money changer in Deutz. Their first girl, Theresia, was born in 1807. Thereafter, at precise two-year intervals, a child was produced until, in 1825, the number of their offspring reached

Isaac Offenbach, the composer's father

ten. Three of their seven daughters showed a partiality in later years for the United States. Perhaps they inherited their father's youthful wanderlust. Isabella and Julia were to end their days in that country. And Henriette became Mrs Jones of Galveston, Texas.

By 1816 an economic slump forced Isaac to take up once again his early trade of bookbinding. Dances were not so frequent and musicians were no longer required to play in casinos. Isaac was bored without music. Bookbinding proved as dull as it had been when he first learned it. He decided to move over the river into Cologne and took his family with him.

In Cologne this gentle man felt happier. He kept his head above water by giving lessons not only on the violin but also in singing, the flute and the guitar. At Number 1, Great Greek Market, he watched over a growing family which neither poverty nor care prevented him increasing with joyous regularity. As well as composing music he wrote poetry, often humorous. One of his verses concerned Jacob's ladder. A rung had been broken, Isaac related, by the heavy tread of the angels. When summonsed for damages, however, the angelic culprits took to their heels. It does not sound much, but in the original German the conceit is amusing.

At the same time he was a profound believer in the religion handed down to him by the Ebersts. His faith was simple and positive. It sustained him in the battle for life. The fiddler who played in taverns also officiated at the synagogue. When he was fifty-one he published a collection of prayers for the use of young Jewish folk.

His seventh child and second son was born at three o'clock in the morning of 20 June 1819. Next day Isaac visited the Lord Mayor's clerk to register the birth and carried the baby with him, as was the custom, to prove that the regulations were not being mocked. A shoemaker and a domestic servant acted as witness. The boy's name, declared Isaac, was to be Jakob.

Jacob soon showed remarkable musical gifts. It was not surprising that Isaac's other children should be musical, given their heredity and an environment in which from morning to night the sound of their father's music lessons filled the house. But Jakob was the quickest of them all. At the age of six he played the violin and, two years later, was composing. It was the 'cello that most attracted him, though his little arms were not yet long enough to handle it properly. He persevered in secret and, whenever his parents were out of the house, worked hard for mastery. One day the family was making music with friends. They thought of attempting a Haydn quartet but lacked a 'cellist. Jakob offered himself and astonished everyone with the assurance of his playing.

The episode was decisive. Isaac presented the boy to a local music teacher, a Herr Alexander as noted for his 'cello technique as for his strict attention to business. This Hoffman-nesque figure with his long flapping coat-tails, great knobbed walking stick and quaint round hat curved at the edges, was known as 'the artist'. Yet however Bohemian his appearance, in the matter of payment he remained inexorable. 'No money, no 'cello,' he would grate.

Alexander also wrote music. Some of it he put before Jakob as practice material. The boy's memory was so sharp that years later, in the Paris theatres, shreds of the old man's compositions were apt to turn up in the middle of Offenbach operettas. He retained everything he heard: melodies from the Hebrew service, popular songs, ditties bawled in the streets during carnival time in Cologne.

Very quickly the skinny child absorbed all that Alexander could tell him. He went on to a more advanced teacher, Bernhard Breuer, a successful writer of carnival songs who initiated him into the techniques of composition. Once again, Jakob soon took in everything this new source of knowledge could provide. In precociousness he was far more advanced than any of his brothers and sisters, clever musicians though they already were. Advertisements began to appear in the Cologne newspaper: 'From today the Offenbach brothers and sister, three children aged 10, 12 and 14, will give musical evenings at the piano, violin and 'cello throughout winter every Sunday and holiday, as also every Thursday. On these occasions Jeandre, at No. 3, Newmarket, will hope to recommend himself by good wines as well as hot and cold meals.'

In order to make Jakob seem even more of an infant prodigy, Isaac used to imply that the musical boy was two years younger than his real age. For the best of his life the composer believed that he had been born in 1821. If he ever doubted this, a natural coquetry inspired him to preserve the illusion of youth. And when he appeared in the taverns, dance halls and beer gardens where he played, the audience readily believed that the thin little virtuoso was no older than his father claimed.

Apart from this small deception, Isaac does not seem to have committed the excesses which tempt the father of a child prodigy. Of course he proudly exhibited his children and was grateful for the much-needed cash their recitals brought in, but he did not drive them. In any case, it would have been impossible to give Jakob too much music. His appetite was limitless. He could never have enough, either playing or composing.

His family background, though often miserably poor, was happy and well-founded. Isaac and Marianne loved their children. They wanted their gifts to be recognised and were prepared to make every sacrifice. In 1833 Isaac decided that Cologne was no longer the place for Jakob and his elder brother Julius. Their best opportunity lay in Paris. For months the family saved hard and put aside every penny that could be spared against the vast expense of the trip to the French capital.

In autumn the local newspaper carried this announcement: 'Today, the 9 October, the undersigned, who intend to go to Paris to complete their training, with the kind support of several distinguished music lovers and the town orchestra, will have the honour of giving a farewell concert in Herr Horst's rooms and will give the art-loving public a pleasant evening. [Signed] The Offenbach brothers.' The concert took place and the modest family treasure profited from the takings.

Next month Isaac and his two sons boarded the stage-coach for Paris. The leave-taking from his wife was painful. Julius, the elder, was eighteen years old and Jakob fourteen. What perils awaited them in that distant city? Marianne Offenbach retreated to her kitchen and wept.

They were on the road for four days and three nights. They had the cheapest and hardest seats on the cumbersome vehicle. The routes across country, especially at the season when they travelled, could turn into a swamp of mud. There were holes, often filled with rainwater, and bumps and loose stones that flew up at the window. Not infrequently the coach dropped a wheel or an axle. Nobody was much surprised when it overturned.

To the jolts and draughts and often terrifying lurches were added the tribulations of the passport. For at that time, when Europe comprised a mosaic of duchies, palatinates and minor kingdoms, it often became necessary to cross two or three frontiers in the same day. On each occasion the customs officials subjected travellers to a rough inspection. The Offenbachs did not feel alarm when their meagre belongings were pawed over. Their bags were unlikely to contain expensive and therefore dutiable objects. What haunted them was the fear that their passports would be inadequate. There were never enough visas or stamps, never enough marks of authority.

The lowering effects of a bad-tempered postillion or a surly driver were compounded by the bleakness of the posting inns. Every eight miles or so the horses were changed at these sprawling establishments. Having paid for his dinner in advance the weary traveller sat down expectantly to his meal. Scarcely had the spoonful of soup reached his lips than the driver bellowed through the doorway that the coach was ready and must dash to make up for lost time. Or if an overnight stay had to be made, the bedroom over the stable was sure to be chill, the sheets would be appalling and the pillow of rock. Dinner invariably consisted of an aged, very aged chicken dressed with hard bits of turnip and metallic slivers of onion.

At last the coach rumbled into Paris. It was still the Paris of the eighteenth century, a large city that enclosed many small towns, a network of small streets bordered by ancient churches, old houses, mediaeval convents. Grandiose mansions stood next to slums. Suddenly, behind a crumbling wall, you glimpsed lovely gardens alive with birds and flowers and sheltered by trees. Already there were boulevards – the one named after Beaumarchais was largely tenanted by second-hand dealers, and the one called the boulevard du Temple presented the façades of theatres, circuses, concert halls and waxwork museums. The place de la Madeleine was little more than a building site, a terrain of wooden fences and half-finished pillars.

A wasteland marked the outlines of the place de la Concorde, peopled still, it was said, by ghosts of the thousands guillotined there. Had not the oxen which, by night, drew vegetable carts to the market, refused, through some intuition, to pass over the spot where the scaffold once stood? A property development company had for the past ten years or so been constructing grand houses along a new district known as the Champs-Élysées. Neuilly was hardly a village, a rural retreat for King Louis-Philippe when he tired of Paris. Cornfields waved in Clichy and people went rabbit hunting there.

The reign of Louis-Philippe was just beginning. This cautious monarch had learned the art of patience during a long exile before coming to the throne. His native prudence had been fortified by the daunting example of his father, who, although a Duke of the Orleans family, took up the Revolutionary cause and even voted for the execution of Louis XVI, only to end himself on the scaffold. The new king was frugal but rich. He steadily enlarged his fortune with shrewd investments. 'Enrich-issez-vous!' was the advice he gave to his subjects. Resources opened up by the recent conquest of Algeria stimulated financial speculation. New opportunities for capital ranged from sugar factories to Mr Macadam's bitumen process. The unwary found themselves invited to get rich quick by contributing to the foundation of guano mines and other enterprising illusions.

Louis-Philippe presented an artfully composed picture of bourgeois unpretentiousness which contrasted with the splendour of monarchs who had gone before him. The solid burgesses of France saw in him a reflection of their own respectable virtues, their thrift and their good sense. He had a handsome, dependable wife, and a quintet of good-looking sons. At the Tuileries he acted to perfection the rôle of citizen king. Often he walked among the Parisian crowds wearing a top hat and carrying an umbrella. He enjoyed gossip and was inclined to fuss. His face had the unmistakeable shape of a pear.

The streets of Paris where he liked to amble, and where Jakob Offenbach soon cast his wondering eye, were noisy and crowded. The air was filled with the cries of itinerant vendors. There were men who sold chickweed, eggs, oysters, feathers and soap. The shout of the chimney sweep mingled with the piercing notes of the old clothes man and the knife sharpener. They competed for attention with the tumblers, the jugglers, the acrobats. A regular sight in the Champs-Élysées was an impoverished quartet of two harps, violin and guitar conducted by a tall character in ragged frock-coat and top hat. They were outdone by the one-man band, a bald-headed ex-soldier with bells attached to his legs, a cymbal inside each knee, on his back a drum which he banged with a stick tied to his elbow, Pan pipes at his mouth, and topping it all a jingling 'chapeau chinois' on his head. And what did he do with his free hands? He played the violin furiously.

Near the jardins du Luxembourg was the regular pitch of the weight-lifter. His speciality was to raise, with the aid of a handkerchief gripped between his teeth, a paving stone of incredible size and weight. One of his fellow-showmen was a long-haired, long-bearded animal trainer who displayed performing rats. The star turn was an intelligent hare that played a drum in perfect rhythm. Here a fortune teller vied for attention. There a sword swallower prepared to demonstrate his craft. Through the crowd marched hawkers of pamphlets which told stories of notorious crimes: in raucous voice they detailed the more bloodcurdling aspect of their wares. The only place of quiet was the corner sometimes known as the *Tombeau des secrets*, where the public letter-writer inscribed messages for inarticulate lovers, budgets of news for distant relatives, or testimonials for domestic servants.

Back and forth along the streets ran carriages, coaches, barrows, delivery carts and sometimes a noble equipage. The public transport system had just been inaugurated with a fleet, a hundred strong, of omnibuses. The charm of their names – the Gazelle, the Hirondelle, the Favorite, and even, inspired by the ballet, the Sylphide and the Eolienne – belied the discomfort of the seats, the cattle-truck dimensions and the gruffness of the coachman, a dour and majestic figure whose invective was as slashing as the crack of his whip.

Perhaps the most ominous persons in this endless carnival of the streets were the water carriers. On them depended the life of each household. They knew their power. Organised with merciless rigidity, they divided the houses of Paris into their own individual territories. The housewife who offended one of them had no alternative but to fetch her own water from a distant fountain. They carried two great buckets suspended from the shoulders on each side. The water slopped everywhere, turning stairs into cataracts and floors into miniature lakes. The carriers, by some ancient tradition, were usually from Auvergne and preserved the gurgling accent of their native region. They

Jacques Offenbach as a child   *His brother Julius, later 'Jules'*

Offenbach the boy virtuoso

were huge, brutal, dark-browed men who roared with laughter at the mess they caused. They could afford to. Whoever crossed them risked dying of thirst or dirt. There may, therefore, have been a more practical reason behind the advice given in a contemporary manual on polite behaviour intended for the guidance of well-bred young ladies: 'Take baths if doctors prescribe them,' it remarked, 'but always with precaution and never more than once a month. Do not linger in your bath under any circumstances. There is something spineless and lazy about lolling in a bath which ill befits the character of a lady.'

2

Halévy and 'the little Jew'

While Jakob eagerly surveyed the strange and sometimes alarming life of the new city, his father took the cheapest rooms he could find and set about launching the two brothers on their musical training. Soon after their arrival he and Jakob went to the Conservatoire. When they had pushed open the heavy gate that frowned upon the traffic rumbling past, they walked together across the courtyard, a cobbled expanse dominated by blackened walls. A spot of faded verdure came from a stunted chestnut tree in a yellow tub. Throughout the early part of the nineteenth century this pathetic little tree tried to spread its branches without success. Its roots cramped permanently inside the tub, its arms regularly snapped off by rampaging students, it never reached the first-floor window at which it aimed. By Easter a few furtive leaves would appear. In June they started to dry up. By July they had shrivelled in the sun. The first winds of Autumn snatched them away and blew them over the wall. In a way the plight of the struggling chestnut symbolised the atmosphere of the Conservatoire. For that institution was bound by the iron régime of its director Cherubini.

Like his fellow expatriate Jean Baptiste Lully, who became the musical power at the court of Louis XIV, Cherubini was a Florentine. Although he never quite achieved the same influence as did Lully, he none the less managed to dominate the official French musical scene for twenty years or so. Was there something about Florence that gave its musical sons a particular strength of character? Cherubini fought hard for success. The ups and downs of his career did not help to improve his irascible temper. Having established himself with some difficulty in Paris, he lost his teaching post at the Conservatoire after the Revolution and, worse still, fell into disfavour with Napoleon. The Emperor disliked both the man and his music. He enjoyed teasing and denigrating him. As Cherubini was the most tactless of men, he returned Napoleon's gibes with interest.

Since all advancement was denied him, Cherubini for a time deserted music and solaced himself with painting and botany. At the fall of the detested Napoleon his fortunes brightened. He was appointed head of the Conservatoire and at last could exercise authority. Largely due to the witty and unforgiving Berlioz, with whom he often clashed, he has come down in history as a figure of fun. In his memoirs Berlioz mocks his Italian accent, his clumsy intrigues, his wild outbursts of temper. Cherubini, he once said, in an access of puritan zeal, ordained that men and women should use separate entrances to the Conservatoire so that all hint of scandalous dalliance be avoided. Berlioz happened one day to enter by the door reserved for women. He tells of the hilarious sequel in which the porter and Cherubini, shouting with passion, chased him round a library table in an attempt to expel the licentious interloper.

Beethoven thought very well of Cherubini. The latter did not reciprocate. Haydn was another admirer. His operas are rarely played now, although their firm classical construction is relieved by a clear thread of romanticism. He was at his best, perhaps, in religious music. The chamber works also are apt to reveal interesting surprises.

Cherubini was seventy-three when the Offenbachs presented themselves at his office. He ran the Conservatoire with an obsessive punctuality. The timetable, his god, had to be observed minutely. He regulated everything by his watch. His first impulse, when approached with a request, was to reject it. He was an inverted Micawber always looking for something to turn down. Life was simpler that way. The task was all the easier in the case of Offenbach since the regulations expressly forbade entry to foreigners.

But he underestimated Isaac's tenacity. Years of poverty, of struggling to keep alive, had bred in Isaac a determination that did not easily flinch. Persuasive, persistent, unruffled, he could draw on a long experience of bargaining with synagogue officials, with authority, with employers. Cherubini scratched his wig. Was he not a foreigner himself? Had he not known the desolate sensation of arriving in a strange land without friends or support?

Whatever arguments Isaac used, Cherubini listened to him. Then he allowed Jakob to play his 'cello. What he heard appears to have convinced him. Before the piece was finished Cherubini held up his hand. 'You are a pupil at the Conservatoire!' said he.

The boy was enrolled in Vaslin's class on 30 November 1833. His birth date appears correctly as 1819, so Isaac must have been honest with Cherubini and not attempted to exaggerate the child prodigy's claims. Even so, Jakob's admission to the Conservatoire was no small achievement. A decade earlier Cherubini had refused to take in the equally gifted foreign child Liszt.

Isaac found his sons an attic in the rue des Martyrs where they could lodge. For over 300 years this long street has wound its weary way up the hill to Montmartre. The burial place of Saint Denis and his companions – he who picked up his head after execution and ascended the hill of the martyrs – is said to be hereabout. The writer Paul Léautaud lived there as a child, in the same house as that which the popular poet Béranger earlier inhabited. At Number 49 the artist Géricault had his studio.

Throughout the next three months Isaac remained in Paris. He arranged for Jakob and Julius to worship at a synagogue choir and earn a little extra money. He himself deputised as cantor, hoping maybe to prepare the way for the rest of his family to join him from Cologne. The plan did not mature. Then he took the road again for the tedious journey home.

Jakob and Julius, henceforward to be known as Jacques and Jules, stayed on in the rue des Martyrs. The two brothers had contrasting personalities. Although Jules was the elder, his ambitions were modest. He happened to have a talent for music, as he might have had for engineering or farming, and he saw it as a means of livelihood. His wish was for steady employment and a regular salary. Jacques, on the other hand, longed for glory. He dreamed of success and reputation. Music would, he was convinced, bring him these things.

The wintry chill of the attic in the rue des Martyrs froze him to the bone. The brothers were too poor to allow themselves the luxury of a fire. In summer the hot sunshine blazed through the uncurtained window and roasted them. They ate little. All around them teemed the life of Paris, that city where they knew no one to begin with and could hardly speak the language. At first even the smallest everyday transaction caused difficulty. To ask the way somewhere, to buy a loaf of bread, posed terrible problems. They contrived with mime and gesture to make themselves understood.

Soon Jacques' quick brain helped him to pick up the language. In time he spoke it fluently, like a native, but he never shook off the clumsy accent which made him say 'bonchour' for 'bonjour', 'gafé' for 'café', 'bedide' for 'petite'. No Frenchman hearing him could have doubted the country of his birth. At school in Cologne the Jewish timbre of his voice had made him a butt. Now, at the Conservatoire, his German accent and the mistakes, often grotesque, which cluttered his precipitate talk inspired an amusement that was not always kind. Neither at home nor in Paris could he escape being called 'the little Jew'.

He looked gaunt and bony. The shabby clothes, worn and unpatched, that he was forced to wear, emphasised his likeness to a scarecrow. The mouth was thin, wide and delicately traced. His fingers were long and dangled awkwardly from sleeves too short to conceal the narrow wrists. His hair tumbled wildly over his collar. The nose was large, fleshy, notably curved.

When classmates laughed at his odd appearance and mocked his grammatical errors he smiled too. Yet in secret the careless jokes wounded him. At the same time they strengthened his ambition. When all the world seemed against him, or at best indifferent to him, there was no alternative but to rise above it or go under. It may be, too, that he remembered Isaac's pride at belonging to the chosen race. All of which explains why Jacques was that little bit quicker, that little bit defter in absorbing information and clarifying a problem than were the young Gentiles around him.

Looking back on those early days of loneliness he once remarked: 'I lived without a care in expectation of the future.' The future was all. It contained the great deeds he was convinced he would achieve. Assuredly the Conservatoire, he soon decided, would be of little help to him in realising them. Although in later years he was to speak well of Cherubini's rule, to praise the discipline and technique it implanted, as a youth he found it dull and frustrating. Just over a year after Isaac had persuaded Cherubini to take him in, the impatient Jacques threw up his studies. On the Conservatoire list of pupils a clerk has added against the name Offenbach: 'Struck off on the 24 December 1834 (left of his own free will).'

He was free to wander the boulevards (he always preferred the rich and fashionable neighbourhoods), free to write the sort of music he liked instead of the cramping fugues Cherubini imposed. He was free, also, to starve. The fifteen-year-old 'cellist looked about him for a job. After playing in several orchestras he was taken on at the Opéra-Comique. Naturally the theatre attracted him. Here was the atmosphere of excitement, colour and warmth his spirit yearned after. Here was the opportunity of success he looked for. Most of all it was the place where his gift of mimicry and his swiftly changing moods made him feel at home. Shaken with helpless laughter at one moment, then suddenly grave as the tomb the next, he had a mercurial personality that reacted on the very instance to people, words, events.

In the orchestra pit, night after night, he bowed over his 'cello and watched alertly everything that passed on stage and in the audience. He saw how effects were gained, how situations were built up and resolved. He learned to gauge audience reaction and to assess just how long a point once made needed to be repeated or emphasised. Even so, once his restless intelligence had seized on all there was to know he quickly became bored with playing the same music over and over again. His partner at the 'cello desk was Hippolyte Seligmann, an excellent player some two years his senior. When they knew the repertory by heart and could play their parts blindfold, they lightened the tedium with practical jokes. Sometimes they would take it in turn to play alternative notes in the same bar. When this palled Offenbach would tie a chair to a music stand and jiggle them about in time to the music. As a result the conductor imposed fines, subtracting the amount for each offence from Offenbach's monthly salary which often shrank much below the agreed figure of eighty-three francs. The impenitent musician preferred near-poverty to boredom.

Soon after he left the Conservatoire an opera called *La Juive* became the sensation of Paris. It was the work of Jacques Fromental Halévy, otherwise Elias Lévy, who had written a dozen operas before achieving the greatest triumph of his career with this lavish production. The leading characters were Eléazar, inspired by Shylock of *The Merchant of Venice*, and a Rachel who came from the Rebecca of Scott's novel *Ivanhoe*.

Never before had the Paris Opera House staged so magnificent a spectacle. The scenery, the dresses, the sparkling armour, the prancing horses, cost the management 150,000 francs. *La Juive* dominated the stage for many years and set the style of French grand opera. It was translated, suitably enough, into both Yiddish and Hebrew. So great was its popularity that even Finns, Letts, Norwegians, Estonians and Lithuanians were able to hear it in their own languages.

Halévy came of that talented family which included his brother Léon, philosopher and antiquarian. His nephew was Ludovic who in years to come worked on many libretti for Offenbach. His daughter married Bizet, one of his students, and unwittingly gave Proust some of the characteristics of the Duchesse de Guermantes. The line continued with Élie, and Daniel, the sons of Ludovic, authors of history, essays and reminiscences. One of the few people who did not succumb to the charms of *La Juive* was the German poet Heine. When asked his opinion of Léon Halévy, he answered: 'He's as dull as if his brother had composed him.'

Halévy's manner, easy-going and almost indolent, concealed great industry. He was to write nearly forty operas. When he died, he was in the middle of composing a piece which had Noah for hero. His son-in-law Bizet completed it. For several decades his music enchanted Parisian audiences and a string of neatly fashioned theatrical successes won him an enviable reputation. He was one of the busiest and most applauded composers of the time. Yet a certain disillusioned reserve, not untypical of Jewish composers, seemed to have made him sceptical of his work and prevented him from reaching greater heights. He taught at the Conservatoire. There he had been a brilliant pupil and a favourite of Cherubini. The latter's textbook on fugue, it was suspected, owed much to Halévy. His friendship with the ill-tempered Italian survived many squalls. At a dress rehearsal Halévy once asked, a little nervously, why Cherubini had said nothing about his new opera. 'I've been listening to you for two hours,' came the morose reply, 'and you've said nothing to *me*.'

Halévy taught at the Conservatoire himself. Though a genial and approachable man, he had little time to spare for his students. With a sigh of relief he would set them counterpoint exercises to do while he caught up with his own heavy work schedule which often entailed delivering two operas in a year. He never turned down a libretto. *La Juive*, which lingered on into our own century as the last production in which Caruso appeared, was followed less than twelve months later by *L'Eclair*. The two works are completely different. The first is resplendent with Meyerbeerian pomp. The second is an intimate, charming piece with a cast of only four. The music is tender and accomplished. It is a pity that, obsessed with Meyerbeer, Halévy did not often return to this attractive vein.

Offenbach played for *L'Eclair* at the Opéra-Comique. At rehearsals Halévy supervised the proceedings and from time to time made suggestions. His little steel-rimmed spectacles glinted in the flickering lights of the stage. From the orchestra pit Offenbach darted up respectful glances at him. Halévy, he noted, spoke with an accent similar to his own. The discovery comforted him.

In Offenbach's eyes Halévy was a great man. Mozart was dead, and Gluck too, but here was a living idol for him to admire. He was fascinated by the stir *La Juive* had caused. What must it feel like to have written an opera everyone was talking about, to be a topic of discussion in newspapers and clubs? Equally important, what did *La Juive* sound like? For a seat at the Opéra was beyond the means of an ill-paid 'cello player.

Early one night he lurked outside the building. He saw Halévy approach and, taking a deep breath, he walked up to him and asked if he might hear *La Juive*. The flustered composer looked at him in surprise. Then, amused by such daring, he agreed. He examined the apparition more closely. There was something about the elongated frame in its flapping overcoat that seemed familiar. Had he not seen those eyes, that nose, before? Had not the boy played the 'cello at rehearsals of *L'Eclair*?

'Come with me,' said Halévy, 'and we'll hear *La Juive* together. You won't see very well from my seats, but it's where I always go when I want to size up the effect, particularly the choruses.'

They went up to a box where, as Offenbach remembered, he listened intently to every note of 'that magnificent score'. The acquaintance did not end there. Halévy quickly sensed the boy's talent. He started giving him lessons. Jules came along too, but it was Jacques who most impressed the composer of *La Juive*. One day in Cologne old Isaac received a letter from Halévy which he was to read and reread over and again: 'I see your two sons quite often: they sometimes come and ask me for advice which I have the greatest pleasure in giving them. I hope you'll be pleased with them: the younger one in particular seems destined, I feel, to genuine success in the career of composer, and I would reckon myself happy to be able to co-operate by encouraging and helping him in his studies and work.'

Three Waltzes before Lunch and a Mazurka after Dinner

Halévy's friendship and support only helped to increase Offenbach's discontent with his existence. The routine of the orchestra pit drove him to distraction. Anything was preferable to the crushing dullness he endured there, even when, dared by a mischievous actor, he climbed onto the stage and incurred the biggest fine yet, one that cut his salary by half. 'I was so bored, so unhappy during the three years I was chained to an orchestra desk,' he said later, 'and I understand so well the irritation that comes from rehearsals under an exacting composer, that I have made it my duty to be as gentle and understanding as possible towards the artists entrusted with playing my music.'

The day when he, as composer, would direct an orchestra in his own music seemed very distant. He was also homesick. Despite two friends from Cologne who had now joined him and his brother in the rue des Martyrs, he felt lonely and deserted. Their poverty depressed him. As the youngest he was usually sent out to do the shopping. Embarrassed by the squalid purchases he made, the lettuce, the potatoes, the cheap wine, he concealed them in an empty violin case. As he walked along the street, the violin case under his arm, he felt he had hidden the shame of these menial chores.

It was not so easy to overcome the unhappiness that swamped him, the frustration, the longing for home. Paris remained obdurate and would not quickly grant her favours. Loneliness hung over him like a pall of anguish. He detested being on his own and was terrified of solitude and quiet. Light, movement, life, were essential to him. In moments of despair he often recalled his childhood days in Cologne and would find himself humming a tune which his mother used to sing as a lullaby; it was a slow waltz. Only the first eight bars remained in his mind, but they were enough to conjure up a whole Proustian world. He saw again

'my father's house and heard the voices of those I
yearned after . . . often my loneliness was bitter to me,
and that waltz eventually came to take on a quite new
significance in my eyes. It was no longer a waltz, it was
almost a prayer which I sang from morn to night, for
myself alone and not to heaven, because I felt that when
I played the tune my loved ones would hear me; and I'd
have sworn that each time it went through my mind
they were answering me.'

The one consolation he had was writing music. The white
paper that lay before him represented a challenge to cover its
blank expanse as swiftly as possible. His pen flew tirelessly back
and forth, dripping notes like fly-specks and scarcely pausing to
dash in the wispy bar lines. The words beneath were scribbled in
a microscopic though legible hand. A friend wrote verse for him
to set. Offenbach had firm ideas about what he wanted, as his
future librettists were to discover. 'Delightful,' he wrote to his
literary colleague, 'but unfortunately not suitable for music. I
would prefer the kind of song where each verse has six or eight
lines, because it's far easier to set to music and sounds more
pleasing. So, dear good old friend, let's have something of that
kind. Something very light that goes well with music – for
instance, the same line returning at the end of each couplet,
which would be nicer so far as the music's concerned.' As an
afterthought he added: 'You can make it sad, too.'

He dashed off songs and dances of every type. His greatest
hope was to have them played by either or both of those kings of
light music at the time, Philippe Musard and Louis Antoine
Jullien. The former had originally been a musician of sober
expectations. He wrote quartets and a treatise on composition.
Even to the quadrilles for which he became notorious, he could
not resist adding some ingenious counterpoint. He discovered a
talent for showmanship. People came as much to watch the
spectacle of his conducting – he performed with hands, arms,
elbows, knees, feet, grimaces – as to hear the music. At the
Opéra ball he dragooned an orchestra of forty-eight violins with
proportionate numbers of violas and 'cellos, fourteen cornets
and twelve trombones. He was particularly fond of trombones
and often gave them the principal melody. 'Napoléon' Musard,
as he was nicknamed, knew what the public wanted. Though

small, sallow and scarred with smallpox, he had a magnetism that could electrify his giant orchestra and a crowd of over 2,000 dancers at a time. His personality whipped them to a pitch of excitement that mounted still higher as the polka galloped to its hysterical conclusion. In the quadrille known as the *Chaise cassée* he would smash a chair at the climax. Sometimes he loosed off a pistol-shot. At the end the dancers would seize him and bear him aloft round the hall.

Jullien depended more on visual effect. His kingdom was the Jardin Turc, a pleasure garden done out in oriental style with chains of coloured lights. He was an exhibitionist who conducted from a gold music stand. When the crescendo was reached he sank back gracefully into an armchair gilded like a throne. His diamond tie-pin flashed hypnotically in the light of two thousand candles. His waistcoats were magnificent, his yellow gloves impeccable. When, in London, he conducted Beethoven, a servant handed him a bejewelled baton and a fresh pair of kid gloves on a silver salver. Despite the exquisite coiffure and the dazzling shirt fronts he was an excellent musician, though it was easy to forget his purely technical skill when panels of light suddenly flared into brilliance around the orchestra, fireworks exploded in sprays of green, red and yellow, and the leader of the revels made his dashing entry, 'all ringleted, oiled, scented, dress-coated, and watered-silk faced, braided, frogged, ringed, jewelled, patent-leathered . . .'. He died in a madhouse at the age of forty-eight. It had always been his ambition to compose a setting of the Lord's Prayer. He never got further than designing the title page:

THE LORD'S PRAYER,
words by
JESUS CHRIST
music by
JULLIEN.

Jullien it was who first played Offenbach's music, perhaps because he too had once a pupil of Halévy and acted on his old teacher's recommendation of the scrawny youth. In 1836 some of these were played at the Jardin Turc and even published at the start of the following year in the *Album Jullien*.

Determined to follow up this first glimmer of celebrity, Offenbach made use of journalistic friendships. Readers of *Le Ménestrel*, a leading music paper, were told: 'M. Offenbach regularly composes three waltzes before his lunch, a mazurka after his dinner and four galops between the two meals. This young prodigy informs us that he has just lost a white handkerchief on which he'd scribbled the music of a waltz. A fair reward is offered to the finder.' Although the note was light-hearted, no more than a puff, the reference to Offenbach's industry was not altogether far-fetched.

Other items were heard at the Jardin Turc. These included a waltz, *Rebecca*, for which Offenbach utilised some old themes from the Hebrew ritual. He did so in all innocence. He could recall his own father, the respectable cantor, introducing opera tunes into the service. What was wrong with reversing the process? This time *Le Ménestrel* criticised him harshly: it was not really necessary to burlesque religious melodies, snapped a correspondent. Already, without intending to, Offenbach had acquired a name for irreverence.

It was probably not the small stir caused by *Rebecca* which estranged Jullien and Offenbach. The dandified conductor would doubtless have welcomed the publicity, and in any case, when set beside his own gigantic bad taste, Offenbach's little waltz appeared a model of decorum. Some disagreement parted them, and the composer took his dance music to other impresarios. He may also, with his shrewd flair, have sensed that Jullien had already begun to slip a little in the public favour.

The popularity of the waltz received an extra boost that year from a visit by Johann Strauss the elder. For a time it was the favourite dance in Paris and Offenbach did well to profit from the vogue. He realised, however, that it did not hold much for the future. A more promising avenue was offered by fashionable drawing-rooms where enterprising musicians could build up useful connections. He made his decision and left for ever the orchestra-pit at the Opéra-Comique.

The man who helped Offenbach launch himself in the salons was a fellow German, the composer Friedrich von Flotow. As the 'von' suggests, he came of a noble family which contained many diplomatists, soldiers and courtiers but never, until Friedrich, a composer. This caused his father some distress.

Though he had a passing affection for the flute, he could not understand why his son wished to take up the ungentlemanly trade of music. In the end Flotow's talent prevailed and he came to Paris. His social gifts made him welcome in many great houses. He knew Chopin, Gounod and Meyerbeer. The year before he met Offenbach he achieved some prominence with his incidental music for a play. His enjoyment of this early triumph was flawed only by the printer's insistence on Gallicising his name as 'Flotteaux' in the programme.

He was to write many operas noted for their instant charm and sweetness. His greatest success was *Martha*, a romantic comedy still performed today. Despite the setting, which is Richmond at the time of Queen Anne, great play is made with the Irish folk tune 'The Last Rose of Summer'. Malice hints that this endearing eccentricity has helped to keep the opera alive. In later years Flotow became Intendant at the Court theatre in Schwerin. During his lifetime *Martha* had over five hundred performances in Vienna. He bore with stoicism the varying fates of his other operas. After all, was he not a member of a family that dated back to the twelfth century? Was he not also Grand-Ducal Chamberlain of Mecklenburg-Schwerin?

Offenbach amused him. He heard with polite incredulousness how his famished compatriot lived in a miserable garret and often could not afford to buy food. The solution to the problem was easy. He must give a concert. First, though, it was necessary to make himself known in the salons, which then provided 'for the ingenious artist a pleasant and practical means of succeeding.' Flotow himself had established his reputation that way. It was simple. Having made yourself known in the drawing-rooms of the great, you then arranged a concert and sent tickets to all the society hostesses you knew. They filled the hall and brought their friends along. After that you went on to a brilliant virtuoso career.

Offenbach admired Flotow. Apart from the pleasure of talking German with him there was the undeniable charm of a man who exuded the promise of success. His confidence tended to rub off on those around him. Such a friendship strengthened morale and allayed self-doubt. The assurance and easy manner of this worldly young gentleman impressed the Jew from the Cologne slums.

Flotow was right. But what could Offenbach play? The dances he wrote for Jullien's flamboyant evenings would not do for the mansions of dukes and viscounts. Flotow helped him put together a few pieces for 'cello and piano. Their first appearance together was in the house of the comtesse Bertin de Vaux, estranged wife of the man who owned that important newspaper the *Journal des Débats* and who worked as a personal associate of Louis-Philippe. Here was Offenbach mingling from the very start in the highest of high society.

However nervous he may have felt, he soon made an excellent impression. His skill at the 'cello, helped by Flotow's sympathetic accompaniment, was remarked on. His lively chatter entertained the people he met. His accent amused them and gave piquancy to what he said. He was quick and ready in conversation. The presence of smartly dressed men and women stimulated him. He loved the atmosphere of wealth and fashion. His eye darted eagerly around the company and took in every detail. They found him a diverting character. 'My friend scored a great success,' wrote Flotow, 'and he soon became a favourite in the salon of the comtesse de Vaux.'

His unruly hair, his lean, lank silhouette, were not forgotten. When, in January 1839, he gave his first public concert, the hall was full. He played, among other things, a slow waltz he had written. One of his admirers was reminded of Chopin. His brother Jules also appeared on this occasion. The wraith-like Jules, condemned for ever to live in the shadow of his brother, eventually left Paris to become conductor at the opera-house in Bordeaux. It was the regular, comfortable job he had always sought.

Just before the concert Offenbach had seen the first of his songs in print. He was paid nothing for them, but publication in itself represented a major advance at this stage. Others followed. These gentle ballads, much to the taste of drawing-room performers, dwelt in conventional style on the subjects of unrequited love, jealousy and sentimental reverie. Several of them voiced a particularly genteel strain suspected to have come from the pen of the comtesse Bertin de Vaux. Salon gossips would not have been averse to suggesting that her 'favourite' now occupied a more intimate place in her affections.

He soon realised that however pure an artist's technique,

Offenbach when young

however refined his musicianship, the way was long and hard in the absence of some little trick that caught the imagination of the general public. It was for this reason that Offenbach tended to play almost anything other than music on his 'cello. He could make the instrument growl, roar and squeak. With it he imitated bagpipes, drums and trombones. He reproduced the lowing of cows, the crowing of cocks and the whinnying of goats. It was not for his virtuosity that a slick journalist dubbed him 'the Liszt of the 'cello' but for his dextrous impressions of barnyard animals. Admiration for his performance mingled with laughter at the irresistibly comic effect. The little talks he gave at the beginning served to break the ice and to put him on familiar terms with his audience. Once he had charmed his hearers with a few jokes and topical references, they were in a mood to be entertained. They could not help liking this odd but attractive young fellow who took such trouble to please them.

His conquest of the salons was rapidly achieved. It was not, by any means, the limit of his ambition. As Flotow had promised, he acquired many contacts likely to be of use in the theatre, where his ultimate aim lay, and he cultivated every possible opening. This was how he made the acquaintance of Anicet Bourgeois, one of the most expert purveyors of melodrama at the time. Bourgeois turned out some three hundred plays which, crude though they were and shrewdly calculated to rejoice the least demanding of mass audiences, were constructed with a skill not altogether to be despised. They anticipated the cowboy films and crime movies of Hollywood. Indeed, Bourgeois would have made an excellent scriptwriter. He specialised in wills destroyed or stolen, in birth certificates lost and found, in poisons and antidotes, in plot and counter-plot. 'Don't turn your head away for a moment,' wrote Théophile Gautier, who as a drama critic sat through many a production of this nature, 'don't fumble in your pocket, don't clean your glasses, don't look at your pretty neighbour; many more extraordinary incidents will have happened in that short space of time than could occur in the life of a patriarch or the duration of a mime in twenty-six scenes, and you'll understand nothing of what follows, so skilled is the author at never allowing your attention a moment's respite. What a remarkable man! He gives neither development nor explanation nor speeches nor dialogue: facts, nothing but facts, and what facts, by Heaven!'

By a wondrous sleight of hand Bourgeois and his collaborators were able to make a stunned audience accept almost anything. 'How comest thou here? And by what miracle? Hast thou not been dead these past eighteen months?' demands one character of another who has been resuscitated because the author can think of no other way of continuing the plot. 'Silence!' comes the answer, 'tis a secret I shall carry back with me to the tomb.' And such was the author's audacity that spectators were bemused into swallowing enormities greater still.

Pascal et Chambord, for which Offenbach was asked to write music, took place during the Napoleonic wars. Bourgeois and his collaborator had cooked up a rich mixture of violence and improbable love. It was first played on 2 March 1839. At the age of twenty Offenbach felt that at last he was realising his ambition. To be associated with a man like Bourgeois, the craftsman upon whom such leading dramatists as Alexandre Dumas were not too proud to depend, was an honour for a young musician as yet unknown in the theatre.

His hopes were disappointed. *Pascal et Chambord* failed miserably. For the veteran Bourgeois this was a temporary setback to be shrugged off while he took up another of the half-dozen projects that at any one time lay on his desk. For Offenbach it was a distressing upset. It had, none the less, the effect of steeling his ambition and making him still more determined to break into the theatre. The stage, he was convinced, must be his life. There could be no other for him.

For the time being he had to keep trundling his 'cello round the salons and giving lessons to reluctant children. How tedious it all seemed by comparison with the brief glamour he had known in the theatre! He went on writing ballads and trifles to be published in those albums so acceptable to parlour entertainers. He quailed at the sight in music dealers' shop-windows of 'the 33,333,444,666 albums destined to beguile the leisure of drawing-rooms dedicated to the ballad during winter.'

Isaac came to Paris with good advice and soothing words. Offenbach wrote a piece for 'cello and dedicated it to him. One evening he played it and the old man listened with tears in his eyes. The two brothers accompanied him on the journey back to Cologne. Marianne Offenbach rushed out into the courtyard to greet them. To Jakob she said: 'I don't know you. Are you my boy?' She fainted in the arms of the strange gaunt creature. 'Yes, mother,' he replied, 'I'm your boy Jakob.'

Trailing a cloud of Parisian glory the brothers gave a concert in their native town. Once more Offenbach's 'cello diverted listeners with antics that implied it had an existence independent of the player who manipulated it. The prophets were honoured in their country with praise for 'the originality which has already attracted a splendid reputation for the two artists.' They returned content to Paris.

Less than a year afterwards they were in Cologne again. Michael, youngest of the ten Offenbach children, died of a cerebral fever at the age of fourteen. His mother, distraught, took to her bed. Jakob and the rest did all they could to cheer her up. Day after day she nursed a melancholy that began to erode her whole system. At one point she seemed to rally. The brothers arranged a concert for which Offenbach wrote a *Grande scène espagnole*. Amid the gloom that shrouded the little house he evoked the sunlight and gaiety of Spain. The piece could not have been more joyful had he composed it in the happiest of moods. Care and worry vanished in the act of creation. It was played to much applause from his fellow townsmen on 10 November 1840.

One week later, on the 17th, Marianne Offenbach died. Her son's efforts to lighten the sorrow that had overwhelmed her were in vain. That bleak November had seen the family twice bereaved. All thought of the salons and the theatre flew from Offenbach's mind. He forgot about his ambitions and remembered only the mother he adored. Like his father, he turned to verse and wrote a poem in honour of Marianne. How she had suffered on earth, he exclaimed, but how, in Heaven, she must be happy. May God be praised, the verse continued, that she had been able to find again her lamented son Michael and to be reunited with him. The style was as commonplace as the feeling was sincere.

Isaac too wrote a poem and gave it to Jacques and his brother as they set off for Paris. It advised them to put their hope in Time, which would dry their tears and eventually bring happiness again. What Isaac failed to realise, however, was that Time does not console. It effaces.

4

'My beautiful Paris'... and Herminie

Back to the drawing-rooms of Paris he came with the 'cello that seemed more like a ventriloquist's dummy than an instrument. Anxiously he hurried to give his services whenever a concert was arranged or a little music made at the house of some rich building contractor, of a government minister or of a duchess. As always he introduced the items on his programme with humorous comments and the latest jokes he'd picked up on the boulevard. What a merry gentleman was Monsieur Offenbach, and how clever on the 'cello!

In 1842 he felt sure enough of himself to give a concert devoted to his own music. It took place at the Salle Hertz, a new hall built by the virtuoso pianist Henri Hertz whose skill at the keyboard was rivalled by an equally inspired touch in business matters. Or was, until his luxurious tastes ruined him. He ran a piano factory as well as the concert hall. His private life was tumultuous. He had been an early lover of the Polish Jewess Thérèse Lachmann. She was known as 'Madame Hertz', a Junoesque beauty who owed to the pianist her introduction to Parisian society. Soon she left him, ruined many lovers, built a vast mansion in the Champs-Elysées, which is now the Travellers' Club, embarked on the career of spy and adventuress, and, as the Marquise de Païva, became the most notorious courtesan of the Second Empire. Hertz, whom she left penniless, went to America, and, in the wilds of California, aspired to make his fortune again by playing to fruit-pickers and miners. They were not even sure what a piano looked like.

At the Salle Hertz, Offenbach presented his new settings of fables by La Fontaine. His 'cello proved an agile commentator on the adventures of the fox and the crow, the grasshopper and the ant, the wolf and the lamb, the town rat and the country rat. The only fable which did not allow the instrument much scope was that of the milkmaid and her pail, although the spilling of the milk gave an excuse for realistic flourishes. The concert had little success. A critic summed up with the tart verdict that Offenbach had forgotten to include the fable about the mountain giving birth to a mouse.

The composer did not surrender. Next year he put on another concert in the same place. Invitations went out to society hostesses and critics, posters materialised on the walls, and paragraphs of a tempting nature were inserted in newspapers. This time, by way of insurance, Offenbach engaged the popular tenor Gustave Roger, whom he had known at the Conservatoire, to share the bill with him. A star both at the Opéra and the Opéra-Comique, Roger sang parts written for him by leading opera composers of the day. He was the principal singer in the first performance of Berlioz' *Damnation de Faust*. Many years later, as an old man, he heard the work again. 'Yes, I sang it way back in 1846,' he remarked, 'but I don't really understand it . . . '

Roger attracted a large audience to Offenbach's concert. He took part in a duet that satirised the Romantic dramas of Victor Hugo. With its mocking side-glances at grand opera, *Le Moine bourru*, as it was called, foreshadows the technique Offenbach was to use in his mature works. It is a complete comic scene in itself. Another item was the Spanish number he had written in Cologne during his mother's last illness. The lilting bolero clung to the audience's memory long after they had gone from the Salle Hertz. Yet the piece, conceived and written in time of sorrow, appeared to have a curse on it. Shortly before this concert where it made its Parisian début, Offenbach's eldest sister Theresia died.

He had by now something of a reputation. Publishers gave him money for his songs instead of printing them without payment. He was talked about in newspapers and did not need to slip discreet bribes to journalists. His glowing eye and domed forehead were becoming known throughout Paris. The mysterious glance that flickered behind his pince-nez was due to long-sightedness, not to any kinship with the devil, though people swore he had the evil eye. It was a legend he encouraged. He seemed to be an odd mixture of brittle gaiety and demoniac dash. There was a frenzied tone about his manner and speech that suggested a character from one of Hoffman's weird tales. It was accentuated when he played. As his matchstick-thin body crouched over the 'cello with dangling arms, as the bony fingers flittered up and down the strings and the sweat sparkled among the straggling hair, the more impressionable of his hearers wondered if he did not take his inspiration from another world. While they laughed at his witty remarks, they were uneasy when he looked at them and anxious to avoid his eye.

Fear of the reputed evil eye did not hamper his success with women. Indeed, it proved to be a help. They were curious to know more, intrigued to find out what its owner was like. Once their interest had been aroused by this strange feature the rest was easy. His wit and his eupeptic personality cast a spell which lasted, usually, for just so long as suited his purpose. His talk was amusing and fanciful. Women excuse a lot to the man who makes them laugh. With Offenbach there was always a great deal of laughter, and a touch of mystery that added spice. His companions felt that here was a man whose talent was quite likely to equal his ambition. They readily overlooked the beaky nose, the skeletal frame and the nasal edge to his voice. These things made them feel quite maternal towards him. And it was not in any case difficult for him to make conquests among the chorus girls and small-part actresses he knew.

At the age of twenty-four he entered a world entirely new to him. Since his arrival in Paris ten years before, his life had been bounded by two extremes: the poverty of his garret and the luxury of the rich houses he visited as a paid entertainer. In between came the sub-world of petty journalism and the lower reaches of the popular theatre. He now penetrated into middle-class circles.

John Mitchell ran the French theatre in London. He also organised concerts and worked as a bookseller. His wife had previously been married to a Spaniard by whom she had two girls, Herminie and Pepito de Alcain. One evening the Mitchells gave a reception for a visiting Spanish general who had lately distinguished himself in the civil war inaugurated by Don Carlos.

The hero of the occasion duly arrived and basked in the admiration of the young ladies. Unfortunately the host had been detained. At last came a ring at the door. But instead of Mr Mitchell the guests beheld an unknown young man with a pince-nez and an excitable manner. To a puzzled Mrs Mitchell he explained that her husband had given him an invitation.

When the first surprise was over Offenbach's charm quickly operated. Valorous though the Spanish general was, his conversational gifts were limited, and there came a point when the eye of even his most respectful listener tended to glaze. Offenbach chatted and joked. He played the piano and sang in a voice which, though harsh, exercised an odd fascination. He brought the evening to life.

Above all he caught the attention of Herminie de Alcain, his host's stepdaughter. She thought him adorable. He put himself out to please her. They were speedily attracted to each other. After that first evening he came many times to the Mitchell home. The atmosphere and quiet taste of the house impressed him. He was absorbed in Herminie. It is true that, optimistic and resilient, he had buoyantly survived until then the ups and downs of the struggle, often bitter, to establish himself. The time had come, though, when he felt a need for stability, for a permanent home. He did not find in his easy love affairs the deeper sort of companionship he had come to want. For, though he was only in his mid-twenties, he had concentrated into a few short years the experience of a much older man.

As a regular visitor to the house he soon knew the family well. Beside the two girls of her marriage to de Alcain, Herminie's mother had a pair of sons and a daughter by John Mitchell. One of the boys grew up to be a well-known journalist and politician. A grandson, Georges Mitchell, trained as an engineer and gained celebrity as a prolific dramatist. His plays satirised corruption in the legal system. Others adopted a moralising vein quite foreign to the light-hearted productions of the uncle he acquired by Offenbach's eventual marriage to Herminie.

This, however, was not yet to be. The Mitchells did not oppose Offenbach's association with Herminie. He had no money to speak of, but it was obvious that he was already launched on a successful career. They just felt that the couple should wait a little longer. To show his good faith Offenbach wrote a ballad called *À toi* which became very fashionable. The title-page bore a dedication to Herminie, and the cover, often to be seen in musical drawing-rooms that year, carried a picture of her. He went to Cologne, gave two more recitals there, and, on his return to Paris, presented the most successful of his concerts yet. For it he composed a fantasy on Rossini's *Moïse* and

Guillaume Tell, having first taken the prudent step of dedicating it to the composer. He played also a *Musette*, a seventeenth-century pastiche in bravura style. Then he wrote an *Elégie* on the premature death of the duc d'Orleans, a son of Louis-Philippe. It brought him a letter of appreciation from the king himself. Proudly he showed it to the Mitchells.

The family imposed two conditions on his marriage to Herminie. He should go on a concert tour to London, which was then a rewarding circuit for travelling virtuosos. Mr Mitchell would help him arrange it. He should also renounce the Jewish faith and embrace Catholicism.

The first of these requirements was the more difficult and challenging. In the spring of 1844 Offenbach arrived in London and on 15 May appeared there for the first time. 'Though this gentleman is very young, he is already a perfect master of his instrument; his tone has all the sweetness of the veteran Lindley, whilst his execution (especially the use of the harmonies) is little short of the marvellous,' observed *The Dramatic and Musical Review*. 'He is on the violoncello what Paganini was on the violin. Mr Offenbach will be a leading feature of this prolific musical season.' For the French he had been a Liszt. For the English he was a Paganini. What other worlds could he conquer?

There was one just outside London. At Windsor Castle on a Thursday he played before Queen Victoria and Prince Albert. Also among the audience were the Emperor of Russia and the King of Bavaria. 'When I come back to Paris,' he crowed humorously in a letter to a friend on 8 June, 'I shan't be able to have much to do with you, accustomed as I am now to associating with lords, dukes, princes, queens, kings, emperors. Emperors, dear friend!!! I can no longer lower myself to talk with an ordinary citizen, but, as you can see, dear friend, I take the opportunity of writing to him . . .' The triumphant 'cellist emerged from this Royal Command performance bearing a diamond ring as an expression of the assembled majesties' appreciation.

He went to a dinner given by a music society whose president was the Duke of Cambridge. After the banquet he played his *Musette*. The guests banged on the table for at least five minutes and shouted 'Encore! Encore!' His triumph had not a flaw in it.

Everywhere he was applauded. Money flowed in. Yet he thought with longing of Paris and Herminie. 'In spite of all the praise I receive here,' he wrote to a comrade, 'I still prefer my beautiful Paris, the company of my true friends and our snug little evenings together. Here everything is grand . . . and cold. In Paris, everything is graceful, dainty . . . and warm, especially when one has a few real friends. And so, dear Emile, I'm impatient to shake you by the hand again and to return to my own dear town which contains all that I hold dear, all that I love. You do understand me, don't you, dear Emile? . . .'

His pocket full of English gold, he saw once again his 'own dear town' and Herminie. A newspaper announced that the famous young 'cellist was to marry 'a young, pretty and rich heiress'. She was certainly young and pretty, but she was not rich. Neither was Offenbach, despite his temporary good fortune. Still, he had done well in London and it only remained for him to clear another hurdle before marriage. He did not find it hard to give up the Jewish faith. Though tender, impulsive and moderately God-fearing, he had never been an ardent worshipper in the Hebrew ritual. His use of old Jewish themes in the *Rebecca* waltz showed that his appreciation of synagogue music was aesthetic rather than mystical. The comtesse Bertin de Vaux acted as his sponsor when he was baptised a Catholic. Isaac Offenbach's attitude to the conversion is unknown.

On 14 August 1844, Jacques married Herminie. He was twenty-five years old. She soon would celebrate her eighteenth birthday. They took an apartment, a very small one, in the passage Saulnier, a narrow alley off the rue Saulnier which runs behind what is now the Folies-Bergère. Nearby is the open-air fruit market, the air odorous with lemons and bruised fruit.

Young though she was, Herminie knew how to give her husband the balance he needed. He veered easily and with disconcerting speed from the height of gaiety to the pit of depression and back again. She put up equably with his changing moods. Her calm and her patience formed a welcome complement to his nervy personality. She had a solid Catholic background which supplied an education and a polish he lacked. Discreetly, lovingly, she guided him with a sure hand. Often he would bring a band of friends back with him to their little home, musicians, journalists, poets, who chattered throughout the night and only left at dawn. She did not complain. When the early morning broke cold and grey over the roof-tops of Paris, Offenbach's high spirits chilled at last and shrivelled into melancholy. He was poor still, unrecognised, no further on the road to success. Herminie was there to comfort him.

The following year, in June, a daughter was born. The arrival of Berthe constricted the narrow limits of the Offenbach home even more. Herminie's task was doubled. It would be hard to say which of the two objects of her affection was the more demanding. She gave them both her unsparing devotion. The problem of handling a temperamental husband and an exigent baby was complicated by an eternal shortage of money. She performed miracles on a house-keeping budget of minute proportions. For the next ten years, years that were the most difficult in Offenbach's life, she was an essential support to him. Without her he might never have survived.

Offenbach at the start of his career

5

Somebody called Beethoven

It looked as if he were doomed to the life of a salon musician without a hope of ever breaking free. It was the only way he could earn enough money – and that was little enough – to keep his family. Yet stubbornly he nourished his ambition for the theatre.

He looked around for an opportunity that would enable him to write one of those burlesques that Paris audiences enjoyed. The subject must be topical and known to everyone. He found it in a new musical work entitled *Le Désert*. This 'ode-symphonie' had been written by Félicien David. From Egypt, where he travelled as a missionary, David brought back a taste for orientalism which he translated into a sort of tone poem depicting the journey of a caravan through the desert. Today it sounds a note of bland exoticism created by a not unskilful handling of colour. In the 1840s *Le Désert* excited keen discussion. It seemed then a very novel piece. Even Berlioz praised it and reflected the general opinion. David went on to exploit the oriental vein with operas like *Lalla-Roukh*, based on Thomas Moore, though he never repeated the success of *Le Désert*. His importance lies in having introduced the oriental strain which was taken up and developed by later French composers.

Offenbach's version poked fun at the solemn romanticism of *Le Désert* and its lyrical evocation of nature's grandeur. The skit was played in the drawing room of the ever-helpful Comtesse Bertin de Vaux. A big audience roared with laughter at the impertinent work. Two months later, on 24 April 1846, Offenbach gave another concert. It included songs, duets and comic scenes. Despite all this activity, he failed to arouse the interest of the management of the Opéra-Comique. It was there, he had resolved, that his destiny lay.

His siege of that institution was resolute and pertinacious. The concerts he organised were only a part of the campaign. He inserted paragraphs in newspapers supporting his claim to be heard at the Opéra-Comique. He sent manuscripts to be read. He called on the director – who never seemed to be at home when Offenbach visited the building. He persuaded mutual acquaintances to put in a good word for him. He failed. The Opéra-Comique had been ready to employ him as one of the rank and file in the orchestra. It would not even look at him as a composer.

He engaged himself yet again on the eternal round of the salons. One of the hostesses who took him under her wing was the Princess Belgiojoso, the Italian patriot whose afternoon receptions were famous. To her came politicians, musicians, literary men and artists. Here conspiracies were hatched and plots contrived to release Lombardy from Austrian rule. None of them succeeded. Another house where Offenbach often played was that of Madame Orfila. So great was the devotion to music in this establishment that on one occasion the son of Louis-Philippe, a prince of the blood, was kept waiting at the door so that a Chopin waltz could be heard to the end without interruption.

The pianist that evening was the American Louis Moreau Gottschalk. His flamboyant career had just begun. Offenbach appeared with him a number of times at Madame Orfila's. Gottschalk played his own exotic showpieces – 'Le Bananier', 'La Savane', 'Bamboula' – and thrilled the audience with these luscious melodies, compacted of nostalgia and traditional Negro rhythms. Once Offenbach performed a 'cello arrangement of 'Le Bananier'. A Gottschalk admirer was indignant: 'How could a man as practical as Offenbach have dared such a desecration when Gottschalk himself could have easily played the piece?'

At last, wearied by Offenbach's importunity, the Opéra-Comique relented. He was given the commission of adapting a one-act play called *L'Alcôve*. Very quickly he wrote the music and secured his old friend, the tenor Gustave Roger, for the main part. The management of the Opéra-Comique remained silent. Again and again Offenbach presented himself at the door. There was never anyone there to receive him. He had already made powerful enemies who chose to act in silence. Moreover, the sort of thing he wrote was not at all in the style of the productions that attracted people to the Opéra-Comique.

He tired of waiting. On 27 April 1847, he produced *L'Alcôve* at his own expense. It had a military theme, lightly treated and sauced with Offenbach's personal brand of humour. The audience liked it. So did a number of critics. Among them was Adolphe Adam, a composer who was also, through occasional necessity, a prolific journalist.

Adam is best remembered today for *Giselle*, which, though it may be third-rate symphonically, belongs to the first class as a ballet. One of his great successes was the opera *Le Postillon de Longjumeau*. (You pass through Longjumeau on the way from Boulogne to Paris. The town is quiet, often deserted. A monument to Adam stands in the main street.) Its popularity inspired a current catch-phrase taken from one of the refrains:

> *Oh! oh! oh! qu'il était beau*
> *Le postillon de Longjumeau.*

He had married the sister of the manager at Covent Garden opera house, which perhaps accounts for the English flavour of his output: *The Dark Diamond, The First Campaign, Falstaff,* and operas on those dim historical figures Perkin Warbeck and Lambert Simnel. His knowledge of English was defective. Once in London he fell ill and tried to make himself understood to an apothecary who knew no French. Fortunately they were able to converse in dog Latin. The apothecary gave him tablets labelled *Capiendum tota nocte*. Adam was horrified at the thought of having to stay up all night swallowing pills. He was reassured when his doctor explained to him that the apothecary had translated literally the English idiom: 'To be taken each night.'

In a purely negative and indirect way Adam owed his knowledge of musical theory to the overworked Halévy, whom we have met before. As a bright student at the Conservatoire he deputised so often for Halévy, who frequently had to dash off elsewhere, that in the end he took over the class entirely, teaching himself at the same time as he taught his fellow pupils, who at any given moment knew almost as much of the textbook as he did. After many successes on the operatic stages in Paris and London, ranging from subjects like Richard the Lionheart to the Brewer of Preston, Adam went into theatrical management. He took over the Théâtre-Lyrique and struggled hard to keep afloat in a sea of mortgages, promissory notes, loans and annuities.

Adam was interested in *L'Alcôve*. He asked Offenbach to write a comic opera which he could put on at the Théâtre-Lyrique. There was talk of engaging Delphine Ugalde, a star soprano. Adam was then in his mid-forties and had had much experience of the stage. It left him cynical but amused. He wrote a lot of music criticism, graceful and readable, to supplement his income. 'Yesterday,' he told Offenbach, 'I reviewed an opera. I heaped the composer with praise and ended my article with the words: "It is almost a masterpiece." He wrote to me this morning: "Your review is perfect. There is only one word too much." Do you think it was the word *masterpiece*? No – it was the word *almost*.'

Offenbach had scarcely had time to start work on the libretto Adam gave him before the Revolution of 1848 upset a startled country. It had, commentators are agreed, a quality of unexpectedness that surprised everyone, not least those who took command of it. For the past few years Louis-Philippe's régime had been uneasy. Bad harvests and growing unemployment darkened the economic scene. There was a flavour of corruption in high places. Two former government ministers were gaoled for bribery. The Duc de Praslin confirmed suspicion about the immorality of the ruling classes by falling in love with an Englishwoman. He then murdered his wife, and his subsequent suicide failed to shake a popular notion that corruptness and debauchery were the favoured occupations of a rotten government.

22 February was dark and rainy. A crowd, vaguely calling for political reform, straggled through Paris. In the Champs-Elysées that evening they made a bonfire out of a heap of chairs. Next day paving-stones were torn up and used for barricades. In the evening a Corsican soldier lost his temper and fired at the rioters. Other men loosed off their rifles too and soon the street was scattered with corpses. The mob grew angrier. By 24 February Louis-Philippe's infantrymen could no longer keep the city in order. A wild throng roared *'Vive Napoléon!'* and surged into the Chamber of Deputies.

The king gave up the throne in favour of his nine-year-old son. He was seventy-four, confused by the speed of events and puzzled by an upheaval which, as one historian remarked, had a spontaneity which it shared with the best earthquakes. He slipped out of Paris with his consort and made an uncomfortable journey across the Channel. At Newhaven the carefully chosen names of 'Mr and Mrs Smith' did not entirely succeed in veiling the identity of a bedraggled Louis-Philippe and a fearful Marie-Amélie.

For Offenbach the Revolution was disastrous. It ruined all hope of mounting his opera at Adam's theatre and put a stop to his activities in Paris. With Herminie and their small daughter Berthe he fled to Cologne. They were poorer than ever. In his native town they rented a furnished room that was meaner even than their Paris home. The revolutionary germ followed them there, for in that year the spirit of revolt flourished throughout Europe. Happily the citizens of Cologne were less vivacious in their demonstrations than the French. They did not strike defiant attitudes on the barricades. They went out in the streets and sang marching songs. Their evenings were spent in cosy session chanting glees and catches of a democratic nature.

Offenbach rushed in to meet this sudden demand for patriots' music. With an entirely straight face he wrote melodies extolling the pure German girl (she had, it was said, none of her Latin sister's wiliness) and jingoistic marches. He celebrated the Fatherland with ballads and sentimental ditties. He took to signing himself 'Jakob' instead of 'Jacques'. He had to live.

On 14 August an elaborate ceremony took place in Cologne cathedral. The foundation stone had been laid 600 years before, and to mark the anniversary Prussia's king and other dignitaries came together there. A choir sang fervently. The assembled company, throned on velvet-covered chairs, next beheld a small thin figure bounce onto the improvised platform in front of the cathedral. It carried a 'cello with which it played a fantasy on operatic melodies by Rossini, probably the one that had already diverted profane ears in the drawing-rooms of Paris. It was heard with the same gravity that had met the Cologne Men's Choir – though perhaps, behind the serious mien of the gentlemen in their ceremonial robes, there beat a faint stirring of relief after all those hearty German choruses. No one seemed to detect the pleasing irony of a 'French' Jew playing Italian music in honour of an essentially German occasion. Offenbach, claimed the local newspaper, 'is one of us, and we are proud of the fact'.

During this strange period he wrote a lot of music, including a fantasy on Meyerbeer's *Robert le Diable* for, it was reputed, seven 'cellos; a Chinese march; 'cello duets for beginners; morsels for piano; salon titbits of a picturesque tendency. His baroque exuberance reached its height in a 'cello solo garnished with an accompaniment of hand-bells. A more substantial piece was the stage work called *Marietta*. Together with a German version of *L'Alcôve* it was presented in Cologne. No more was heard of either.

Back in Paris the Second Republic had been proclaimed. It did not last for long. From the shadows emerged the slow, dull-eyed figure of Louis-Napoléon, nephew to Bonaparte and touched, for many Frenchmen, with something of his uncle's glory. By the end of the year he was President of France. The theatres opened up again. Restaurants began to cater once more for the elegant crowds who returned to the boulevards. The Comtesse Bertin de Vaux and hostesses like her resumed their sway over society.

Offenbach had been a year in Cologne. It was time to take up the threads in Paris. He appeared at rich houses, witty and amusing and on the mark as always with his topical jokes. It was as if he had never been away and the tiresome inconvenience of a Revolution had never spoiled the fun. There were signs that the new régime would govern with more sense of style than had the insufferably middle-class Louis-Philippe. One of Offenbach's influential friends – the comtesse? – obtained an invitation for him to a Presidential reception. For the first time they met, Offenbach and the Louis-Napoléon whose later reign was to be identified in history with the popular one-time 'cellist. Most definitely his wife, the beautiful Eugénie, did not appreciate music.

When Offenbach was presented to her at a first night she made gracious small talk. Monsieur Offenbach was a Rhine-lander? He was indeed, Madame. He came from Bonn, did he not?

'Ah no, Madame, I was born in Cologne. The composer who was born in Bonn was called – let me see . . . ' Offenbach tried hard to think of the name. Some early nineteenth-century musician, wasn't it? At last he remembered – a man who'd written only a single opera. 'Ah yes, Madame, he was somebody called Beethoven.'

PART II

HIS OWN THEATRE

6

At the Comédie-Française

In April 1850, Isaac Offenbach died. A notice in the Cologne newspaper said: 'The death of our much loved and never to be forgotten father, father-in-law and grandfather, Isaac Offenbach, which took place on the 26th of this month, is announced to relatives and friends. He died, seventy-one years old, of the weakness of age. Those left behind ask for silent sympathy.'

Isaac's death caught Offenbach at a time when he was least able to bear it. His fortunes were low and his career had reached a full stop. Nostalgia for childhood flooded into his mind, and with it the melody of that tantalising waltz which represented for him his father's house and the voices of those he loved. On one of his visits to Cologne he had startled Isaac by humming the eight bars that alone remained in his memory.

'Good heavens:' said Isaac. 'Do you still remember Zimmer's waltz?'

Rudolph Zimmer, he explained, had been a young and promising composer. One day he abruptly vanished and nothing had been heard of him since. Unfortunately Isaac could not remember how the waltz ended. Neither did they succeed in finding the music of it anywhere. The tune preserved its mystery intact.

Towards the end of the month, sad and frustrated, Offenbach sat listlessly in one of the cafés much used by theatrical folk. A man with an immaculate beard and wavy moustache swept in. His coat was beautifully cut and fashionably narrow at the chest. From his exquisite cravat there depended an expensive eye-glass. He was Arsène Houssaye, poet, man about town and director of the Comédie-Française.

Houssaye's present renown contrasted with his origins. He had been born in a country village. In 1815, when the Allies invaded France to defeat Napoléon, a Russian regiment was billeted near his home. Arsène was five months old. Cossack officers with a brutal sense of humour forced his mother to dance for over two hours while his father, encouraged by whips, accompanied her on the violin. As the boy grew up he read books avidly and wrote poetry. His father was outraged to find him scribbling verse, forbade him to do so and threw all his papers and books on the fire. Whoever has attempted the inhuman task of reading Houssaye's poetry will agree with his father's verdict. The tinsel has long ago faded to leave a deposit of implacable banality.

At the age of fifteen Houssaye ran away from home and joined a band of travelling players. He arrived in Paris and found a hotel where, to his surprise, the proprietor invited him to take a whole floor. The latter's forty-eight guests had died in a cholera epidemic. 'Stay here,' he cheerfully advised Houssaye. 'Death believes there's no one left in the place.'

Houssaye established himself in literary and theatrical circles. As a journalist he was alert and quick to seize the main chance. He had the luck to be taken up by the omnipotent Dr Véron, who, with a fortune built on patent medicines, ran the Paris Opéra and became the only man to coin huge sums of money from it. His flawless instinct for profit helped him make another fortune in newspapers. 'Do you keep horses?' he asked Houssaye. 'No, I haven't even enough money to go on foot.' 'Keep horses, believe me, they put you on your mettle. At least you're always kept busy earning the hay they eat. People who walk never get anywhere.' It was advice the young man did not forget.

His talent, he soon discovered, was not for poetry or novels (he wrote over sixteen of them) but for managing people, for all the subtle tactics that are needed to harmonise rival personalities. Nowhere could he have found a greater challenge to his toughness than the venerable Comédie-Française. The actress Rachel, herself a formidable intriguer and probably his mistress, had brought about his appointment as director there. The actors promptly went on strike. Legal summonses showered about him like autumn leaves. Unperturbed, he threw out mouldering costumes and replaced them with new ones, freshened up the scenery and renovated the auditorium. Theatre-goers started coming back to the place. At the end of the year Houssaye blandly offered the squabbling troupe a share in the profits – something that had not been known for many years.

He remembered Offenbach from having heard him play at

musical evenings. Here, he thought, was a useful recruit. Music at the Comédie-Française consisted then of a wretched quartet that mechanically ground out interludes and accompaniments, usually drowned in the chatter of an indifferent audience. Offenbach's personality and musicianship were what he needed to stir things up.

'Would you like to revolutionise the Comédie-Française?'

'By all means. I'm a great one for making a noise.'

At a salary of 6,000 francs, not wealth but at least a regular income for a family man, Offenbach was to be responsible for all matters musical at the Comédie-Française. Transported with instant enthusiasm he rushed about engaging players. His mind hummed with all sorts of plans. He had forgotten about the actors, their touchiness and their jealousies. When he sought to enlarge the orchestra pit by taking out a few stalls, the mummers stridently objected. Their share of receipts would be lessened if the number of paying places were reduced. They disliked his other ideas as well. Did not words, after all, count for more than music in the theatre?

'Scarcely had I taken up my post when I saw that I would be fighting in vain against the prejudice at the Comédie-Française which insisted that the music must be impossible and the orchestra appalling; the players, most of all, were unworried by this state of affairs,' wrote Offenbach later. 'I'd arranged for the curtain to go up only after the bell had rung, which is what happens even in the most second-rate theatres, but every night insuperable difficulties were created as a result. Once the players were on stage they refused to wait; the call-boy, for his part, refused to take up the curtain, having had strict instructions from M. Houssaye. There were endless petty annoyances, arguments and wrangling.'

Offenbach struggled on. He added a touch of dignity by wearing evening dress and white gloves in the orchestra pit. The music he conducted now had some relevance to what happened on stage. It was intelligently chosen and arranged with care. The musicians could always rely on Offenbach to fight for improvements to their pay and conditions. Often he would lend them money from his own salary.

In time the actors and actresses came to accept him, though not with any great warmth. An armed truce was quietly agreed between them. At least Houssaye appreciated all he had achieved. 'Offenbach did wonders,' he said afterwards. 'How many operas and operettas did he not play during intervals!' He liked Offenbach as well as he respected his professional skill. Both men had a natural gaity and an absorbing interest in women.

Houssaye allowed his musical director to have a piano in his office. It was here one day that a shifty-eyed, rather unsteady man with a hoarse voice and shaking hand made his appearance. Houssaye greeted him warmly. It was the poet Alfred de Musset, once a dandy, lover of George Sand, author of exquisite verse, but now a dishevelled alcoholic. He did not drink to be happy, said a friend of his. He drank so that he might escape into another existence, strange and fantastic, in which he was utterly alone.

Houssaye was about to produce Musset's comedy *Le Chandelier*, a graceful piece featuring a heroine who, to distract her husband's suspicions about her affair with a handsome officer, pretends that she is adored by the humble young clerk Fortunio. Such are his genuine innocence and admiration for her that she, in the end, truly falls in love with him. There is a song Fortunio sings to her which helps arouse her affection and Offenbach was asked to write the music. He produced it the same day, a wistful little melody in the vein of his drawing-room ballads.

The actor who played Fortunio had a warm and musical speaking voice. When he came to sing, however, his tone emerged as a gruff bass. After a few performances the disappointed composer had to drop the song, but it did not go to waste, because eleven years later Offenbach used it among the material for his operetta *La Chanson de Fortunio*. He never met Alfred de Musset again. The poet, sometimes to be glimpsed staggering drunkenly in the street, took Offenbach for a bird of ill-omen. He really believed the popular legend about the evil eye. The sight of the composer made him turn away with a quick shudder.

Another disappointment was the production of *Ulysse*, a neo-classical drama by that master of constipated verse François Ponsard. The incidental music was written, not by Offenbach but by Gounod, then a rising young composer. His early opera *Sapho* had caught the attention of Ponsard, who asked him as a result to illustrate *Ulysse* with his bland sonorities. The production was elaborate, gorgeous scenery was constructed, and extra forces were engaged to play the music. Offenbach had only a minor rôle as conductor. He must have felt at home with the chorus invoking Bacchus. It goes with the swing of a full-blown café-concert waltz.

On 2 December 1851, which happened to be the anniversary of Napoleon's victory at Austerlitz, France awoke to find that his nephew had seized absolute power. The effect was almost as surprising as the one achieved by the equally abrupt appearance of the Second Republic three years earlier. There was not much fuss. A number of people were shot and others deported. Louis-Napoléon rode through the streets and was met neither with great hostility nor overwhelming enthusiasm. In the following December he was proclaimed Emperor.

The scene was set, also, for Offenbach's reign. The Second Empire had begun, that period which, as observers never weary of pointing out with a shade of satisfied disapproval, was notorious for debauch, luxury, and shameless immorality. It would seem, from their remarks, that every other age had been a golden epoch of sobriety and clean living when compared with the disgraceful lubriciousness of the Second Empire. But was it really worse than any other? On a Sunday in 1864 the Tuileries gardens were filled with people listening to the brass-band that played there every week. A group of three young women, pretty and dressed in charming fashions, became suddenly the object of scandalised attention. Respectable persons rose from their chairs and called the park keepers. The three young ladies were seized and handed over to the police who immediately expelled them from the gardens. What had been their crime? Were their dresses cut too low? Had their conduct been too lively? No – they had committed the horrible offence of smoking cigarettes in public.

7

Zing-zing boom boom on the Champs-Elysées

Although Offenbach at the Comédie-Française was on the edge of the theatrical world, he still did not properly belong to it. He was so discouraged that for a time he thought of emigrating to America. Two of his sisters had already gone there and a third was to follow.

He wrote to a sister in Cologne:

'Last year I sent you a confidential letter about my situation ... Unfortunately it hasn't improved since, I'd almost say it's got still worse, because all that's happened is that I'm six months older: the golden future I dreamed of doesn't materialise, and each day takes away that little bit more of hope. Believe me, dear Netta, I'm not exaggerating my position ... The cost of living increases every day here and money's getting scarce ... In spite of everything, this letter will be unnecessary if I tell you that the plan I've had in my head for years to go to America for some time will probably materialise at the beginning of September. So my wife will go to Marseille to stay with her father and the children, and I'll put my furniture away in some room or other so that it can be got out again and I don't have to buy any if I come back to Europe – which I doubt ...'

'If I come back to Europe ...!' His mind was made up. America promised all the things he had failed to achieve at the time he wrote this letter at the age of thirty-five. He was getting older. His career to date had little of distinction about it. America must surely be the place where his talents would be rewarded. Yet, at the last minute, he wavered. Paris had him in her thrall. When the final step had to be taken – it was only a small step, too, for all the arrangements were made – he suddenly drew back. Paris had won. Paris was his home.

In the meantime, several small triumphs came his way. At the Comédie-Française a schottische he had composed won the

approval of Prince Jérôme Bonaparte. Jérôme was the son of
Napoléon's youngest brother, a frivol whom the dictator had
made ruler of the short-lived comic opera kingdom which he
knocked up for him and called Westphalia. Like his father,
Jérôme belongs among the least attractive spawn produced by
that extraordinary family. He owed a lot to his cousin, the
Emperor Louis-Napoléon, and so could never forgive him. In
the frigid pomp of his mansion beside the avenue Montaigne his
guests were treated to frequent envious diatribes and much foul
language aimed at the Emperor.

He enjoyed Offenbach's little dance number so much that he
called for an encore. Next morning he sent the composer an
appreciative letter and a diamond stock-pin. His sister, Princess
Mathilde, was a slightly more cultured figure in society. She
presided over a salon frequented by leading authors whom she
tyrannised with all the force of her powerful character. Offenbach
dedicated to her a collection of his songs. It does not seem to
have provoked the same flattering reaction as had come from
her brother.

The composer renewed his siege of the Opéra-Comique. At
the Salle Hertz he produced a little comic opera entitled *Le
Trésor à Mathurin*. The cast was drawn from singers regularly
employed at the theatre itself. The director of the Opéra-
Comique remained unimpressed. The battle thickened: Offenbach prefaced his next piece with an obsequious dedication to
the director's wife, but even this blatant move failed.

The operetta so hopefully but vainly inscribed was called
Pépito. The librettists included Jules Moinaux, a brusque and
irritable man who, like many comic writers, presented a façade
of impenetrable gloom. His character was difficult. He was
known to be painfully honest and sincere to the point of
brutality. From Tours, his birthplace, he came to Paris and
clerked in a bank, but soon found the work he really wanted
when the job of court reporter on a popular newspaper fell
vacant and Moinaux took it. (His predecessor was notorious for
his drinking habits. When he had drunk himself into oblivion his
colleagues would roll him into the street and leave him there
with a lantern poised on his stomach as a warning to traffic.)
Moinaux discovered in the law courts a plentiful supply of
material for his books. 'You draw on an inexhaustible source of

perversity, or rather human stupidity,' said Alexandre Dumas *fils* to him, 'for what causes evil in this world isn't wickedness but stupidity.' Moinaux would still have his niche in literature even if he had not been the father of that great humorist Georges Courteline, who inherited so many of his characteristics.

Pépito was an early model for those curtain-raisers featuring two or three players which Offenbach was to write in profusion. It recounted the love affairs of a young Spanish dandy and resolved his problems with a slick curtain line. The audience applauded and critics were favourable. Offenbach seems to have been fond of it since he later had one of his daughters christened Pépita. It was his first complete and personal success in the theatre. Still ignored by the Opéra-Comique, he arranged a performance of *Pépito* at home a few months later. Some 200 guests poured into the tiny rooms in the passage Saulnier to hear Offenbach himself, in an impossibly raucous voice, chanting the leading rôle. He adored evenings like this when he was surrounded by musicians, actors and writers; when the talk was fast and allusive in the best Parisian manner; when he could mimic and amuse with a ceaseless flow of exuberance; and when he had the satisfaction of reducing his listeners to helpless laughter. What power he felt then, and what a delicious feeling it was to be able to control an audience!

In 1855, impressed by the success of the Great Exhibition in London, the Emperor decreed a similar but more grandiose event for Paris. His Prefect of the Seine, the ruthless and hard-drinking Haussman, was ordered to build a vast Palace of Industry. It was the first task assumed by the man who in a few short years was to transform the face of Paris with majestic boulevards and stately perspectives. The Exhibition would demonstrate conclusively the vigour and brilliance of the new régime. Europe was invited to wonder and admire.

Many thousands of tourists and visitors would be coming to Paris, eager for diversion and in a mood to be entertained. What an opportunity, thought Offenbach, for the asking! He knew exactly what he could give them, and he would do so in his own theatre. 'At that time, faced with the continued impossibility of getting my work produced by others, I conceived the idea of founding my own musical theatre,' he recorded. 'I said to myself that the Opéra-Comique was no longer the home of comic opera, and that truly funny, gay and witty music was gradually being forgotten. The composers who worked for the Opéra-Comique wrote *miniature grand operas*. I realised that something could be done for young musicians who, like myself, were cooling their heels at the door of the lyric theatre.' But how was he to set about it?

Someone had, indeed, already put this idea into practice. At the little Théâtre des Folies-Nouvelles, a pocket establishment in the boulevard du Temple, the composer Hervé had launched a very successful line in vaudevilles and musical farces. He began life as Florimond Ronger, a choirboy who never wholly lost his taste for religious music. Although his widowed mother could not afford to give him a musical education, he contrived to have a few lessons from a teacher at the Conservatoire and from Auber, the composer of *Fra Diavolo*. The rest he quickly acquired through his own remarkable aptitude. One Spring morning – he was fourteen years old at the time – he went for a stroll on the outskirts of Paris. The sound of an organ caught his ear. It came from the church of Bicêtre, originally a hospice for the crippled soldiers of Louis XIII but then, as now, a lunatic asylum. The mass came to an end and Florimond entered the empty church. He persuaded the organ blower to stay at his work and, his short legs dangling from the stool, he began to play. The priest came in. Astonished by such musicianship, he offered the child the post of organist at 150 francs a year all found. They also needed someone for the laundry, he added. Would the boy's mother accept the job at 240 francs, again all found? The name of this excellent man, it is good to know, was the abbé Paradis.

At Bicêtre the organist watched the behaviour of the unfortunate inmates with curiosity. There he initiated what must have been one of the earliest experiments in musical therapy. Having first convinced the management that he had not himself lost his reason, he produced a little vaudeville cast entirely from among the patients. With sympathy and forbearance he rehearsed them. Under the nervous eye of the medical staff they performed delightfully. From then onwards music classes formed a part of the routine.

An understanding grew up between Florimond and Mademoiselle Groseille, the granddaughter of one of the supervisors.

He gave the lie to her name (it means gooseberry) by marrying her. Then he was appointed organist at Saint-Eustache, one of the most important churches in Paris. The passion for the stage which he indulged at Bicêtre began to occupy him. He took the pseudonym of Hervé and started writing operettas. As Florimund Ronger, though, he still kept his hand in by composing masses and motets.

When he gave up the organ loft for good he founded his own theatre and soon drew large audiences with burlesques of fashionable operas, satirical revues, vaudevilles and operettas, and in a good year put on as many as seventeen of them. His industry was terrifying: he wrote the music, and often the words, of a hundred and twenty entertainments. He sang and acted in them and, when necessary, conducted the orchestra. And all this he did besides engaging singers and players, directing productions, supervising the box office and generally managing his theatre. The music he wrote under these conditions was often surprisingly good. Somebody once played an anonymous chorus to Vincent d'Indy, that venerable and distinguished composer. It wasn't Wagner, opined d'Indy, nor yet Berlioz. Certainly it came from the theatre, observed someone else, perhaps Meyerbeer on a good day? Or even Lully? suggested a third. It was the druids' chorus from Hervé's *Chilpéric*.

As a performer Hervé could win over the dullest audience. Off stage he was tall, fair moustached and blue-eyed, always elegant. In the theatre, where he brought to many different rôles a chameleon skill, he was unrecognisable save for the straight-faced, almost wintry calm with which he delivered the most uproarious lines. Puns, topical allusions, catchphrases and absurdities were shot over the footlights in a cool impassive manner that dared the audience to laugh. They nearly always did.[1]

Hervé's manifold activity extended across the Channel. He

[1] A sample of alliterative quick firing from *Caracalla*, 'a tragedy almost in verse':

Géta	... Hier, Caracalla
	Sur un cheval fougueux, dit-on, caracola?
Livia.	Eh! quoi! Caracalla, dis-tu, caracola?
Géta.	Qui caracolerait, sinon Caracalla?
	etc.

several times played and conducted at the Empire Theatre in London. His *Petit Faust*, one of the cleverest parodies of Gounod's opera, was very well received here, and so was *Aladdin the Second*. He even popped up at a Promenade Concert to direct a work improbably entitled *The Ashantee War* and described as 'a heroic symphony'.

His productions were not always successful. Some inevitably collapsed beneath the jeers of a disappointed audience. He took his failures with a wry stoicism, and in the merciless jungle of the commercial theatre preserved his good nature. One of his most amiable characteristics was a readiness to help the young, and it was Hervé who gave Delibes his first chance on the stage. When Offenbach came to see him with a newly composed operetta he listened sympathetically. Within a day or so Hervé accepted it for his Théâtre des Folies-Nouvelles.

Offenbach had acted shrewdly. He was not at the time in a position to rival the owner of the Folies-Nouvelles, but he could at least attach himself to his coat-tails. Naturally he lavished many a flattering compliment on his new patron, but Hervé was too experienced to be blinded with sweet words. He recognised Offenbach's talent for the stage, and that was why he agreed to put on the new piece.

Oyayaie, ou la Reine des Iles had a libretto which was once again by Jules Moinaux. Sub-titled 'Cannibalism in music', it featured a double-bass player called '*Râcle-à-mort*' ('Scrape to death') who is wrecked on a desert island. The local cannibals seize him, divest him of everything save his collar, tie and shoes, and lead him to their queen Oyayaie. They order him to amuse her. He sets her laundry bill to music and sings it. She eyes him hungrily. He gives her a recital on his double-bass. She enjoys it but still hungers after him. In desperation he plays the Jew's Harp. She is charmed by his efforts but even so he cannot take the edge off her appetite. The only solution is escape. Using his double-bass as canoe and a handkerchief as sail, he puts to sea and vanishes over the horizon while cocking a snook at the queen of the islands.

Hervé himself played and sang the part of Oyayaie (the name comes from an idiomatic interjection perhaps best rendered by 'Blimey O'Riley!') with a characteristic solemnity that emphasised the zany humour of the piece. During performances

Offenbach watched from the auditorium. He noted reactions, estimated the volume of laughter, judged how effects came off. For a theatrical performance was a living thing that changed according to many different factors, and the audience was an essential partner in the game to which the players had invited it. During his time in the pit at the Opéra-Comique, and as conductor at the Comédie-Française, Offenbach had stored up many a valuable lesson. Now he was learning the most precious of all. It was one that could only come from seeing his own work tried out in the theatre.

The laughter he heard nightly at the Folies-Nouvelles convinced Offenbach that he was on the right path. There was no time to be lost. Preparations for the Exhibition of 1855 were nearly complete. He must act quickly if he were to have his theatre. Somebody told him about a place that had become vacant among the plane trees of the Champs-Elysées. He hurried off to see it and found a tiny dilapidated building constructed of wooden planks. The owner was a conjuror fallen on hard times. His magic had lost its potency and his dusty little kingdom grew more woebegone as each day passed. Normally Offenbach would not have been interested. But the grimy shack had one superb advantage: it lay close to the Palace of Industry, centrepiece of the Exhibition, and would inevitably be seen by thousands of visitors on their way to and from the building.

In February he applied for an official permit to install his theatre there. Twenty people had already done the same. Offenbach was the twenty-first. In the past few years he had made influential acquaintances who would be useful to him in his application. There were Arsène Houssaye, of course, and Rachel. He could count on the support of Jérôme Bonaparte who admired his Schottische. And another very powerful friend, the most powerful of all, was the Comte, later Duc, de Morny.

Morny was the Emperor's closest collaborator. He was also his illegitimate half-brother. As the great-grandson of Louis XV, grandson of Talleyrand and the son of Queen Hortense, Morny summed up his position by remarking: 'I address my father as "comte", my brother as "sire", and my daughter as "princess", which is all perfectly natural.'

He owed his name to an obscure couple named Demorny

who, for a consideration, allowed themselves to be registered as his parents. At the age of fifteen, with the connivance of a pliable clerk in the civil service, he gave himself a noble particle by cutting the name in half as 'de Morny'. Such an enterprising boy must go far. Soon he built up an enormous fortune through speculation. The obvious next step was parliament, where he combined the pleasures of high office with the excitement of financial adventures which, as a private citizen, even he had until then been unable to enjoy. He was cynical and wholly unscrupulous. At the same time he was undoubtedly the most able and far-seeing of all the Emperor's entourage. His early death in 1865 robbed Louis-Napoléon of an adviser who might have helped avert the tragedies that closed in on the Second Empire at the end.

For all his shady commercial deals, Morny was an irresistible charmer. The faint air of scandal that hung over him helped to increase his attractiveness. Perhaps he inherited from his grandfather Talleyrand the grace and diplomatic ease of manner that made him so delightful a host as well as a guest. He was never at a loss. The receptions he gave were sumptuous occasions. Women adored him. His mansion in the Champs-Elysées was nicknamed 'le petit coin d'amour'. He was as fascinated by them as he was by the stage. Like that earlier politician Richelieu, he loved the theatre and would dearly have liked to be associated with it in some way. He had met Offenbach, had liked the man and his music. It was only natural that he should put in a good word for him with authority.

For several weeks Offenbach lived in a state of fevered anxiety. The days seemed endless. His application moved slowly from department to department, from official to official. His nerves shredded down to the quick. On 4 June the prefect of police gave his authorisation. Monsieur Offenbach was licensed to open his theatre and there to perform harlequinades, pantomimes, comic scenes, conjuring tricks, dances, shadow shows, puppet plays, songs . . .

He would call it the Bouffes-Parisiens. Painters, decorators and carpenters moved in. The wooden theatre echoed to the noise of hammers and saws. Through the shavings and around the bales of carpets danced the lean figure of the composer, ordering, pleading, gesticulating. A company was formed that would pay him a fixed salary plus royalties. One of the partners was Hippolyte de Villemessant, once a bankrupt, now the director of *Le Figaro*, a newspaper which he was turning into a gold-mine based on a formula of sharp gossip and personal chat. '*Le Figaro* was for me,'he reminisced nostalgically, 'what the Bouffes-Parisiens were for Offenbach. Born at the same time, the newspaper and the theatre were similar in nature and aimed at the same public . . .'

Villemessant was a giant of a man, short-haired, gross-lipped, double-chinned. He had, said a friend, the face of a prison warder stuck on the shoulders of a navvy. This Balzacian character had been chorus singer, poacher, insurance agent, actor. In the 1840s he launched an early magazine for women. The pages were scented. Then he went in for scandal sheets. *Le Figaro* was his great creation. In the name of conservatism and good morals the paper led a nimble campaign against the Second Empire and earned for itself the description of 'a holy water basin full of vitriol'. Villemessant had a genius for publicity. His flair enabled him to capitalise hugely on *Le Figaro* as an advertisement medium and to make it a commercial power in a society increasingly dominated by mass-production. Crude of speech and habit, endowed with reserves of primitive energy, he knew talent when he saw it. Emile Zola was one of his early journalistic discoveries. In Offenbach he recognised a determination to succeed that resembled his own.

Having settled the business arrangements and supervised the renovation of the theatre, Offenbach had just under three weeks left in which to compose, cast and produce the items that made up the bill for his first night on 5 July. Jules Moinaux wrote for him a one-act piece called *Les Deux Aveugles.* Another librettist provided *Une Nuit blanche*. Since *Arlequin barbier* was a pantomime, (a dumb show, that is to say, and not a spectacle in the English sense), Offenbach had no need for words and could polish off the music at speed. The curtain-raiser with which he hoped to open the show, however, caused a lot of trouble. First one librettist and then another had to withdraw through pressures of work. He was left with a hundred or so lines of dialogue and the words of a song. Who would come to the rescue? He thought of a young man called Ludovic Halévy who, he had heard, wrote for the theatre. Perhaps he would be the one to complete *Zing-zing, boom boom on the Champs-Elysées*, as the piece was originally called.

Halévy was then twenty-one years old. Offenbach already knew the family, since from Ludovic's uncle, the composer Fromental, he had received early help and encouragement. Ludovic was a son of Léon the antiquarian. He had entered the civil service and became secretary to a high-ranking adminis-trator. From time to time his chief went on a tour of inspection throughout France to 'assess the state of the public mood', as instructions put it. This dignitary had an insatiable passion for whist. Halévy's first task on arriving at a Prefect's office was to arrange the evening's whist game. 'Have you any good players in the town?' he would ask. When they had recovered from their initial astonishment, the local officials were usually able to oblige the visiting grandee with a player to match his cunning at the game. After many an exciting contest on his journey through sixteen counties the administrator wrote in his report: 'The mood of the public is excellent! Excellent!'

While his superior tested out the whist-playing skill of municipal employees throughout France, Halévy sat writing plays in his hotel bedroom. He had been fascinated by the theatre from his earliest youth. In his bottom-drawer the number of unperformed comedies mounted up with dispiriting ease. 'What do you expect?' said his father. 'You can't succeed straight off. If only you knew how many tragedies I'd written . . .'

Ludovic was to become one of the leading dramatic figures of the Second Empire. In partnership with Henri Meilhac he supplied libretti for many composers and a number of well-crafted plays. On his own he wrote valuable memoirs and several entertaining novels. Among the latter was *La Famille Cardinal*, later turned into an operetta by Arthur Honegger and Jacques Ibert. The original is full of delicious irony. It concerns the efforts of Madame Cardinal to find rich husbands for her two daughters who are in the Paris Opéra ballet troupe, a domain where opportunities were unlimited for girls whose worldliness, or that of their mothers, equalled their beauty. A wealthy Italian marquis falls in love with one of the Cardinal sisters. He declares his passion to the mother and father. Monsieur Cardinal wags a finger and makes the following superb speech: 'Don't say that sort of thing in front of me, monsieur le marquis, because I'll have nothing to do with it . . . I don't know what you mean; I must not know what you mean; and anyway, I have an appointment at four o'clock, I am expected. I go, I depart, but I leave with the hope of saying to you, not goodbye, but *au revoir*.

Offenbach shot into Halévy's office at the ministry and presented himself. 'Of course I know you, Monsieur Offenbach,' said Halévy. He had noticed him often at the Comédie-Française. Indeed, since that theatre was a State institution, all the people at the ministry had free passes and he saw Offenbach nearly every evening. It was an unwritten convention that when Rachel did not appear the men from the ministry should attend to fill the empty seats. And as Rachel hardly ever did appear . . .

The composer lavished breathless compliments on him. Halévy was amused and interested. Then Offenbach explained the situation. Halévy's job would be, in effect, to cobble up the unfinished scraps of *Zing-zing, Boom boom*. It was not a very exciting commission. Offenbach charmed and wheedled. Halévy agreed. After all, the piece would at least be staged, which was more than could be said of his other plays so far. The partnership was forged.

At the last minute the title was changed to the more sedate *Entrez, Messieurs, Mesdames*! Otherwise everything went as planned. At the dress rehearsal there were qualms about *Les Deux aveugles*. It featured two beggars who, pretending to be blind, quarrel over a coin tossed their way by a kindly citizen. They play a game of cards, both cheating madly, to decide who shall have the alms. But another prospective donor approaches and they hastily fall back into their accustomed pose as blind victims of fate. Villemessant, of all people, thought it too cynical. Halévy felt uncomfortable about it and suggested it be dropped.

Jules Moinaux, implacably honest as usual, told Offenbach: 'My *Deux aveugles* aren't up to much, but your music is charming; I don't want you to have written it in vain. Take it back. You won't have any trouble in using it for another libretto . . . And here are a hundred francs I'm giving you by way of compensation; it's all I can do.'

Offenbach laughed. 'Keep your money, my friend. I don't understand what happened last night, but I'll guarantee you its success.

He was right. *Les Deux Aveugles*, with its two grotesque

heroes Patachon and Giraffier, made stars of the comedians who played it and it ran for at least a year. Offenbach's music robbed the theme of any offensive quality that might have disturbed sensitive tastes.

The quaint little theatre in the Champs-Elysées became instantly famous. The odd strain in human nature which drove later generations of pleasure-seekers to huddle within the narrow fetid confines of nightclubs encouraged Second Empire theatre-goers to squeeze delightedly into the Bouffes-Parisiens. That it was fashionable to do so, palliated the acute discomfort of overflowing onto your neighbour's lap. The effect, said a newspaper, was of a ladder, so steep were the rows of seats, with spectators clinging to the rungs. In the boxes, if you wished to take your coat off you had to open both the door and the window.

A few months later, in September, Offenbach resigned from the Comédie-Française. His new venture, he explained, was taking up all his time. To the members of that theatre, with whom he had had so many furious arguments in the past, he wrote diplomatically: 'But in leaving you I do not hope to become a stranger to you: my sympathies and my support remain the property of the Comédie-Française, and every time it thinks fit to call upon my feeble talents, as composer or as performer, I shall always fulfil its commands with alacrity.' There was no point in reviving old grievances. And he needed all the friends he could get.

Even before the new theatre opened Halévy had begun to receive that flow of letters with which Offenbach ceaselessly peppered him over the next twenty years. The red seal bore the composer's mark: the initials J.O. worked into each side panel of a 'cello. The writing was small and cursive. The words often ran together in Offenbach's devouring haste.

'I shall need it tomorrow at the latest, so try to make it this evening, if at all possible, we'd go into rehearsal the day after tomorrow . . .' 'I need from your white hand a charming little piece, amusing, droll, comic, gay, phew!!! for my friend Jonas. As quickly as possible would be best because I want to put it on immediately it's done . . .' The tyranny was unrelenting.

Offenbach was now arrived at the point he had been dreaming of for years. With the current flowing his way at last he did not

Offenbach the man-about-town

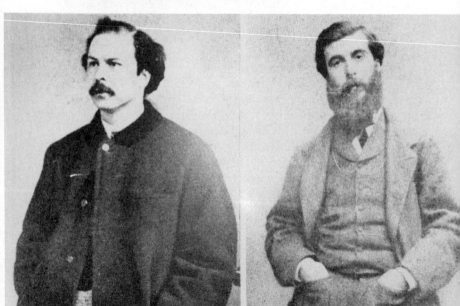

Henri Meilhac and Ludovic Halévy

want to lose a second. At the end of July he added two more attractions to his bill, another pantomime called *Pierrot-Clown* and a comic number, *Le Rêve d'une nuit d'été*, about two Englishmen on holiday in Paris. Pantomimes, he found, were losing their vogue. What audiences wanted was operetta. Words and music were the thing. Off went more scribbled notes to Halévy.

When the accounts for the first month were drawn up, the Théâtre des Bouffes-Parisiens showed a clear profit of 11,000 francs. The result was far from surprising. The house was crammed every night with solid paying audiences. Had not Offenbach's wife herself been forced to sit on the stairs when she wanted to see the show?

8

The Coming of Hortense

Once upon a time in the place Dauphine at Bordeaux there lived a tailor whose name was Schneider. Like Offenbach he had first seen the light of day in Cologne and spoke French with a German accent. On 30th April 1833 he was in a prickly mood. His wife had just given birth, not to the boy he wanted but to a girl. This was almost an affront to the man who had once tailored uniforms for the soldiers of Napoleon's army. At least, though, he could pay a muffled tribute to the Bonaparte family. He would give the infant the name of Hortense, after the stepdaughter of Napoleon.

As the years passed his annoyance mellowed. Hortense grew into an engaging child. At the age of three she yodelled prettily the songs he taught her. When she was six she fell in love with the theatre. Before she reached her teens she paraded one evening in fancy dress before her stupefied parents and acted out the principal scenes of a melodrama she had recently attended. 'I want to become a famous actress, do you understand?' she declared. If, she announced, her parents tried to oppose her, she would kill herself.

She would be a singer, observed her mother pacifically. No – a dancer, said her father. 'Actress, singer *and* dancer,' concluded Hortense majestically.

Eight years later, still obsessed by the stage, she joined a touring company. She was to play in tragedy, comedy, drama, melodrama, curtain-raiser, pantomime, opera and comic opera. All costumes and accessories were to be supplied at her own expense and she had to pay for the words of her rôles to be copied out. Without the director's permission she could not leave the boundaries of any town where the company happened to be playing. At each performance, whether she was involved that evening or not, she must be present at curtain-rise. During a period of six weeks she acted in fifteen different operas and plays.

She came to Paris. One of the singers in *Les Deux Aveugles* took her up as his mistress. He liked her voice, too, and arranged an audition for her with Offenbach. They mounted the stairs to his apartment in the passage Saulnier. The composer looked her up and down. He saw a fair-haired girl, slim, twenty-two years old with fine shoulders and promising eyes. Before she had finished her song he slammed the piano shut. Where had she learned to sing? he enquired excitedly. Was she still having lessons from a teacher? She was.

'Little wretch! If you're crazy enough to go on with them I'll kick you in a tender spot and tear up your contract. Because I'm engaging you, do you understand, at 200 francs a month!'

Hortense made her début on 31 August 1855, just a month or so after the Bouffes-Parisiens had established itself. A curtain-raiser, *Une pleine eau*, with music by two composers unknown to history, opened the programme. The words came from the pen of 'Jules Servières', a pseudonym chosen by Ludovic Halévy who had begun to feel a little anxious about his dignity as a civil servant. He stood that night in the wings, curious to see how Offenbach's new discovery would turn out.

She was terrified. However much experience she had garnered in the rough school of a provincial touring company, her nerve crumbled at her first contact with a Parisian audience. She had known stage-fright before, but the emotion she felt now was entirely, devastatingly new. It weighted her legs and crept to the pit of her stomach. Her arms quivered, her whole body shook.

'You're on, Mademoiselle,' said the stage manager. She took one hesitating step forward and then one back. Halévy came up behind her. 'Get on stage and play your part!' he hissed. With a vigour that surprised him, he grasped her shoulders and gave her a hearty push. She stumbled out behind the footlights and for a moment stood there, blinking and confused.

Even before she opened her mouth a round of applause broke out. In her glittering costume – she was supposed to be the wife of a Doge of Venice – she looked beautiful. With the theatre so small, so crammed, the audience could relish every detail of her shapely figure and her dazzling looks. The enthusiastic reception helped her to regain her nerve. From then on she acted and sang with mounting confidence.

The triumph that set the seal on her overnight reputation

Jules Barbier

Hortense Schneider

came later that evening with *Le Violoneux*. The librettists had taken an old Breton story about a village fiddler and made it into a one-act operetta, by turns comic and moving. 'Le père Mathieu' was played by one of the company's most experienced character actors. Hortense appeared as the rustic heroine, and her sweetheart was none other than the actor from *Les Deux Aveugles* who in real life was her lover. There were encores for several of her numbers, particularly the duet 'Le clairon sonne'. It had a military 'Ra-ta-plan' ('Rub-a-dub') refrain of the sort Offenbach was to use many times in his operettas.

Not a single discordant note could be found in the reviews next day. All the critics agreed that a new star had been discovered. 'As for Mademoiselle Schneider, whom the provinces have sent us and whom Paris had naturalised at her first attempt,' wrote one of them summing up the general view, 'it would be impossible to show more grace, refinement, sprightliness and wit.' They decided that no other jewel fitted so well into the setting of the Bouffes-Parisiens.

It must be admitted that the legendary beauty of Hortense Schneider was not unflawed. Her lips tended to be narrow and her chin had a certain imperfection. One of her hands was slightly deformed. Yet she contrived to hide these drawbacks very cleverly. The eyes and their magnetic gaze distracted attention from lips and chin, and she kept her hand folded in the discreetest possible way. Both on and off the stage her personality created an atmosphere, a sensual radiance that bewitched those who saw her. Her presence inspired an excitement that blinded people to minor defects.

The girl from Bordeaux quickly learned the ways of Paris. She soon discarded the actor who had provided her lucky introduction to Offenbach. There were lovers far richer and more influential, and ones better placed to reward her talents. It is a tribute to her versatility that argument may centre upon whether she achieved greater distinction as an actress or as a whore. A few years later, when foreign royalty crowded into Paris for yet another of those Expositions Universelles, a malicious competitor gave her a nickname taken from that thoroughfare which links one of the boulevards with the rue de Richelieu: the 'Passage des Princes'.

The duc de Morny, who was everyone's lover, did not neglect

Hortense. (The paternity of several distinguished names is attributed to him. 'Morny soit qui mal y pense' was the pleasing epigram that went the rounds when yet another child was born to some fashionable beauty.) With Hortense he found a second youth. She became so regular a visitor at his mansion in the Champs-Elysées that from addressing her as 'la Schneider' he progressed to calling her plain 'Schneider'. One evening, after a heavy afternoon's work in Parliament, he felt a need for relaxation. He rang for a servant and ordered 'Schneider' to be brought to him in the small drawing-room. (Or so the story goes. Another version features the Khedive of Egypt as hero.) The servant hastened away. Flowers were culled and tastefully arranged, musky scent was sprayed throughout the room and a luxurious bed was prepared. Morny, bathed and shaved, reclined expectantly. The servant announced Schneider. His employer gazed incredulously at what he saw. There, in the doorway, stood the unlovely and corpulent person of Monsieur Paul Schneider, owner of the famous steel business.

9

Monkey Tricks

By the autumn of 1855 the trees around the Théâtre des Bouffes-Parisiens had begun to shed their leaves. Icy winds crept in between the uneven planks that formed its walls. Rain trickled through the ceiling. The Bouffes would not last the winter. Offenbach looked around for more substantial premises.

He found what he wanted in the passage Choiseul, a little way off from what is now the avenue de l'Opéra. The passage Choiseul had been built some thirty years previously and was to survive Haussmann's replanning. Today it is surrounded by streets appropriately named after Lully, Rameau, Monsigny, Dalayrac and Cherubini. (The ladies of the night who used to patrol the rue Hippolyte Lebas thought the name referred to an 'Hippolyte' who lived further down the street.)

In the passage Choiseul stood a theatre founded in 1812 by the physician and ventriloquist Louis Comte. He gave there healthy and wholesome entertainments for the young. Mothers could take their daughters to the Théâtre des Jeunes Élèves confident that the fairy tales and moral dramas presented by the respectable Monsieur Comte would bring a blush to no female cheek. The spectacle usually ended with a demonstration by the impresario himself of magic, conjuring and ventriloquism. One evening while he was performing, his wife, who lived with him in an apartment on the premises, gave birth to a child. At that moment Comte was on stage producing doves from a top hat. The news was passed to him. There came a brief pause in his act. And from the same top hat he suddenly, before an astonished audience, drew out his new-born son.

The child who almost literally came into the world behind the footlights grew up, as to be expected, a man of the theatre – not on the stage where he had made his first appearance, but behind the scenes as an administrator. Charles was alert in business, a cunning negotiator and a master of those sub-clauses which make a contract unbreakable. His carefulness over money was blessed by his partners and derided by his enemies. When Offenbach purchased the Théâtre des Jeunes Élèves from him he was attracted by his charm and organising talents. The young man started advising him on business matters. In time their relationship drew still closer, for Charles also caught the interest of Berthe Offenbach. Some years later he became the composer's son-in-law.

Not much larger than the picturesque summer-house in the Champs-Elysées, the newly acquired theatre inherited the name of the Bouffes-Parisiens. The contract of sale was drawn up by Charles Comte. He received 10,000 francs in advance on the 25,000 he agreed to accept for relinquishing the licence to Offenbach. There were another 20,000 to be found for a year's rent. The building accounted for 30,000. Taking into consideration all the other items, Offenbach had to raise 80,000 francs in cash. This he somehow did. He readily committed himself to huge outlays of which he did not have a penny. An example of his inspired business methods occurred in the matter of renovation. The estimate was for 60,000 francs. Having originally asked for a deposit of 30,000, the builder then reduced the figure to 20,000. Offenbach jubilated. This meant, he reasoned, that he had another 10,000 to spend immediately!

Fortified with his three-year lease he turned the decrepit theatre into a place of glamour. It shone with gilt and sparkled with chandeliers. He had all the seats upholstered in thick, luxurious velvet of a rich colour. 'Offenbach must be particularly sure of his programme's attractions to offer his audience seats where you could sleep soundly,' remarked a journalist.

The same restrictions under the terms of his licence applied here as elsewhere. He was allowed to produce the usual pantomimes, harlequinades and dances for a specified number of performers. In one-act pieces he was limited to a cast of four at most. This regulation dated back to the first Napoléon. The Emperor could not keep his hands out of anything nor resist the temptation, however bizarre, to regulate in the smallest detail the lives of his unfortunate subjects. In 1807 he laid down a hierarchy for the Paris theatres. At the top stood the Comédie-Française, home of tragedy and comedy, and its subsidiary the Odéon. Next came the Opéra where spectacles 'entirely in music' and ballets 'of the noble and graceful sort' were to be the speciality of the house. The Opéra-Comique was to perform comedies and dramas in which songs, arias and concerted numbers mingled with speech. No other theatres were allowed to put on music given there until five years after the first performance. The remaining playhouses were designated 'secondary theatres' and kept to the number of eight only.

The rule originally did not permit more than three characters to appear on the stage at minor theatres. Hervé showed ingenuity at evading it. When he wanted a chorus to take part in his *Agamemnon* (sub-titled 'The Camel with Two Humps'), he had a troop of Greek soldiers painted on the back of a revolving flat. At the required moment he switched round the scenery and displayed it to the audience while an off-stage choir sang the music, after which the painted batten turned again and showed its former vista of rose bushes. Another of his tricks was to bring on a cardboard camel worked by two actors playing the front and the back respectively. The camel then split up and each half exchanged dialogue with the other before joining up and trotting off whole. The height of this enterprising musician's invention was achieved in his playing of the regulation three parts himself. Strictly speaking, he had only one rôle. But he 'died' at various stages in the plot, only to reappear almost immediately as a different character. Thus he impersonated one after another a husband, his wife's lover and his servant. At one point a trio was sung by the wife, her lover and a corpse with his head tucked beneath his arm. A multiplicity of false panels and hidden trapdoors enabled Hervé to contrive apparently endless permutations. Who could argue that a corpse was a character within the meaning of the act? In such a way did the great and good Napoleon unwittingly contribute to the growth of operetta and the gaiety of nations.

Another distinctive feature at Hervé's theatre was the refreshment peddled during the interval. He was the first to introduce barley sugar sticks flavoured with absinthe. These pungent lollipops became extremely fashionable. To be seen nibbling one proved that you were up-to-date. 'Syrup, lemonade, beer!' called out the vendors. 'Barley-sugar, chocolate, sweets!' Everyone, of course, rushed for the barley-sugar. It sold for five sous instead of the usual two charged for other flavours. Hervé's competitors adopted the idea and increased their takings. At the

Hervé, an early rival

first night of the new Bouffes-Parisiens on 29th December 1855, the acrid whiff of absinthe and barley-sugar could unmistakeably be sensed in the auditorium.

The attraction was *Ba-ta-clan*, a one-act '*chinoiserie musicale*' for which Halévy wrote the words. '*Chinoiserie*', though it refers both to the setting and to the mode for Chinese things, encouraged by the Exhibition earlier that year, also signifies a monkey trick. Add to this a title roughly equivalent to 'the whole damned shoot' and you have the impression, rightly, of a joke with all the stops pulled out, and even thrown away. Fé-ni-han (fainéant = lazybones, ne'er do well) is the ruler of a vaguely Chinese kingdom numbering twenty-seven subjects. He wishes to honour five of them. Unfortunately, his knowledge of the Chinese language being defective, his remarks are construed as a death sentence. The honorands, upright and innocent burgesses, are impaled. It is not surprising that Fé-ni-han lacks acquaintance with Mandarin, for he is really a Parisian. So are two others at his court, a dilapidated rake and a fading music-hall singer. All three pine for their native capital. They come to an arrangement with Ko-ko-ri-ko (cock-a-doodle-doo), a high official who has designs on the throne. In exchange for the granting of his ambition he lets them return to Paris.

The prelude opens with a delirious gabble of phrases in which the orchestra blows some monstrous raspberries. There are pauses where the boom of the big drum is guaranteed to wake the doziest spectator and to still the noisiest chatterers in the audience. The music satirises romantic opera and, in particular, the Meyerbeerian grand manner, with incidental gibes at the Italian style. In the final 'Ba-ta-clan' ensemble there is one of those brassy tunes which are Offenbach's speciality. It is played on the trumpet and takes over from the vocal line, a perky, irrepressible motif which embeds itself in the mind and, until it is finally exorcised, drives the sufferer to the edge of madness. The frenzied rhythms pound on with untiring zest. There is no relaxation. Everything is keyed up to the highest pitch of excitement. Never is the audience's attention allowed to wander. Offenbach attacks with all his guns blazing from start to finish.

The result was an even greater success than *Les Deux Aveugles.* Encores were demanded of the trio 'I ask for a chair' ('He asks for a chair, He asks for a chair'), a number where

Offenbach juggles deftly with a short phrase and builds it up into a musically satisfying whole. The Meyerbeer parody, which included genuine extracts from *Les Huguenots*, was adorned with verse written in a Franco-Italo-Chinese jargon which added force to its mockery of grand opera.

The political satire is there, of course, but it is by no means the chief ingredient. While dictatorship is laughed at for its ability to do the wrong thing for the wrong reasons, Halévy is not really concerned to bring down the régime. His comments are framed in the style of a worldly-wise boulevardier. The main purpose of *Ba-ta-clan* was to create laughter. This it still does, and the music on its own remains more than enough to exhilarate and amuse. The operetta made such an impression that a café-concert was named after it. In time the place became a music hall where, among others, Mistinguett wriggled her shapely legs. Then it was turned into a cinema. But Offenbach's gaiety survives the years unchanged.

The tunes were heard everywhere in Paris. People sang them, danced to them, hummed them. Queues jostled each night in the passage Choiseul. Offenbach did not rest on his laurels. Three weeks later he staged *Elodie* to a libretto by Hector Crémieux who eventually collaborated with Halévy on *Orphée aux enfers*. Crémieux, a hard-working journeyman of the theatre, dramatised one of Halévy's novels, *L'Abbé Constantin*. It is, apart from some of the things he did for Offenbach, the only one of his plays to survive and for a long time was a hardy perennial at the Comédie-Française. In *Elodie* the heroine is suspected by her husband of having drowned an illegitimate child of hers one night. What emerges, after the usual misunderstandings, is that in fact it was her doggy she threw into the river because, heartless creature, she baulked at paying the new tax on canines.

After this 'comic melodrama', at an interval of another three weeks, came *Le Postillon en gage*. It was overshadowed, on 3 April, by the success of *Trombalcazar*, a buffoonery in which a timid hotel keeper is mistaken for a bandit chief. Hortense Schneider danced a gypsy bolero and aroused Prince Jérôme Bonaparte to a more than passing interest. By special command she and her colleagues performed *Trombalcazar* at his home. The 'Passage des Princes' was already earning her nickname.

Receipts at the Bouffes-Parisiens were healthier than those at any other theatre. The business manager Charles Comte looked over the takings and exulted: the boxes were full at six francs each (or two pounds in current English money), and so were the stalls at three francs. During the interval the audience surged into the tiny gas-lit foyer. A clock which never told the right time stood against the wall. It was the only thing in the Bouffes-Parisiens that did not work well. All else functioned admirably. Attendants sold the absinthe flavoured lollipops and oranges by the basketful. The reek of those oranges hung so heavy in the auditorium, it was said, that they stifled the scent of any other perfume. And always, at first nights and on most other evenings, there were celebrities to be glimpsed in the stuffy, over-crowded, very fashionable atmosphere.

One of them was Meyerbeer himself. He bore no grudge against Offenbach. The witty parodies of his work, he knew, were good publicity. Through modesty, perhaps, he did not come to the first performance of a new operetta, but turned up invariably at the second. The routine was that he arrived at the box-office, showed his ticket, and was ushered into a box that had been kept for him. During the performance Offenbach would visit him. Compliments were exchanged, often in the form of veiled witticisms.

The duc de Morny attended regularly, as did other high society figures of the same calibre. For visiting foreigners the Théâtre des Bouffes-Parisiens was an essential part of their tour. The English novelist Thackeray saw a programme that included *Le Savetier et le financier* which Offenbach had worked up from his earlier recital number based on the La Fontaine fable. The composer, decided the author of *Vanity Fair*, 'had a great future'. One evening the earnest features of Tolstoy, no less, were seen at the Bouffes. He was young then and still permitted himself to visit haunts of iniquity. 'It is truly French,' he wrote; 'the comedy is so good-natured and spont-aneous that everything is allowed it.'

Towards the end of 1856 Offenbach's reputation was formally acknowledged. Louis-Napoléon invited the company to the Tuileries, home of the Imperial court, and there in the great drawing-room *Les Deux aveugles* entertained the royal assembly. Next day the players went to the home of the duc de Morny and gave him *Ba-ta-clan*.

Now that Offenbach had established himself he felt he deserved a little treat. As a change from his own music he thought he would put on several works by other composers he had always held in affection. At the top of the list came his admired Mozart. After a good deal of trouble he managed to track down the score of *The Impresario* in Germany. Halévy and others helped him adapt the libretto of what was then an unfamiliar piece. It enchanted him to do this. 'You ask for something new, good, amusing,' he declared proudly to journalists. 'I give you Mozart. What do you say to that?'

Another favourite piece was that little opera by Rossini called *Il Signor Bruschino*. Apart from a few revivals, the overture is all that is heard of it these days. At its first performance, over forty years previously at carnival time in Venice, the audience had failed to appreciate a trick Rossini played. He instructed the second violins to tap out the rhythm in several passages with their bows. The Venetians did not approve of this, thought they were being laughed at, and in any case found the libretto stupid and illogical. Offenbach liked *Bruschino* and planned to revive it. Rossini had for long been living out his comfortable retirement in Paris. He heard Offenbach's plan benevolently. The two composers had much in common, not least a disabused sense of humour. For Rossini, Offenbach was 'the Mozart of the Champs-Elysées'. The Italian gave his permission, though he refused to attend any performances. He had incurred a heavy enough responsibility in letting Offenbach go ahead, he remarked mischievously. There was no need for him to act as accomplice.

Rossini's discretion was justified. *Il Signor Bruschino* met with no greater success in Paris. Compared with Offenbach's own lively works it seemed staid and slow-moving to regular patrons of the Bouffes-Parisiens. An even greater curiosity Offenbach sought to disinter was *Le Devin du village* by the philosopher Jean-Jacques Rousseau. Better known as the author of advanced theories on education and as the father of illegitimate children whom he was reputed to dislike and to have bundled off to a foundlings' hospital as soon as they were born, Rousseau had also a deep interest in music. He wrote a treatise on notation, engaged in polemic with Rameau, and compiled a musical dictionary as full of errors as it is of valuable information about the state of French and Italian music in the eighteenth century. *Le Devin du village* is one of several trifles he composed for the stage, and Offenbach, when he proposed to give it, was sharply reminded that the work belonged to the repertory of the Opéra-Comique. It therefore came 'under the protection of the higher administration' and could not be transferred 'to a theatre of the secondary rank'. The official decision seemed unaware that the Opéra-Comique, despite its claim to *Le Devin du village*, had never paid it the honour of performance.

Ideas gushed so liberally from the director of the Bouffes-Parisiens that as soon as one had been fulfilled or rejected there were half a dozen others jostling for expression. A terrible flood disaster that claimed many victims and caused much suffering worried his tender heart for days. He suggested a massive charitable function to raise money on behalf of the stricken. Carried away with enthusiasm he envisaged a great concert in the Palace of Industry. Meyerbeer, Verdi, Berlioz and Gounod would conduct. There would be a vast ball for 100,000 dancers with music directed by Strauss, Musard and Jullien. Virtuosi such as Liszt would give recitals. Trains would carry passengers at reduced prices and special accommodation would be arranged. So exciting did the whole thing look on paper that Offenbach decided to make it into a yearly festival. Cooler heads examined the project. It was pointed out that expenses alone would amount to at least three times the receipts envisaged.

A better scheme and one that brought definite advantages was a competition Offenbach launched in the July of 1856. He had exact notions about the genre he did so much to create. The reduced dimensions of opéra-bouffe did not mean that it was easy to write. Like Hervé, Offenbach found that the official restriction on the number of characters allowed in a work a spur rather than a drawback. (It was not lifted until 1864.) With a small cast, a small orchestra and a time span as brief as forty minutes or less, there was no room for the self-indulgence possible in more inflated forms like grand opera. Good ideas and good tunes were essential. The challenge of writing for a small combination, where awkwardness and error showed up instantly, was greater than when scoring for a large body where they could be drowned out. Offenbach echoed Voltaire on prose when he spoke of a stream, bright and clear, whose transparent water revealed its bed, whereas the depths of a broad river were apt to be obscured by unknown quantities of sludge. He called for a return to the spirit of the French eighteenth-century comic opera and its qualities of gaiety, sincerity and grace.

'The Théâtre des Bouffes-Parisiens wants to revive the true, original style,' Offenbach announced. He invited young composers to 'a little musical tournament'. Three things only were asked of them: aptitude, knowledge and ideas. A committee of illustrious musicians was formed to judge the entries. The chairman was Auber, veteran composer of some fifty operas which began with *L'Erreur d'un moment* and ended, still on the same note, with *Rêve d'amour*. The busy librettist Eugène Scribe, who had written the words of his *Fra Diavolo* and many of his other successful works, also joined the committee which included, as well, Fromental Halévy and Gounod.

Seventy-eight competitors took part. They had first to write a song for voice and piano, score it for orchestra and then compose a piece for orchestra alone. Once they had passed these initial tests they were to set a libretto called *Le Docteur Miracle* which Ludovic Halévy and a colleague had thrown together for the occasion. The preliminaries reduced the number of contestants to six. Among them were Georges Bizet and Charles Lecocq.

Bizet was then eighteen years old, a prodigy who had already written the brilliant Symphony in C. His talent and his warm personality made him a favourite with Fromental Halévy and Gounod, whose admiring friendship was a tribute to his gifts. Lecocq was his senior by six years. His early life had been hard and shadowed by poverty. Crippled in childhood by a deformity of the hip and ruthlessly teased by schoolmates, he withdrew to find consolation in music. He lacked the social grace of a Bizet. His teachers, even the genial Halévy, found him, though talented, a dull dog. He could not help feeling embittered by the long struggle for recognition. The aim of his life was to be a great composer. Instead, a perverse fate had endowed him with an admirable facility for writing light music.

The committee of judges awarded the palm equally to Bizet and Lecocq. The latter discovered afterwards that, but for Halévy's insistence on behalf of his favourite pupil, 'I would have had the prize all to myself.' The two versions of *Le Docteur Miracle* were performed on alternate nights at the Bouffes-Parisiens. The composers drew lots to see which should be played first. Lecocq won and his version inaugurated the series of eleven performances each that the works received. Offenbach was delighted. The committee's novel decision stimulated public interest in operetta and brought useful publicity for his theatre. But Lecocq, understandably, felt that life had snubbed him with yet another disappointment. He nursed his rancour in silence and bided his time.

10

In Search of a Hit

The Bouffes-Parisiens continued on its irresistibly successful way. If the popularity of an attraction started to flag, Offenbach withdrew it and had no trouble at all in replacing it immediately. His eye for the topical remained unerring. On 12 June 1856, the Bouffes played *Les Dragées de baptême* to celebrate the christening of the Prince Imperial born to Louis-Napoléon and his beautiful Empress Eugénie. The composer was no less adept than Molière at writing *pièces de circonstance* to flatter and amuse the ruling house.

The same programme featured Schneider as *La Rose de Saint Flour*. It is a tradition to represent the Auvergnat with his comic accent as a figure of fun. 'We were neither men nor women,' runs the final chorus in acknowledgement of this, 'we were . . . Auvergnats.' Much robust amusement is drawn from the Auvergnat's habit of pronouncing 's' as 'j' or 'ch'. Solicited for her favour by two competing suitors, one a blacksmith who offers her a pot and the other a cobbler who presents her with a pair of shoes in homage, Schneider as Pierette sang:

> 'Entre les deux mon coeur se balanche
> Je ne chais lequel épouja!
> Pour chelui-chi quand mon coeur penche,
> Il penche aussi pour chelui-là.'

The blacksmith, 'with passion' and to a series of elaborate scales and turns, indicates that his pot will be ideal for brewing up cabbage soup. He threatens to slash the cobbler into twenty pieces: 'Ha ha ha il tremble il me chemble'. The situation is resolved in an elegant trio that presages *Trial by Jury* and the song that begins 'With a sense of deep emotion'. Perhaps Sullivan knew *La Rose de Saint Flour*. It was done in England as *The Rose of Auvergne*, and its success was great enough to justify a published translation complete with full production details.

La Rose de Saint Flour set a style in peasant comedies which

Offenbach and his imitators frequently exploited. It was a notable contrast with *Les Trois Baisers du diable* which he put on the following year. This departed sharply from the formulas he had established to date. An eerie little melodrama, it carried a foretaste of the *Contes d'Hoffmann*. Audiences did not like this musical piece and it had to be quickly taken off.

The replacement, *Croquefer*, or 'The last of the Paladins', brought the public back. It was a satire on knightly romance during the Middle Ages, 'a thing of inconceivable insanity' decided the Goncourt brothers. They were alone in their opinion, since *Croquefer* had capacity bookings nightly. Here Offenbach once again mocked the casting restrictions. When officials objected to the presence of a fifth character, the resourceful musician turned him into a warrior whose tongue had been cut out in battle with the Saracens. This hero was accompanied on stage by attendants who unrolled sheets of paper bearing the remarks he wanted to make. His speeches, ribald and inconsequential, therefore evoked more laughter than if they had been spoken. The part he would have sung in the quintet was replaced with yells and barks.

Offenbach's ridicule of the convention had its effect on government attitudes. Eventually the rule was lifted and he was allowed to increase the number of characters, although it was still some time before he had complete freedom. The one-acter he produced six weeks after *Croquefer* kept to the established usage with a cast of four. *Dragonette* was an eighteenth-century comedy about the fife player Julien who suddenly vanishes at the height of battle. He is suspected of desertion but returns in triumph bearing the flag which he has bravely snatched from the enemy. The finale, 'Vive la France!', a brisk 2/4 measure, brought the audience to its feet in a storm of patriotic applause. The German Jew who wrote it had assimilated himself so closely to the country of his adoption that he was more of a chauvinist than the proudest Frenchman.

Dragonette flourished at the box-office as did most of the other spectacles Offenbach mounted with a lavish, even too lavish hand. The problem was that he overspent, sometimes in excess of receipts. Nothing was too good for his beloved theatre. He wanted the best scenery, the best costumes, the best furnishings for the auditorium. His purchase of silk and velvet alone swallowed the profits. Neither could he resist the hard-luck stories of actors out of a job or musicians come by hard times. The cash was there, in the box-office, so why not spend it? It is no wonder that, faced with Offenbach's prodigality and the threatening visits of grim-faced creditors, his manager Charles Comte fell ill. Comte was an able businessman, but the whims of his mercurial colleague were enough to unseat the most stolid, and financial catastrophe hovered over the little theatre. Offenbach decided to recoup his fortunes with an English tour. He knew there was money to be made over there. The scenery, costumes, instruments and music of his last four productions were packed up and sent across the Channel. Offenbach travelled with them.

In the summer of 1857 the company arrived in London and played a short season at the St James's Theatre. They had almost as warm a reception as they were accustomed to at the Bouffes-Parisiens. Takings were good in the financial terms of the age and ranged from fifty-six pounds an evening to sixty-four. Offenbach himself had a benefit night and played the 'cello in some of the numbers with which, 'a perfect master of his instrument', he had pleased London audiences thirteen years before.

On 17 June he took his company down to Richmond. Here lived Queen Amélie, widow of Louis-Philippe who had died in 1850, and her sons. *Dragonette* was among the pieces given at a command performance. Inevitably the 'Vive la France!' chorus reduced the exiled queen to tears. Aware that his visit to the family of Louis-Philippe might create unwelcome political reactions in France, Offenbach wrote to Charles Comte warning him against those whom he ironically described as 'my good friends in Paris' – those, that is to say, who, jealous of his success, might seize the opportunity to make trouble in official quarters which at the moment were favourable towards him. Imprudent though he may have been in financial matters, he never forgot the importance of diplomacy.

One evening Queen Victoria sat in the theatre. She had, Offenbach reported, been very keen to see the show, 'and you can easily understand how delighted I am.' Royal approval meant excellent business front of house. Yet even while the English visit went from success to success Offenbach was busy planning future triumphs. In between writing music he sent long letters to Comte explaining the arrangements for a provincial French tour. Not a detail escaped him. Times, dates, rehearsals, hotel bookings and prices, were outlined with precision. He gave specific instructions about the items to be transported: the two guitars for *Les Deux aveugles*, the comedian's wig and blue waistcoat, the heroine's costume and bouquet for *Le Savetier et le financier*, the exact number and type of instruments required by the orchestra . . . He had considered every need, provided for every risk that might be foreseen.

The travellers returned to Paris, embarked on the tour and came back to the Bouffes-Parisiens, but for all their wanderings, for all the cheering audiences, the balance-sheet still lurched dismally on the wrong side. In August Offenbach had to withdraw half of the 10,000 francs deposited as a bond when he launched the Bouffes. Summer is a bad time for theatres, he explained. 'The excessive heat this year has made it ruinous for mine.'

Things grew worse. Later in the year, and again in 1858, he had to vanish over the border and take refuge in Brussels. Had he shown his face at the Bouffes his creditors would have seized him. Within a few days the 5,000 francs had gone and income was again threatened by debts with bankruptcy in their train.

What he needed was obviously a bigger theatre where he could operate on a more reasonable scale. He looked at a property in the boulevard de Sébastopol. A petition went to the minister responsible. It passed from department to department and was quietly filed.

The most urgent necessity, of course, was a new hit. Would it be *Une Demoiselle en loterie*? He had great hopes of his new discovery, an actress and singer called Lise Tautin. She played the part of a circus rider who, desperate for money, puts herself up as a prize in a lottery. The man who wins and unwittingly marries her turns out to be a cousin. He had previously cheated her of an inheritance which, for the sake of dramatic neatness, was the same figure as he had paid in the lottery. As the heroine— 'aged more than twenty-one and less than thirty . . . military gentleman can buy their tickets at half-price' – Lise Tautin proved agreeable to the audience, especially in an attractive gypsy bolero number. But her success was yet to come, and the talent that soon made her a formidable rival to Schneider still called for something more substantial to aid its flowering.

Or would *Le Mariage aux lanternes*, which came after *Une Demoiselle en loterie*, be the saviour of the Bouffes? It had much in its favour. The plot concerns a farmer and his cousin, mutually in love and neither daring to reveal the secret to the other. An uncle tells the farmer to go when the angelus rings and to dig for buried treasure at the foot of a tree. There he finds his cousin, his 'treasure' waiting for him. They are married by the light of lanterns carried by peasants whom the rumour of hidden gold had attracted. Rossini liked the piece very much. It had a Mozartian resonance and a tenderness which up to then rarely featured in the knockabout humour associated with the Bouffes. *Le Mariage aux lanternes* is nearer to the spirit of operetta than opéra-bouffe, and there is a freedom and a naturalness about it which can only partly be attributed to the chorus which Offenbach was using for the first time in one of his productions. He saw his new piece as a tribute to Mozart, a composer whose biography was one of his favourite bedside books.

Lise Tautin sang the part of cousin Denise and once again impressed the growing band of admirers who filled the theatre when her name appeared on the posters. But expenses still outpaced receipts. *Les Deux pêcheurs* failed to remedy the situation, even though one of its exchanges became for a time part of contemporary lore.

'Given a ship leaving Smyrna with a draught of twenty feet, what is the age of the captain?'

'This can't be worked out until the ship approaches Marseille.'

'Why?'

'Because the captain will be in quarantine (*quarantaine*).'

Despite this elaborate witticism, or perhaps because of it, *Les Deux pêcheurs* sank with all hands on deck. It was succeeded by *Mesdames de la Halle*, a salty comedy set in the Paris fruit and vegetable market. The market women are all in love with the swaggering drum major Raflafla. (When a letter is handed to him he remarks: 'I can't read, I haven't got my stick with me.') He turns out to be the father of Ciboulette, played by Lise Tautin, who sang with charm a Meyerbeerian bolero entitled 'I'm the little fruit girl'. The real importance of *Mesdames de la*

Halle was that here, at last, Offenbach enjoyed the liberty of using as many characters as he liked. He could also deploy a full chorus. For the latter he incorporated street cries which, often heard in his youth, must have survived long afterwards. They included one that sharp ears have detected as a leading motif in Gustave Charpentier's *Louise*, the opera about Montmartre low life which came out nearly half a century later.

In the middle of summer 1858 Offenbach decided it was time for him again to vanish discreetly from Paris. Writs fell in a constant drizzle onto the Théâtre des Bouffes-Parisiens. He was obliged to avoid places he usually frequented and take routes across Paris where duns were unlikely to interrupt him with their tiresome demands. It was impossible for him to understand the economics of business: if a stall or two in the theatre happened to be slightly damaged, he would have the entire seating torn out and re-upholstered in costly velvet. He spent lavishly on costumes and sets for *Mesdames de la Halle*. Did not those penny-pinching tradesmen realise that he was creating something far more beautiful, more magical than dull balance-sheets?

And he was suffering from rheumatism. On the verge, like the captain of the boat from Smyrna, of reaching forty, he experienced the first pangs of an ailment which for the rest of his life was to grip him with a lancinating pain that increased as the years went by. He would go to Ems and seek relief by taking the waters there, but before he left he added a new item to the programme. *La chatte métamorphosée en femme*, based on a Scribe farce, told of a cat turned into a woman by the magic of the Indies. It emphasised this useful advice to be found in the sacred Brahmin writings (Book Three, Verse the First): 'Don't upset people. Let well alone.' In spite of which the spell is cast and the feline becomes a woman to take part in a 'Miaow Song'.

Once the cat was launched Offenbach jumped on the train for Ems. He liked it there and was often to return. Most important of all, he could write in comparative tranquillity. No bailiff hammered on his door, no accountant badgered him with sets of figures. When he remembered he took the waters. The greater part of the time found him with his lean figure robed in a voluminous dressing-gown, scribbling page after page in tireless handwriting. Early in July he wrote to Halévy: 'I won't talk to you about all my ailments, you must already have heard of them. I'll only tell you that the piece is nearly complete . . .' For several years he had been thinking of an operetta with Orpheus as the hero. Now it would soon be ready for production.

PART III

A FRENCHMAN AT LAST

11

Jacques' Fridays

Offenbach refused to let business worries cloud his private life.
His natural gaiety repulsed dark thought, his brittle high spirits
deflected melancholy. The Goncourt brothers described him in
the summer of 1858 as 'a skeleton with pince-nez who looks as if
he's raping a 'cello.'

Round about this time he moved from his cramped home in
the passage Saulnier and took a large, airy apartment on the
fourth floor of Number 11 in the rue Laffitte. This street in the
Opéra neighbourhood runs from the boulevard des Italiens over
the rue Lafayette to the church of Notre Dame de Lorette. At
one point it crosses the boulevard Haussmann, named after the
Emperor's architect, who, remodelling Paris with his bold
design, in the course of his activities was eventually to demolish
the building where Offenbach lived.

The composer and his wife Herminie now had four daughters
ranging from the eldest Berthe, by way of Marie and Pépita, to
the infant Jacqueline. The new quarters in the rue Laffitte were
big enough to take them all, as well as the visitors who climbed
the stairs in a ceaseless procession. The doorbell jingled
perpetually as authors, dramatists, unemployed musicians,
singers and aspiring librettists addressed themselves hopefully
to the capital's most successful and popular musician. According
to their status they were asked to wait in the hall, the dining-
room or the drawing-room. Offenbach saw them all, his moods
flashing quickly from laughter to irritation, from calm to
jumpiness. During intervals between callers he wrote music,
breaking off half-way through a bar to argue with a tradesman,
or leaving a melodic line in the air to discuss a tricky point with a
collaborator.

His first visitor of the day, and to Offenbach one of the most
important, was Coquillard the hairdresser. Every morning
Coquillard attended to give his hair those waves and curls which
all Paris thought, or which Offenbach liked to think it thought,

were natural. For the composer was a dandy with an obsessive care about his appearance. He owned innumerable pairs of trousers complemented by spats cut in the same shade and material. The tailor Dusautoy, one of the city's most fashionable and expensive, knew that his client could never resist the alluring samples spread out before him. Since Offenbach wore sober ties of black satin he felt that his dandyism should show itself in his choice of trousers. They filled his wardrobe in every type of pattern and colour.

Another preoccupation was shoes. He had dozens of pairs and his choice for the day was only reached after long and careful thought. Then his daughter Marie, or 'Mimi' as she was known, had the duty of helping him put them on. His left foot, badly affected by gout, needed particular care when being eased into a shoe. He did not wish to entrust the delicate operation to his valet. So, every day until she married, the gentle Mimi lovingly encased the aching foot in its elegant armour.

Once his toilette was over and he could present his neatly shaven, well-coiffed person to the world, Offenbach was in a state to receive. Some of his callers were there in response to urgent summonses. Others came seeking favours and these were the most difficult to handle. They included musicians anxious for help, eager to take on any libretti Offenbach had turned down and he always felt obliged to do something on their behalf. Yet there were times when his generosity was tried beyond the limit. 'Can't you see I'm not at home?' he screamed in desperation at one of the most importunate. 'Because I'm working!'

His correspondence mounted to vast proportions. He either answered letters immediately or not at all. Between a fitting for a new suit and a consultation with his doctor – gout and rheumatism were the prevailing topics – he dashed off quick missives often embellished with musical notes by his flying pen. 'Come and see me . . . I need you: come . . . I need *you* tomorrow morning at half-past nine . . . Unfortunately I left the second and third acts with you, naturally you've kept them and I can't work . . . Wretch, come to my home at nine o'clock: it is absolutely essential to complete the finale of the second act . . .' Sometimes, exasperated by what, to such a fast worker, seemed the endless dawdling of a librettist, he signed off in mock anger

'Not at all yours,' or 'Accept, dear Sir, my less than friendly greetings.'

The morning passed in this fashion with the master of the house commanding, ordering, pleading, arguing, discussing. Lunch time arrived, but however tempting the dishes, however appetising the fare, he ate very little. His slimness was skeletal and he never weighed, at any time in his life, much more than six and a half stone. The slight bony figure, just a shade over five feet tall, was the delight of caricaturists, and it stayed that way. Though he was often hungry he always lacked an appetite. The lunch brought to him consisted of a boiled egg, a lamb cutlet, potatoes and fruit. After three spoonfuls of egg, a morsel of lamb, a mouthful of potato and a quarter of fruit, he pushed it all away and lit the cigar which gave him more satisfaction than any food.

These tiny repasts were taken at the nearby Café Riche or at one of the other then fashionable restaurants where he kept a table permanently reserved. There he was joined by a court of admirers and spongers. If it were a business lunch with impresarios or managers or collaborators, he would take a private room, which he called a 'cabineto particolioso'. Once, at the restaurant Peters, as he sat at his table nursing his gout and savouring a cigar, a performing bear suddenly appeared and wandered about, soliciting tit-bits. Offenbach, with a quivering hand, offered a lump of sugar. As soon as the bear turned away the composer's legs, despite their rheumatic stiffness, propelled him speedily out of the place and into his carriage. His friends tried to reassure him of the bear's pacific intentions but he did not believe them. A few days later the bear, which had been engaged as a novelty attraction, cuffed a waiter. It had to be put down. The proprietor of the restaurant invited Offenbach to sample a rare dish: bear's paws. Offenbach returned, savoured a shred or two, lit his cigar, and became a regular customer again.

When he did not go out he had his lunch sent up from the Café Riche. This was done to avoid upsetting the household routine since he had to leave early for rehearsals in the afternoon. His daughters took it in turn to attend at these meals. The duty was fought over and whoever presided had the privilege of finishing up the copious remains that he left – most of the egg, nearly all the cutlet and sometimes asparagus, cherries and strawberries. Once he had an urge for peaches out of season. These were hastily procured at twenty francs each but by the time they arrived his whim had passed and he did not touch them. The girls fell on them delightedly.

There was the time when, just as the family were sitting down to a meal, he felt like tasting sole. Again it was speedily brought in from a shop. He took a few gulps, lost interest and picked up a cigar. These he smoked continually; around the house boxes were scattered which he offered to his friends; but for himself he kept an Italian cabinet inlaid with marqueterie, which contained fifteen drawers, wherein he preserved his best Havanas, to be caressed and smoked with voluptuous pleasure. The visitor who was invited to enjoy one of these had received a very high favour indeed.

But there was not time to linger, even to enjoy the rich clouds of Havana. With a familiar gesture Offenbach would draw from his waistcoat pocket the watch that accompanied him everywhere. He was ruled by its dictatorial hands, those little black knives that sliced away the time remorselessly and commanded his routine with unforgiving precision. Punctuality obsessed him. He was always the first to arrive at rehearsals. 'Yet we shan't be able to start on time,' he would grumble to his coachman Mathurin, 'because so-and-so's bound not to be there.'

Often of an afternoon he would rehearse, one after another, as many as three different productions in three different theatres. If a current attraction wasn't doing good business the wary Charles Comte, after a depressed glance at the figures, would ask him for something new. Offenbach would sort out the pile of libretti he always kept to hand, and having chosen the least mediocre, he started composing on the spot.

It was for this reason, and to save valuable time, that he had a desk installed in his brougham. While being driven from theatre to theatre he could work on the operetta that currently engaged him. As the vehicle jerked and lumbered through the Paris traffic he sketched out a scene, orchestrated an overture, filled in a quartet, oblivious to the oaths of carters and cabbies, the grind of iron-shod wheels, the lurching of the carriage. When night fell or the weather was dark, the wavering gleam of a candle lit up his manuscript as wax dripped and sputtered over the heedless composer.

He was usually in a good humour when he opened rehearsals, although he warned the company: 'My dear friends, before we start I ask your forgiveness, *in advance*, for all the unpleasant things I shan't fail to say to you in a moment.'

And then they were away. Almost immediately his bad temper flared out. 'That's not it!' They started again. He beat time with his stick, croaked tunelessly with the singers, danced with the chorus, led the cancan, worked up the pace with increasing verve until, as the last notes of the finale died away, everyone collapsed exhausted and he himself fell panting into a chair. His smile returned. His voice was gentle.

'It was very good this time, girls and boys, in fact it was extremely good . . . *BUT IT STILL ISN'T WHAT'S WANTED.*'

Again the weary troupe threw itself into action, goaded and harassed by the dictator. 'Oh, these blasted rehearsals!' he would moan. 'Man proposes and rehearsals indispose.' The joke restored his good humour. When the scene was finished the singers and orchestra, with blessed relief, saw him vanish into Comte's office. Here he inspected the wording of poster proofs, examined designs for sets, approved or altered press releases, checked the takings, ordered repairs. The Bouffes-Parisiens was his own creation. The close attention he gave to every detail, great and small, was responsible for the legend that, to make sure everything was done as well as possible, Offenbach stamped the tickets, sat in the box-office during the interval and issued passes, dressed his usherettes and, himself, stood outside the door to be the first person in the queue.

His bulletins were drawn up with military exactness. One such order of the day read; 'Sunday rehearsal: nymphs and clerks, less need for the chorus. First act, scenes from the second and especially the third. The parts in the fourth must be copied in time for reading on Sunday; I'll answer for production on the 27th or 28th. It's the third, the third, the third, the third, the third that must be worked at. Let me have the clerks on stage, the nymphs in the third act. There must be four rehearsals tomorrow of the third act so that the artists can memorise. All the clerks on stage, during their rehearsal, after their entrance. Then lessons for them in the foyer, after which they come back on stage for the finale, because we have to do it four times tomorrow.'

Around five o'clock in the afternoon Offenbach had finished for the day. He went home, shut himself up in his room, and, crouched over his little table, wrote more music. The piano stood close by so that he could try out phrases to the extent that his gouty fingers would allow. Sometimes he whistled an accompaniment to the melodies that grew on paper.

'Herminie! Herminie!' Frequently he called his wife to give judgement. She was frank in her opinions. 'Very good, my dear,' he would say when her criticism was adverse. 'I thank you and I'm extremely sorry to have disturbed you to no good purpose. *But you don't know the first thing about it.*'

After a few moments' thought and some more tinkling, he would call her back: 'Look, Herminie, perhaps you'd prefer this?'

This time she approved. And, often, when he discussed his music with other people, he would declare passionately: 'Herminie was right!' The remark became a family joke.

On the other hand, she would sometimes murmur: 'It seems to me, Jacques, that I've heard it somewhere before.'

He was ready for this one and had his answer pat: 'That could very well be. But so many of my dear colleagues have taken their inspiration from me ... or won't fail to do so in the future, that I don't suppose I'm forbidden to plagiarise myself a bit.'

Then he noticed an unaccustomed silence. 'What are the children up to? I can't hear them. You know I like to hear them chatting and laughing. I need their noise to work. That's why I forbid them to talk quietly. What distracts me is all this whispering. Is there a dead body in the house then?' Without the constant background of household noises and children at play he felt unable to concentrate – just as he needed the din of traffic to inspire him while writing in his carriage.

He worked so fast that he could never remember which tune he had used and where. If somebody whistled a familiar melody to him, he would scratch his head and say: 'What's that you're whistling? I know it's one of mine but I can't recall which score it comes from.'

For all his vagueness about past work, he knew exactly what he was doing when writing his current piece. The same neurotic care for detail that he showed in administering his theatre also dictated his method of composing. As a scene developed on paper he kept in his mind's eye a clear picture of what was happening on stage. He knew from bar to bar the exact positions of singers, chorus and walk-ons. When the time came for rehearsals it was invariably found that he had provided the right amount of music, just enough and no more, to allow the singers to move from place to place or carry out what 'business' was needed. Once the piece had been tested against the reactions of a live audience he was ready to adjust and tailor where necessary. Any effect that did not succeed was instantly dropped. He cut and slashed ruthlessly. His collaborators knew only too well that ominous verdict which in his Germanic accent sounded even more threatening: '*Une bedide goupure* . . . ' It was Offenbach's version of death by a thousand cuts.

At about six o'clock he had his first rest of the day. Into a drawing-room usually crowded with people he limped cheerfully and made for his favourite seat. This was a grandiloquent piece of furniture in gilt wood decorated with carving and upholstered in red velvet, more like a throne than a chair. Another, slightly smaller, was reserved for Herminie. Once, when the Shah of Persia was to attend an official reception and a spare throne was needed, the duc de Morny, a frequent guest in the rue Laffitte, borrowed Offenbach's famous chair for the emergency.

Lulled by the hum of conservation, the composer then dropped off into a brief siesta. But it was never so deep that he failed to realise what was going on around him. The story is told that on one such occasion while returning to consciousness he overheard a guest speaking disdainfully of his latest work.

'How right you are, dear friend,' he beamed, 'to find my music light. All to the good! If it's as light as all that there's less chance of it falling down.'

In the evening, if he felt well enough, he would visit the theatres where his operettas were being performed. It was very rare for him to go to see other people's work. But most often he stayed at home playing endless games of bezique.

Friday was a very special day. *Les vendredis de Jacques* were famous throughout Paris. He had a superstitious veneration for that time of the week, and if it were possible to give a première on Friday he would gladly do so. He never went out on Friday evening, which was always reserved for family dinner and afterwards he kept open house for his friends who were exhorted to come and enjoy themselves. Those who, for some reason or other, failed to turn up were sadly rebuked and warned to mend their ways in future.

One of his dearest friends was Nadar, the photographer whose portraits of contempories, including Offenbach, are now of historic value. The Impressionists held their first exhibition in his studio. An Offenbach letter to Nadar illustrates the composer's awareness of how, in his busy life, he was prone to forget appointments: 'On Tuesday I'll come to your house at half-past twelve to pose for the sake of my ugly face . . . P.S. All the same, let me have a note on Monday to remind me . . .'

Another was the writer Edmond About who enjoyed a brilliant reputation, now vanished, for witty novelettes and, even more, for articles on social and religious problems. For one of Offenbach's 'Fridays' he wrote a skit that ended with the company dancing a noisy farandole through every room in the apartment and out on to the stairs. About, the author of that profound study, *La Question Romaine*, also distinguished himself in the part of an executioner, his axe dripping horribly with red-currant jam.

Musicians were there in plenty, notably Bizet, who had gained Offenbach's friendship with *Le Docteur Miracle*. Delibes was another young composer taken under the host's wing. Not yet the famous creator of *Sylvia*, he had written music criticism, including a notice of *Mesdames de la Halle*, and soon became a well-known figure at the Bouffes-Parisiens where Offenbach gave him his opportunity and most of his early operettas were produced, while two others, thanks to Offenbach's influence at Ems, were played in that favourite spa.

Though shy and, in some ways, too sensitive and gentle a spirit for the rough and tumble of the theatre, Delibes among friends was a gay and uninhibited companion. His brilliant musicianship gained respect, his loveable nature won affection.

He danced, on one uproarious Friday evening, a polka with himself, the large black beard fluttering nobly, the corpulent frame spinning round and around with unexpected agility. This was the star turn of the gala arranged to celebrate 'the approaching end of the world'.

He was a prominent member of the 'Society for self-help against boredom' founded by Offenbach. In a scratch *Farmyard*

Symphony he gave a realistic impression of a dog whose paw had been trodden on. For a parody of *Il Trovatore*, Offenbach Italianised him into Léo Delibestino. Edmond About became Edmondo Abutti. Bizet was metamorphosed into *il maestro Bizetto*. The host appeared as Jacomo Offenbacchio.

There was a fancy dress ball where the artist Gustave Doré, later to design the sets for *Orphée aux enfers*, made his entry as an acrobat walking on his hands. Another artist friend, the painter Edouard Detaille, who produced hugely successful battle scenes, designed for Offenbach an elaborate gamekeeper's suit. Bizet and Nadar came as babies and the soldier in the corner with his gaiters and cap turned out to be Delibes. A figure half-pierrot, half-King's guard was the librettist Hector Crémieux. The bulky shape of Villemessant, director of *Figaro*, presented the unbelievable complexion of a Red Indian.

Charades, little revues, burlesques and parodies of grand opera were the main events of these Friday evenings. In between were games of whist and bezique. Gossip, laughter and champagne supplied the lubricant. At the centre of it all was Offenbach. As the hours grew shorter his exuberance increased. He would pass round caricatures of himself which had lately featured in the press. His person, he knew, was heaven-sent for cartoonists and it delighted him to see what extremes they could draw from his tiny stature, his thick nose, his slender body and skinny legs.

At midnight everyone rushed to the larder. It was stocked, as ever, with supplies of hard-boiled eggs, ham, salads, cold leg of lamb and fruit. Tables were set up. Corks popped. Offenbach circulated among the guests waving his cigar and urging them to eat up.

The latest anecdotes, the newest scandal would pass from mouth to mouth. Halévy would tell of a conversation recently overheard in the theatre. Said one actress to another: 'You disgust me. It's shameful to live as you do and to give yourself to men for money.' To which her colleague replied: 'It's more honourable than giving yourself for nothing.'

Someone else would recount the story of the leading lady who became involved with a stagehand. The manager interrupted them one afternoon at a crucial moment in their relationship.

'Mademoiselle,' cried the manager angrily, 'you are forgetting

Offenbach as 'cellist

yourself in the company of a common scene-shifter.'

'I place my affections where I choose,' came the answer.

'Well, in future kindly do not place them on my staircase.'

Such tales were told discreetly: Herminie and those of the girls old enough to stay up late did not hear them, because Offenbach, where his family was concerned, had a ferocious propriety. He discouraged his daughters from attending his own theatre and rigorously secluded them from any hint of immorality. He knew only too well what the world, and especially the world of the theatre, was like. By an amusing irony this composer of 'naughty' operettas, this famous impresario who had his pick, and took it, of the loveliest actresses in Paris, was the most stern and the most moral of family men.

By early morning the final guest had departed and Offenbach went reluctantly to bed. He spent money without heed entertaining his friends and gave generously to anyone in need of cash. He made large sums and dissipated them almost immediately but in one respect he was curiously mean: it is not infrequent, as worried housewives know, for men to begrudge the necessary expense of running a house, and while Offenbach would gladly fritter away everything he had on champagne and copious meals for his acquaintances, he loathed being called on for housekeeping money. He would rather surprise Herminie with a piece of jewellery than give her enough to pay the grocer's bill.

So when he was asleep or otherwise occupied, Mimi would surreptitiously go through his wallet and pockets. In time she reduced to a fine art the process of taking sums that were small enough not to be noticed by her adoring father. Herminie, too, became adept at the trick.

It was as well for Offenbach that Herminie possessed the thrifty habits of the traditional French housewife. While she cossetted her Jacques and fell in with his hospitable ways, she surveyed minutely every item of the household budget, buying vegetables at the lowest price, hunting out the most advantageous discounts and watching her cook with the eye of a predatory bird. By keeping expenditure to a minimum and counting every halfpenny, she was able to build up a reserve fund. Often her spendthrift husband would bless her economy. When he was short of ready cash he turned to Herminie and the miracle always happened. She could produce, out of thin air so it seemed to him, a few welcome bundles of thousand-franc notes. How did she do it? he wondered. What, he thought in his careless innocence, what an amazing woman Herminie was!

12

Orpheus triumphant

On 8 July 1858, Offenbach wrote from Ems to Ludovic Halévy: 'What's all this about you're not being able to finish *Orphée*? . . . Can such a thing be possible? If you must and will become a serious man and write no more plays, you ought at least to end your career as author with a masterpiece. A masterpiece *Orphée* will be and it'll have two hundred performances. The music is coming on wonderfully, so I won't let you go.'

It was maddening. Now that authority permitted him as large a cast as he wished and he could go ahead with his idea for a satire on Orpheus and the gods and goddesses, here was Ludo becoming difficult. Lately promoted to Secretary for Algerian affairs in the government administration, Halévy felt it was undignified, in his exalted station, to go on writing frivolous libretti. Offenbach pleaded and cajoled. At last Halévy agreed to supply various passages on condition that his name was left unprinted. Offenbach contrived to acknowledge his assistance by dedicating the score to him.

The composer's other librettist was Hector Crémieux. They had worked together before. Unfortunately Crémieux wrote at an exceedingly slow pace. His laborious methods irritated Offenbach beyond measure. What a contrast with dear Ludo! Crémieux, furthermore, had excessive notions of his own importance. He, like Halévy, was a civil servant with an itch for the theatre. In later years, proud of his association with Offenbach, he would describe himself as 'the father of operetta'. Once, in the presence of the composer, he spoke with much self-satisfaction about the words he had written for *Orphée*. At that moment a street organ began to grind out a popular quadrille based on the finale which could be heard in every Paris dance-hall and in every French drawing-room where there was a piano. Offenbach was unable to resist malice.

'Listen to that,' he crowed. 'Your words are pretty, aren't they?'

It was Crémieux who, generally speaking, elaborated and filled in the original scenario provided by Halévy. The legend of Orpheus, in Gluck's well-known opera, has for hero the musician whose playing of the lyre was so beautiful that it even cast a spell over wild animals. Deeply in love with his wife Eurydice, he determines to recover her from the infernal regions where she has gone after dying of a serpent sting. He charms Pluto with his music and is allowed to return with Eurydice, provided he does not look back at her until he comes up from the underworld. The loving husband forgets, turns round, and Eurydice is for ever lost to him.

In the Offenbach version Eurydice is a flouncing coquette bored to death by her husband's scraping on the violin. He keeps trying to play her his latest concerto, which, he proudly says, lasts an hour and a quarter. 'For pity's sake!' she exclaims. We only hear a few bars of it, a pretty little tune with delicate accompaniment by woodwind, horns and then strings. Both husband and wife pray to their respective gods that they may be delivered of each other.

Eurydice is having an affair with the honey-maker Aristeus, (none other than Pluto, master of the underworld, in disguise), and later with Jupiter himself. Her third lover in this situation worthy of a Tristan Bernard farce is John Styx, Pluto's servant (=*domestyx* = *domestique*). When, much against the will of both partners concerned, Orpheus is coming back from the underworld accompanied by his reluctant spouse, Jupiter delivers an Olympian flash of lightning up his behind. Startled, he looks round and Eurydice vanishes. Everyone is happy. 'But it's not in the legend,' says Pluto. 'Very well then, ' replies Jupiter, 'we'll change it.' And the gods carry Eurydice to the waiting arms of Bacchus.

The tone of the piece is resolutely disrespectful towards a legend which people agreed, though for reasons they could not quite define, to be profound and moving. In Offenbach's day, and even until quite recently in France as a whole, the classics were a part of every literate person's education. It came as a shock to hear Orpheus calling his wife the French equivalent of 'ducky', or Minerva and friends teasing Jupiter about his love life with the staccato chorus 'Don't try to sweet-talk us, we know your little game, Jupy.' Even more outrageous was the spectacle of gods and goddesses dancing a cancan, although the less classically-minded pointed out thoughtfully that it gave you a much better view of Diana's legs. Worse still, Mercury acts as conductor on a bus that carries away the older immortals of Olympus. Its signboard reads: 'Ligne P.Y. [A pun on the French pronunciation of those letters which emerges as *Pays grec*, or country of Greece.] Champs-Elysées – Barrière des Enfers. [Elysian Fields – Hell's Gate.]'

Musicians also were annoyed by the apparent slight on Gluck. One of the greatest arias in his opera, Orpheus' plaint at the loss of Eurydice, turns up on the most incongruous occasions. Today, in a world that has largely forgotten the classics and no longer in fact cares much about anything else either, the libretto fails to disconcert. It is the music, as Offenbach sharply observed to Crémieux, which preserved *Orphée* from the nether regions to which it would otherwise have vanished.

Those parts of the score which upset contemporaries have mellowed now. Jupiter dances a minuet which sounds no more than an elegant pastiche full of nostalgia. The cancan itself is a brisk and bracing galop, innocently high-spirited. Some moments are positively sentimental. Orpheus' 'concerto' is one. The aria sung by John Styx is another. Here he recalls in a wistful elegy memories of his previous existence. The humming chorus which opens the second scene is yet another agreeable example of Offenbach in contemplative mood. The clarinet solo introducing Act I creates a pastoral flavour which returns from time to time as a quiet refreshment amid the boisterous action.

The libretto, though not yet up to the standard of later works, is an improvement on the sort of thing Offenbach had had to deal with until then. We may be sure that, as usual, he took a large part in it, snipping, adjusting, revising and making those 'bedides goupures' of his. An amusing innovation is the character called Public Opinion who replaces the Chorus of the old Greek plays. 'The ancient Chorus,' he explains, 'undertook in confidence to explain to people what, when they were intelligent, they'd understood in advance. I do better. I take part in the action myself.' When Orpheus protests at the unwelcome news that Eurydice must rejoin him, Public Opinion is there to warn him: 'For the edification of posterity we need at least one example of a husband who's wanted to get his wife back.'

The metrical schemes are slick and workmanlike. The number where the goddesses laugh at Jupiter – '*Ah! ah! ah! ah! ah! ah! Ne prends plus l'air patelin, On connaît tes farces, Jupin!*' – is set to one of those nervous, racy tunes that were Offenbach's speciality.[1] Minerva reminds Jupiter that when he seduced Alkmena he disguised himself as her husband. 'I know many women,' she remarks, 'with whom a trick like that wouldn't have worked!' For his seduction of Europa, sings Diana, he assumed the shape of a bull – with horns! she adds. (Horns being the sign of the cuckold, that immemorial figure of fun on the Latin stage.) Pluto sums up this torrent of disrespect: 'What do all these disguises prove? That you're so ugly that to make yourself loved you dare not show the face you were born with!'

Too much emphasis should not be laid on the political satire in *Orphée aux enfers*. Offenbach wanted to make audiences laugh, to entertain them, to fill his theatre. He was no more a subversive than Noël Coward. When the gods and demi-gods cry 'To arms! Down with this tyranny! The régime irks us!' the strains of the Marseillaise are woven into their music. That revolutionary *chant de massacre* was unwelcome to the régime of Louis-Napoléon. Yet Offenbach got away with it because he had hit on an idea that amused by virtue of its impertinence. The Olympians complain they are fed up with nectar because it makes them sick. They don't want any more of that wishy-washy ambrosia, either. Let's rise up, they say, against the tyrant Jupiter who pushes it down our throats. This was no anarchist attacking the rule of Napoléon III. This was a boulevard entertainer skating on thin ice as he was expected to do, a court jester taking people's breath away with his smiling audacity. The last thing Offenbach planned was the destruction of a society which applauded his music and flocked to his theatre.

He was convinced that *Orphée* would provide the big success he needed. He engaged new singers, added to the chorus and augmented the orchestra. His friend Gustave Doré, one of the most highly paid artists of the time, designed the sets and lavish

---

1 Originally it read: 'Oui, l'on sait ce qu'a fait Jupin/Qui prend des airs de capucin.' Official censorship, nervous of anti-clericalism, deleted the *capucin* reference. Unwittingly, it helped the librettist to improve his couplet.

costumes. Casting the piece was difficult. For the name part Offenbach took on an actor who, having begun life as a violinist, had strayed into vaudeville and operetta. Unfortunately Schneider was no longer available to play Eurydice. Conscious of her own value she had demanded a salary of five hundred francs a month. Offenbach refused. She swept angrily out of the Bouffes. In any case, she would not have been able to perform. At the moment she was living discreetly retired at her parents' home in Bordeaux where she had just given birth to a baby. It was the child of the duc de Gramont-Caderousse, a young, handsome, cold-eyed debauchee who when he met her had already lost a million francs at the gambling tables. For the only time in his life he fell in love. Hortense resourcefully assisted him in throwing away millions more of his inheritance. He killed a man in a duel and thereafter enjoyed that special respect of men and the admiration of women that only a murderer can command. Tuberculosis brought his own death in the early thirties. The boy born of his love for Schneider turned out to be a mongol.

Lise Tautin was chosen to play Eurydice. Ever since Offenbach had discovered her in Brussels and launched her quaint personality with his *Une Demoiselle en loterie*, he had watched, benignly, her steady rise to fame. She had a funny little face and an adorable smile. Her manner was an odd combination of naïveté and boldness. As Eurydice, especially in the short skirts she wore for the cancan, she was to triumph brilliantly and seemed on the verge of a great career, but for some reason no such part came her way again. Schneider eclipsed her, and Tautin was reduced to hoping against hope that one day her rival would fall ill so that she, Lise, would come forward and regain her lost admirers. Fortune turned against her. She retired to Italy and died, still very young, in Bologna.

An actor who became free at the time and whom Offenbach eagerly snapped up was the eccentric Bache. The composer wrote the part of John Styx especially for him. Bache had once been a provincial lawyer. He married a wife of surpassing ugliness and by her had several daughters. One of them, a fourteen-year-old, he would sometimes take on his lap and lifting her skirts would chuckle: 'And how are we going to keep Daddy when he's old, eh?' And, with a slap on the bottom, he would put her down.

He delivered his lines in a way peculiar to himself alone. Some of his speeches he drawled interminably and others he spoke at top speed. His physical and vocal mannerisms prophesied those of Louis Jouvet. Tall, thin, lugubrious, he resembled a giraffe and his behaviour was as original off stage as on. He was often seen carrying a large kitchen knife about with him, which it appeared, was because he had found that no implement, in restaurants or friends' houses where he dined, ever cut sharply enough to his satisfaction. Once, while strolling through the church of Notre Dame, he was taken by a verger to be an archaeologist and the helpful official asked if he would like to visit the crypt. Bache turned gravely towards him. 'I go into churches to meditate,' he observed, 'and I would ask you to be kind enought not to get on my tits with your interfering bloody rubbish.'

The role of John Styx was tailor-made for this bizarre personage. While adapting it to the notorious oddity of his character, Offenbach infused it with something that bordered on a gentle melancholy. In '*Quand j'étais roi de Béotie*' John Styx remembers his life before he went down to Hades. He had been king of Boeotia, that region of Greece where people were noted for their stupidity. (Though Plutarch and Democritus came from there). So it was natural for him to be associated with loutishness. Yet even a buffoon has feelings. When his regrets become too much for him he makes himself drunk . . . on pure water, the water of forgetfulness which he draws from the river Lethe. His song wavers to a desolating close. Bache with his gangling manner was so good at conveying the blend of pathos and clowning that Offenbach instantly doubled his salary. 'In doing this, my dear Bache,' he added cynically, 'believe me, I have only one aim: that of creating yet another ungrateful person.'

The afternoon of 21 October 1858, was frantic. Offenbach worked in his room at the Bouffes, adding last-minute touches to the score, while from the auditorium came snatches of the dress rehearsal which was taking place on stage. It was a pleasant little room with an open piano and, in a corner, a double-bass. Scores, libretti and sketches for costumes sprawled over the table. On a divan lay an unknown woman's hat. Scene designs embellished the walls and Offenbach's friend Nadar watched the proceedings. The composer set to work on the piccolo part; it needed many changes.

Suddenly the costumier irrupted. The costumes, he blazed, were impossible: he needed a lot more money to do the thing properly; he washed his hands of the whole affair. Scarcely had he slammed the door than Charles Comte appeared, with crisis written on his face. Lise Tautin, he reported, was demanding a real tiger's skin to wear in the second act finale. 'Yes,' replied Offenbach absently, 'a real one would be better.' He returned to his score. Comte vanished, on the edge of apoplexy.

Then an unknown gentleman came in who was, he explained, a fellow-native of Cologne. Could he have a ticket for this evening? Had he realised it, the mention of Cologne was enough to damn him in Offenbach's eyes and he did not get his ticket. On going out he passed the stage manager, who arrived to announce that the actor playing Comus was drunk again and would have to be replaced by the next evening. But where were they to find their new Comus? 'Wherever you like. But leave me in peace,' replied Offenbach.

More Germans in quest of free tickets elbowed their way into the room, and were joined by a dirty little man trying to sell shoe varnish. While Offenbach was scribbling on his score he felt something at his feet and looking down he saw the dirty little man trying to varnish his shoes. '*Verfluch!*' screamed the harassed composer and he was angrily chasing the varnish king around the table when the conductor rushed in to tell him that the piccolo player was ill in bed and couldn't perform.

And so the hellish afternoon wore on: a trio of creditors materialised, breathing ominous threats; an anonymous letter was delivered, promising that the writer, an unsuccessful composer, would wreck Offenbach's first night; another German importuned for a seat. Suddenly a caretaker broke the news that the gas pipe in the street had fractured and it looked as if the theatre would be in darkness that evening. Mademoiselle Tautin complained that Mademoiselle Garnier's part was too long and Mademoiselle Garnier complained that Mademoiselle Tautin's part wasn't short enough. A gentleman called to ask if Offenbach would act as his second in a duel. The maid from the rue Laffitte entered worriedly: the eldest Offenbach girl had just caught measles. Would Monsieur Offenbach come home instantly?

As Orpheus

Offenbach was alone in believing that *Orphée aux enfers* would be a great triumph. His publisher Heugel bought the score a fortnight before the première. The price was low, but Offenbach could not refuse it. His faith in *Orphée* remained unshaken. The house at the first performance amounted to nearly 1,000 francs, which compared with average takings of 500 odd for other programmes earlier in the month. By the end of October *Orphée* was drawing over 1,600 francs a night. Next month the figure had risen to over 2,000, and on 8 March *Orphée* took the highest sum ever recorded at the Bouffes until then.

Offenbach was still unsatisfied. He felt in his bones that *Orphée* could be better, and he did all he could to make it catch fire. Without mercy he subjected it to his 'bedides goupures'. A whole scene vanished. Lines were dropped and replaced with others. New music was hurriedly written. In February he was still revising.

Then, weeks after the first night, an unexpected piece of luck came his way. A critic of the time who wrote for the important *Journal des Débats* declared, in the petulant tones of a Peter Hoy, that *Orphée* amounted to sacrilege. His name was Jules Janin. Offenbach and Crémieux were delighted. Janin had fallen into the trap, for they had mischievously taken from the pompous critic's own articles a passage of faded classical tralala and used it as one of Pluto's speeches. It was full of the obligatory references to gentle Olympus, blue skies, the scent of myrtle and verbena, the cooing of doves, the smell of nectar and ambrosia, the perfume of the Graces and of the Muses. 'Have you finished with the scent-shop yet?' enquires Jupiter.

In reply to Janin's onslaught Offenbach revealed the source of the borrowing. The critic was silenced. On the following Monday he avoided the delicate question of words and limited himself to denigrating the music. 'Oh Janin! my worthy Janin!' said Offenbach, 'how grateful I am to you for attacking me every Monday as you do!'

This was no mere witticism. Offenbach felt real gratitude towards Janin. His attack stimulated controversy. It had come at just the right time. As every publicist knows, there is nothing that sells quite so effectively as a charge of scandal or obscenity. People were curious and bookings increased abruptly. One admirer liked *Orphée* so much that he reserved the same seat forty-five times running. Receipts in March alone spiralled to over 62,000 francs.

Offenbach's faith was vindicated. By way of celebration he organised one of his super parties. 'Annual General Meeting of Shareholders in the Company of M. & Mme. Jacques Offenbach,' announced the invitation. 'Head Office at 11 rue Laffitte. Guests whose memory is treacherous have only to think of the host's legs to remember the number.' His Excellency Marshal Offenbach was to present a Grand Revue of the past year. During the evening guests were allowed to address each other as 'Prince' for a fee of five francs. 'My Lord the Duke' cost four francs fifty, and the scale descended via 'General' and 'Dear Master'. 'Ducky' and 'Old Cock' were rated at fifteen centimes.

Orphée began to travel abroad. Soon it was being heard throughout Europe. Offenbach admitted that 'my Parisian's heart was very flattered' by the enthusiastic reception his opéra-bouffe had in Berlin. He travelled there with the company for the opening. It was a piquant situation. If he spoke French with a throaty German accent, he now found that his German had a distinct Gallic flavour.

'I shall bear an eternal grudge against my former compatriots for having lumbered me with such an accent,' he said. This was not the only complaint he made about the land of his birth. His feelings toward Cologne were mixed. He seemed to be torn between the natural pride of the townsman who has won success in a bigger world and dislike of the place where he had known poverty as a child. When his German publishers told him that Cologne was very eager to put on *Orphée*, he answered in a mixture of French and German. The alternation of languages betrayed his conflicting sentiments.

'You know I'm not mad keen on my native town,' he wrote. 'You also know why. For this reason I do not wish my operas, if possible, to be produced there; the inhabitants of Cologne have, for those of their fellow-countrymen who've achieved fame, *so wenig ubrig*, and it's best to leave them quietly drinking their beer ...'

In May 1859, *Orphée* reached its 150th performance at the Bouffes-Parisiens. On 5 June it ended its run for the time being. Orpheus had lost his Eurydice no less than 228 times. The production was taken off, not because people no longer wanted to see it but because the cast had arrived at a point of simple exhaustion. Offenbach kept the piece in reserve and was later to revive it in times of emergency. It was like money in the bank.

A few weeks later, when the Emperor's troops came back from their victory over the Austrians at Magenta, they marched to the tunes of *Orphée*. On 14 January 1860 an official decree granting Offenbach French naturalisation was published in the *Bulletin des Lois*. There had been a little trouble behind the scenes. The bureaucrat instructed by the Emperor to carry out this piece of business at first had the request turned down. A sharp and unambiguous direction from the Emperor's office rectified the mistake. And the worried musician at last was assured that 'M. Offenbach, Jacques, composer of music, director of the Théâtre des Bouffes-Parisiens, born on 20 June 1819, in Cologne (Prussia), living in Paris, is admitted to enjoyment of the rights of a French citizen in conformity with Article 2 of the Law of 3 December 1849.'

Louis-Napoléon, as if to underline this, ordered a command performance of *Orphée aux enfers* in April. It was given at the Théâtre des Italiens where the fight to obtain seats, once people had heard the Emperor planned to attend, reached desperate proportions. The box-office collected 22,000 francs. Even more delightful to Offenbach was the handsome bronze Louis-Napoléon sent him. On the base was inscribed: 'From the Emperor to Jacques Offenbach.' With it came a letter, 'I shall never forget', wrote the Imperial hand, 'the dazzling evening *Orphée aux enfers* enabled me to spend at the Théâtre des Italiens.'

13

A Butterfly and a Dog

Offenbach's daemon never rested, even when *Orphée* could have served as an excuse for a holiday. A one-acter, *Un Mari à la porte*, gave Lise Tautin, as a friend of the lady with a husband at the door, a chance to sing a waltz-song that kept the town humming for several months. Bache was not forgotten either, and in *Les Vivandières de la Grande Armée*, a very topical piece about the Italian campaign, he had a more or less serious part which tested the considerable abilities that lay beneath his comic mask.

The 1859 season was rounded off with *Geneviève de Brabant*. After satirising classical antiquity in *Orphée,* why not move on to mediaeval French history? So the old legend of Saint Geneviève, her suspicious husband and the villainous courtier Sifroy, was taken out, brushed up and sauced with jokes about the Crusades. The censor proved troublesome over fun poked at gendarmes. (*'Ah! qu'il est beau d'être gendarme!'*) They were a respectable body of men. But, the librettists replied, we weren't laughing at the gendarme. Yet you give them three-cornered hats to wear, riposted the censor. Yes, but they're hats of the time. Ah, one of your gendarmes calls another 'corporal': there were no corporals in the Middle Ages. Very well, we'll call him 'sergeant'. Respect for lawful institutions was preserved. If the authors of the piece at last managed to please the censor, they did not succeed so well with audiences. A delicate spinning song and the beauty of Lise Tautin failed to draw. One feels that Erik Satie's version of *Geneviève de Brabant*, a little operetta written some forty years later for a puppet theatre, shows more aptitude for generating naïf humour.

The search for variety led Offenbach once more onto the terrain of *Orphée.* Some of the latter's pastoral charm emerges again from a score he based on the old legend of Daphnis and Chloe, half a century before Ravel turned it into one of the most sumptuous pieces in the French orchestral repertory. Another novelty was the inauguration of classical concerts at the Bouffes, for which he knocked up *La Symphonie*.

Neither of these pieces created such a stir as the satire he directed at Wagner in *Le Carnaval des Revues*. The German musician was at the time living in Paris and had won notoriety as a composer of music that aroused intense argument. After many struggles and long delays, a performance of *Tannhäuser* at the Opéra was given to jeers and catcalls. The fiasco made him well known. 'God give me a failure like that!' murmured Gounod. On the other hand, Offenbach expressed many people's feeling when he wrote: 'To be learned and boring isn't art; it's better to be pungent and tuneful.'

Even before the passing failure of *Tannhäuser*, Wagner's humourless intensity and egocentric belief in his own propaganda had given him a reputation which, for a time, seemed to attract literary men in particular. Baudelaire was a fanatical admirer. The poet Théophile Gautier also fell into the net, and Offenbach cannot have been surprised to see that his adversary Jules Janin, who was incapable of distinguishing between boredom and profundity, figured largely in the train of Wagner.

Offenbach's little sketch, *Le Musicien de l'avenir*, came out in February 1860, during the carnival period. It had already appeared the previous year at the gala to mark the 150th performance of *Orphée*. Now it reached a wider public as part of *Le Carnaval des Revues*. The characters in the skit included Weber, Grétry, Gluck, Mozart and 'the Musician of the Future'. The last-named bustles on exclaiming: 'Here I am! Here I am! I'm the Composer of the Future and I trample on you all, you the Past, you the commonplace! I'm a Revolution in myself alone! No more notes, no more harmony; no more unison! no more scales! no more flats! no more sharps! no more naturals! no more forte! no more piano!'

'And no more music?' enquires Gluck.

The Composer of the Future plays a Wedding March of his own composition. Then, despite the protests of his eminent colleagues, he performs a 'Yodel of the Future'. They push him off while he shouts: 'Throw me out! Insult me! You won't make me any less the composer of the future!'

It is all very unsubtle stuff, which went down well with the noisy carnival crowd. Wagner never forgave Offenbach. His attitude changed from one of patronising good will into hatred. The years he spent in Paris were among the unhappiest of his life and he did not forget the snubs he endured there. The memory nourished his loathing of France and kept it green. He rejoiced at the humiliations the country experienced after 1870 and its defeat by German troops. In 1873 he wrote *A Capitulation* which enabled him to pay off old scores. Here he gave full expression to his rancour in a squib that fell even lower than *Le Musicien de l'avenir*. Victor Hugo was buried under a pile of childish invective and Offenbach was not forgotten either. With leaden Teutonic irony Wagner wrote:

> Crack! Crack! Crack, crack, crack!
> Oh magnificent Jack Offenbach!

In a calmer mood, though still obsessed by the excremental imagery that informs *A Capitulation*, he had remarked: 'Offenbach possesses a warmth that Auber lacks; but it's the warmth of the dunghill; all the pigs in Europe have wallowed there.'

After this exchange of compliments *Le Papillon* struck a sweeter note. The only full-length ballet Offenbach ever wrote, it came into being under very distinguished auspices. The choreographer was none other than Marie Taglioni, the great Romantic ballerina. Though now in retirement, she had been excited enough by the talent of a young dancer called Emma Livry to create a ballet especially for this bright new star. Moreover, *Le Papillon* was to be given at the Opéra, the shrine that Offenbach had longed to enter for many years. Perhaps now, he would be accepted as a 'respectable' composer?

The scenario is of a winning absurdity. Its high campery includes – and the reader is perfectly free to believe this or not – a wicked old fairy with a magic crutch. Pantomime is represented by a handsome Prince and a court of spirits furnished with golden harps. Yet the baroque involvements of the plot were forgotten in the beauty of Emma Livry's dancing as the butterfly of the title. One critic praised her soaring elevation and thought he could almost hear the quiver of wings on her shoulders. Another compared her to a feather, a snowflake.

Offenbach's music is buoyant and very danceable. It is alive, airy, headlong. It switches quickly from nonchalance to unexpect-

edly warm emotion. The '*valse des rayons*', which accompanies
the swarm of butterflies in Act I, survived to have an existence
independent of the ballet itself. Offenbach was to use it again in
other work. It would have been a pity to waste such an
exhilarating number. More strangely still, in 1908 it gained a
new lease of life in a revue at the Moulin Rouge. Re-named 'The
Apach's Dance' [*sic*] it became a *valse chaloupée*, a waltz
performed in a series of swooping dives by two performers who
later became famous. The one who devised it was Max Dearly.
His voice, which recalled the sound of a not very efficient gravel-
crushing machine, and his face, which resembled a flat-iron,
adorned many French films of the nineteen-thirties. The
partner who glided sinuously over the stage with him was
Mistinguett, she of the popping eyes, large teeth and admired
legs. The career which led her eventually to be classified as a
national monument had just begun.

Despite the apparent success of *Le Papillon* – it achieved
forty-two performances and made the name of Emma Livry – an
air of melancholy surrounds it. The young ballerina started,
with the help of Taglioni, to prepare for her next production.
She happened one day to be dancing at the Opéra. Her wispy
skirt fluttered dangerously near a gaslight and immediately she
was dwarfed in huge flames. The firemen threw a soaking
blanket over her. The Goncourts, with their appetite for the
macabre detail, recorded that underneath the blanket Livry
struggled to her knees and prayed. She lingered on for more than
eight months until death released her from the agony of her
terrible burns.

The ballet in which she danced her way to an ephemeral glory
also signalled the end of the Romantic era that began with
Taglioni. It was never revived and Offenbach never wrote
another one. The reasons were a mixture of circumstance and
personal disappointment. Although critics spoke favourably of
his music, there were others who thought it disgraceful that a
composer of opéra-bouffe should be allowed inside an institution
which belonged more properly to the grand operas of Meyerbeer
and Halévy. Now Offenbach was the professional of professionals
and he had long since learned to put up with adverse criticism; a
satirist himself, he knew how to accept the barbs which he
despatched so light-heartedly against others. Yet there were

times when the sting of a malevolent enemy went deep. He was hurt by the contempt that *Le Papillon* evoked in certain quarters and even more wounded by the furore that greeted *Barkouf*, his next operetta.

This opened on Christmas Eve 1860 at the Opéra-Comique, at whose door the young Offenbach had long knocked in vain. The plot, contrived by the prolific Eugène Scribe and his inevitable assistant, features a dog which, because of its magic powers, is sent by the Grand Mogul to keep the seditious people of Lahore in order. Whenever trouble threatens, the dog has only to bark for the rioters to disperse in terror. So as not to profane the stage of the Opéra-Comique with the actual presence of a dog, Barkouf growled his part from the wings.

Reactions were unanimous. *Barkouf*, said a prominent critic, was 'wretched, shameful for those who collaborated on it and unworthy of being performed in front of a public which has the right to be respected.' Berlioz, who wrote for the *Journal des Débats*, had every reason to dislike it.[1] As an impassioned admirer of Gluck he could never forgive the disrespect shown his idol in *Orphée*. The popular theatre he regarded, in any case, as indistinguishable from houses of ill-fame, and he saw Offenbach as the high priest of a barbarous revel peddling stupidities, empty blare and naked flesh for sale. The chaste muse could not set foot there without a shiver. (Though Berlioz would not have disdained a theatre ready to perform his own ambitious operas.) At meetings of the Institut, where he attended as a member of the Academie des Beaux-Arts, he scribbled on his writing-pad: '*Barkouf = Merde*'. And he wrote the impolite word in Greek letters.

In his review, however, he was more careful. He knew that Offenbach had important protectors like the duc de Morny, who had ignored his own *Les Troyens*, and that he should try not to make more enemies than he already had. So he watered down his views a little. *Barkouf*, he remarked, belonged to the type of thing popular in 'those theatres I cannot name'. But why present it at the Opéra-Comique? Its defenders would say it was intended to amuse. 'Thank you! You drop razor blades in my

---

[1] Though in the early eighteen-fifties, when Offenbach was still at the Comédie-Française, Berlioz had given him a friendly letter of introduction to the critic Jules Janin, also destined to be an adversary.

coat pocket at the moment when I put my hand in it; you offer me a seat and whisk it away when I'm about to sit down . . . You cut the stuffing out of my mattress, you squirt ink at me through the key-hole of my door, and then you come to me and say: "It's a laugh! It's funny! Ah, what a good joke . . . " I'd prefer to live with an undertaker's mute.'

Offenbach defended himself in *Figaro*. There were people, he said, who did not like his music. That was their right. There were others who thought it sacrilege for him to leave the Bouffes-Parisiens and dare to write for the Opéra and the Opéra-Comique. 'The crusade began with *Le Papillon*, and I do not think that any ballet music has ever had the honour of being listened to with so much curiosity and so great a desire to find it bad. I can foresee a similar storm over *Barkouf* and you can guess so well what people are going to say that I ask your permission to reply in advance . . .'

He pointed out, rightly, that the article had been labelled 'Opéra-bouffe' and not 'opéra-comique'; that the theatre had lost the secret of laughter and strayed into a hybrid genre described as 'imitation' grand opera; that while he did not defend his own music he would certainly stand up for the genre to which it belonged; and that it was being unfairly judged by the wrong standards. All of which was quite justified. Unfortunately his case in this instance rested on frail support. There is no doubt that *Barkouf* was one of his most inferior scores. The drama's laws which, in Johnson's phrase, the drama's patrons give, conceded this maligned piece a derisory run of seven performances.

Yet so resilient were Offenbach's powers that the operetta with which he followed it presented an amazing contrast by its finesse. Even while *Barkouf* wallowed at the Opéra-Comique he was deep in the score of *La Chanson de Fortunio*. It took him a week to write and a week to produce. A fortnight after *Barkouf* started its short life the romance of Maître Fortunio had such a delighted reception at the Bouffes that it was encored in full the same evening and would have been played a third time but for police regulations governing the closure of theatres at night.

The piece was based on Musset's comedy *Le Chandelier*, for which, so long ago, Offenbach had written a song on its production at the Comédie-Française. The incident was a part of his youth and he had always had an affection for the play. Crémieux and Halévy wrote a libretto which presented a Fortunio grown old, an elderly lawyer who has forgotten the song he used to sing, that little melody which no woman, it was said, could ever resist. But it is rediscovered one day and its romantic power is found to be as strong as ever.

La Chanson de Fortunio helped its composer to put the humiliation of *Barkouf* behind him. Themes from it were made into a popular quadrille by Strauss. There was a Fortunio Polka and a Fortunio Waltz. Many arrangements for drawing-room pianos, as duet or solo, testified to the success of what Offenbach described as an 'Opéra-comique'. He was determined that it should not be confused with his more broad-grained operettas.

The song of the title has a flowing tune with a sweet chromatic fall. Oboe and clarinet add soft touches of colour in the unobtrusive accompaniment. A contrast is provided by the vigorous drinking song and a waltz that Fortunio's clerks roar out with youthful vim. They declare, outrageous in their masculine pride, that 'All women belong to us.'

Three weeks later Offenbach collaborated with Delibes and several other composers on a New Year carnival farce, *Les Musiciens de l'orchestre*, in which the actors, posted throughout the auditorium and up in the gallery, exchanged quips. His next work, *Le Pont des soupirs*, although more conventional in that all the action passed on the stage, had just as much the air of a carnival. The Doge Cornarino Cornarini disguises himself as a beggar to investigate the activities of his wife, who, he suspects, is on the point of yielding her virtue to Malatromba. An opening chorus praises the beauty of Venice: in the evening it sparkles, by day it smiles, at night it sings. A barcarolle starts on its lilting way. 'In beautiful Venice what do we seek?' enquires Cornarino. And, instantly pricking the bubble of romance which has been created, his servant answers: 'A wife who's faithful to her husband.'

Le Pont des soupirs has nothing to do with the melancholy Bridge of Sighs whence it borrows the title. A guitar serenade and a 'complainte', delivered at rollicking high speed by Cornarini, are among the novelties which brought applause for Lise Tautin and Bache in the main rôles. At one point, in the lively chorus '*Vive Malatromba!*' Offenbach coolly inserts a famous theme from Auber's *Masaniello*.

Halévy and Crémieux were the librettists of *Le Pont des soupirs*. As soon as it went into production Offenbach was harrying them for more. 'Good Lord,' he wrote to Halévy, 'what a dreary life I lead without work to do. And it's your fault, both of you. When shall I have the libretto? . . . And my piece for the Opéra-Comique? My friendly curse to Hector and to you. Yours never again, J.O.'

While Offenbach fumed at his collaborators, Herminie went out to a rare first night with the wife of one of them and was glimpsed by the Goncourt brothers at an Alexandre Dumas play. 'A sympathetic face,' they wrote of Herminie, 'witty, inclining to plumpness; enormous ear-rings that stuck out beneath her hat. Beside her, Madame Hector Crémieux, with her face like an Oriental slave, her fixed attitude, her snake-like eyes . . .'

On 15 August 1861, the Emperor's Birthday Honours List included Offenbach among recipients of the *Légion d'honneur*. Officially, now, his Frenchness was unassailable. He joined with Guy de Maupassant and the fashionable novelist Alphonse Karr in revealing to other Frenchmen the neglected charms of Étretat, a little fishing village on the Norman coast. Here he established his seaside house. Though he rather spoiled the effect by ever mispronouncing the name as 'Étertat'.

14

The Alcazar beside the Sea

At the gare Saint-Lazare he would be decanted painfully from his brougham and helped into a reserved compartment. There he was propped up with cushions, his gouty legs wrapped in furs. By the time the train passed through Rouen he had recovered enough to look out of the window and sniff the air. His spirits rose even higher at Beuzeville and he was able to change trains with something like alacrity. Cushions and furs became increasingly neglected. At the end of the line, the aches of Paris forgotten, he jumped lightly into a rattle-trap vehicle for the ten-mile journey to the 'Villa Orphée' at Étretat.

Here he found, he said, 'a balm for my ailments.' Built with the aid of royalties from *Orphée aux enfers*, the sprawl of verandahs, wooden balconies and tall chimney-pots was Offenbach's joy. It stood on the side of a hill before a garden where he played hide-and-seek with the children and where, one evening, he conjured from his 'cello for the first time that tender aria in which the Grand Duchess of Gérolstein reveals her love.

For a week servants had been preparing against the owner's arrival. Once there he made a quick tour of the garden, inspected the gates that bore his monogram J.O., looked over the house, played a few bars on the piano – it had been a gift from his publisher Heugel to mark the success of *Orphée*—and went gratefully to bed where he could sleep off the fatigues of the journey from Paris. Each of the bedrooms in the house was to be named after one of his operettas. In time he could boast that he slept (if this may be said without impropriety) in *La Belle Hélène*.

Next morning, at the house perched high up on the towering cliffs above Étretat, the host marshalled his family and guests for the ritual trip to the beach. The walk down took not much more than ten minutes. But the return journey was uphill and exhausting. So Offenbach had a special charabanc designed on the model of the Empress Eugénie's own conveyance which she used when the Court went rustic. Offenbach's coachman,

Mathurin, filled the driver's seat. Next to him, with a favourite dog at his feet, sat the composer. The girls each took their appointed place under the eye of Herminie and were joined by whatever friends happened to be staying. They all set off like the gods in the omnibus from *Orphée*. The vehicle rolled through Étretat accompanied by tinkling bells and the crack of Mathurin's whip.

Once on the beach the company divided into loungers and bathers. Some preferred to sit and read the newspapers and gossip. Others plunged into the sea. Offenbach, nursing his gout and his rheumatism, stayed on the pebbly shore. He had only been known to brave the Channel when, on a still, moonlit evening, he sat in a fishing boat and, as it glided beneath the stars, improvised at the 'cello.

He would sometimes arrange good humoured practical jokes. With Delibes he wrote a cantata for unaccompanied voices to greet his friend Villemessant when the latter emerged to take a dip. The journalist was large and corpulent, his attributes ludicrously emphasised by the bathing costume. As he advanced ponderously over the beach, the choir struck up in solemn tones:

'Il est si gros, il est si gras, il est si frais, il est si rond
Qu'il fait craquer son pantalon...'

Other guests were likewise saluted with good-humoured aubades, and each year new verses, new bars were added to the established musical honours.

After an hour or so Offenbach gave the signal to depart. It was time to gossip on the Casino terrace. At about half-past eleven Mathurin arrived with the charabanc to drive back to the Villa Orphée. There were always more passengers for the return journey than there had been on the outward trip. Distant acquaintances and those not even known to Offenbach at all squeezed in, hoping that if they condensed their persons their presence would not be noticed.

Lunch and dinner were stage-managed with all the care Offenbach gave to his stage productions. A first stroke of the bell announced that the meal was ready. At the second ring everyone was expected to make for the dining room. Those who were late received frowns of displeasure. One of Offenbach's nephews sinned repeatedly. He would arrive, dishevelled and dirty, long after the bell had sounded. The reasons he gave for his unpunctuality were elaborate and showed a gift of invention that was later to make him a successful playwright. Offenbach would listen in silence, curious perhaps to hear what flights of fantasy the young man achieved next. One day the host himself was late and the second stroke of the bell was heard in his absence. A message arrived that lunch should begin. Suddenly, at the omelette stage, the doors swung open and Offenbach appeared, magnificent in dazzling starched shirt, full evening dress, white tied, white gloved. Gravely, in silence, he took his place at table, convinced that he had given his nephew a lesson in etiquette.

All around the Villa Orphée were holiday homes owned by Parisian celebrities. Many of them were actresses and opera singers whom Offenbach knew well – sometimes very well. When his mood was low and there were no guests for him to organise at home, Herminie would write to a neighbour: 'Come quickly, please . . . he's unbearable. You're the only one who can calm him . . .' Or Offenbach himself would plead with one of the few women who knew how to handle him in his moments of depression: 'Thérèse, I love you. You're a *bitch*. All the same, come and play a hand of bezique with your old friend.'

Though bezique was his favourite, all card games were allowed except for patience. Offenbach loathed it and considered it to be an anti-social offence. Once when he found his sister-in-law indulging in patience, and what is more, occupying his favourite place at the card table, he was furious. He stormed. He threatened. She grinned and held fast to the cards he tried to snatch away. Only desperate measures, he could see, had a chance of success. He lowered his trousers and, like an insolent little boy, flipped out on to the table the thinnest portion of his thin anatomy. His sister replied with the only possible answer to such naughtiness: a vigorous fusillade on the bottom that had at the same time become exposed to attack.

He was a tyrant who demanded a constant background of people, laughter, excitement. His invitations had the air of a summons, a command, mixed with puns and light cajolery. Ludovic Halévy's mother he addressed as 'Marquise'. 'If everything can be arranged,' he wrote to her after a chain of word play that defies translation, 'we have the honour of asking you to be kind enough to come for a pretty little ride with Madame Offenbach and her lady-in-waiting at about two forty-five (or a quarter to three, or nearly three, or an hour to four) in my magnificent brake, braique, brayk, braic. I have the honour to accept only a unanimous yes. I throw myself at your feet, dear Marquise, but not at the feet of others.'

These trips in the 'brake' with Mathurin at the reins usually meant a call on 'la belle Ernestine', the handsome and popular hostess of a tavern where artists, writers and musicians gathered regularly. They not only drank her wines. They confided in her as well and took her advice. She kept a visitors' book which her famous patrons inscribed with their autographs. When Offenbach wrote in it he added an ingenious rhyme:

> *A vos yeux, belle Ernestine,*
> *Je devine*
> *Que vous voulez un autographe:*
> *Le voilà . . . phe . . .*

Days at the Villa Orphée melted into a whirl of charades, pleasure jaunts and amateur theatricals. On summer nights there were entertainments devised by Offenbach with the aid of artist friends like Doré and Detaille. They were presented, with music and elaborate costumes, in what the leader of the revels called the 'Alcazar d'Étretat', a name inspired by the Alcazar d'été, a famous café-concert in the Champs-Elysées. Posters were designed, arresting, colourful, to spread the news. One such announced that the 'actors in ordinary to Madame Offenbach' would be giving the first performance of a 'grand opera, revue and fairy pantomime in one act, two tableaux and a prologue mixed with dances, stage effects, surprises and transformations.' The sting came later: the authors were described as 'a group of Academicians' . . . and the music as being written 'by Richard Wagner'.

Other posters advertised a parody of Rossini's *Guillaume Tell* with J. Offenbach playing the father of the hero's fellow conspirator. Since the Shah of Persia was at that moment on a State Visit to France, he too figured in the cast.

Sometimes Offenbach would arrange the first performance of one of his own operettas before introducing it at the Bouffes. But more often, the programmes at the 'Alcazar d'Étretat' were intended only for home consumption, containing jokes about the family and about the friends who came to stay or who had their own villas nearby: Dumas father and son, Halévy, Delibes and Bizet, Nadar, the singer Faure, Detaille and Doré. Anything served as an excuse – a birthday, a departure, an arrival, a family event. They set up the stage in the billiard saloon which was cut off from the main drawing-room by sliding doors. These latter served as curtains. The artists designed and painted the scenery. It was the rehearsals everyone enjoyed most. Although Offenbach frequently swore he would have nothing to do with these escapades, inevitably he ended up by taking charge and shouldering responsibility for the production. There were times when, forgetting that he had amateurs to deal with, he became as irritable and demanding as when he rehearsed professionals at the Bouffes.

Occasionally they gave performances in aid of charity. At one of these a difference of opinion arose between the town council and the benevolent amateurs of the Villa d'Orphée. It was finally resolved, but, exasperated by the pettifogging attitude of the town hall bureaucrats, Offenbach and his friends decorated the walls of Étretat with a poster that read as follows:

Grande Symphonie
de la
MER DE
Jacques Offenbach
POUR
les malades
avec la permission de
L'AUTORITÉ

If the words in capitals alone are read they are seen to spell out an extremely rude message to 'authority' in the shape of the town council.

Until Offenbach's death some twenty years later, Étretat remained a place of happiness, a welcome retreat from the hectic life of Paris. And if the existence he led there seemed only a fraction less animated, it was because his eternally vivacious character found relaxation only in a change of excitement. Where other people might need rest in peace and quiet,

Offenbach needed it in the form of different activity, however intensive this might be.

Today he is remembered in 'Étertat', as he always called it, by a street named after him. It runs in the direction of Fécamp, parallel to the one that commemorates Guy de Maupassant. The rue Alphonse Karr and the rue Isabey recall others who helped to put Étretat on the map during the nineteenth century. It was, however, no simple matter to persuade the council, that council with whom the master of the Villa Orphée had already crossed swords in the matter of the charity performance, that Offenbach deserved his street. A son-in-law of his, who for eighteen years was mayor of the place and who himself is remembered by the rue P. Brindejont, met with resistance when he proposed a change of name for the street that passes by the Villa Orphée. Offenbach? The worthy councillors frowned. Was he not, they claimed sternly but with an uncertain grasp of history, the personification of the Empire, a notorious Bonapartist? How could they, who were true and faithful Republicans, agree to such an idea?

Patiently, the mayor accepted their decision. Then he returned to the attack. Suppose they called the street after the composer's wife Herminie? Again they shook their heads. After more discussion they at last agreed. New plaques were fitted bearing the legend 'rue H. Offenbach'. Tourists paused and stared in wonderment at the glistening enamel. Presumably the Norman spelling of the musician's name was 'Hoffenbach'? Many years were to pass before a later council redressed the balance and gave the thoroughfare its title of rue J. Offenbach.

15

Adventures

In the Autumn of 1861 a carriage often parked outside the stage door of the Théâtre des Bouffes-Parisiens. The panel shone with a lustrous coat of arms. The attendants wore splendid livery. The equipage belonged to the duc de Morny who was finally, with Offenbach's aid, on the point of realizing his ambition to become a dramatic author.

A year or so previously Morny had asked Offenbach to find him a libretto. The composer, without mentioning the source of the request, prevailed upon Halévy to fulfil it. Halévy's father lent a hand and the result was *Un mari sans le savoir*. Offenbach provided music and rehearsals began immediately. Then Morny spoke to Offenbach again. He wanted the piece to be produced at one of his grand receptions, but it was not long enough to provide an evening's traffic of the stage. An idea for another *bouffonnerie* had just struck him and he wanted someone to develop it.

Offenbach and Halévy went to see him at his office on the quai d'Orsay. Morny looked out at them from behind his massive desk. Embarrassment hung in the air. For Halévy, the civil servant, this was his first encounter with Morny, and but for his activity in the theatre the meeting would probably not have taken place. 'Your Excellency . . .,' said he to the second most powerful man in France. There was another pause.

If the truth were known, Morny felt just as ill at ease as his two callers. The politician who could stage a *coup d'état*, make fortunes on the stock exchange and shape the government of France, became as nervous as a young girl where his theatrical ambitions were concerned.

He put his hand on a drawer. Timidly, he said: 'I wanted to see you. It's about a manuscript I have here.'

Out came the bundle of paper at last. Morny recounted his plot. A newly-rich businessman, a Monsieur Choufleuri, is anxious to rise in society. He plans a magnificent *soirée* at which three famous Italian opera stars will sing. Invitations go out to all the best people. At the last minute the singers fail to appear. Monsieur Choufleuri is in despair. His daughter comes to the rescue. Why not replace the missing trio with herself, her father . . . and the impoverished young composer whom she loves? Monsieur Choufleuri agrees. The evening is a complete success and the daughter receives her reward: a dowry and her father's permission to marry.

Composer and librettist genuinely liked the idea. It gave excellent scope for satire of Italian grand opera. The collaborators soon finished *Monsieur Choufleuri restera chez lui.*

This dabbling in operetta by a major government figure has sometimes been quoted as evidence of the régime's frivolity. It does not seem, however, any more reprehensible than the usual pursuit of fornication and wealth followed by men who have attained power. And many 20th century politicians have made fools of themselves for greater vanity.

Monsieur Choufleuri restera chez lui gratified Morny's hopes and at the same time aided the career of 'cher Ludo'. While ambassadors and ministers cooled their heels in the waiting room, Halévy was trying out verses at the piano with Morny. A few months later the ministry to which Halévy belonged was suppressed and he asked Morny for help. The posts offered him by way of replacement were unattractive, so why should he not, he suggested, become Morny's secretary? Morny agreed. Halévy, from then on, had a place at the very centre of things, a position he owed chiefly to Offenbach. In later years he tended to forget this.

Anxious, on edge like any tyro dramatist, Morny watched over the preparations for his operetta. It was given one brilliant evening at the presidential palace itself. Everyone knew that the 'M. de Saint-Rémy' whose name appeared on the programme was none other than Morny himself. Before the curtain rose he checked, with nervous care, all the props and accessories. One of the characters needed a snuff box for some essential 'business'. 'That's not at all the sort of thing a well-off Parisian would have,' said Morny when he saw the object. 'This is what you want.' He handed over a gold snuff box inlaid with precious stones and engraved with the actor's own initials.

The comedian Bache added to the gaiety of the occasion. He

grumbled comically about the makeshift dressing-room allotted him. With licensed daring he grasped Morny's lapel and croaked: 'And you'd do well, old boy, to lash out with a few biscuits and a good bottle of wine, the best, mind you, as if it were for yourself.'

Later the piece did well in a double bill at what the Goncourt brothers called 'that big little theatre, the *Figaro* of theatres, the Bouffes.' They did not like Hector Crémieux, who also lent a hand with *Monsieur Choufleuri*, and described him as one who 'rises and rises, makes money with plays he doesn't write, a mountebank combined with a Jewish clown, a buffoon who jobs in manufactured verse.' They abominated the circle that went 'from Halévy to that Crémieux, from Crémieux to Villemessant, from Villemessant to Offenbach, chevalier in the *Légion d'honneur* – engaged in shady deals, selling a bit of everything, their wives to a certain extent included . . . and to Morny, Offenbach's patron, the amateur musician, the prototype man of the Empire, immersed and rotted in every sort of Parisian corruptness . . .'

Yet however much the Goncourts raged, Morny's little piece flourished on the curiosity of theatregoers intrigued to view the handiwork of 'M. de Saint-Rémy'. A month later it was joined in the repertory by *Apothicaire et perruquier*. The music, written by another composer, had been submitted to Offenbach some time before. He promptly lost it. Assailed with complaints and threats of legal action by the disappointed musician, he wrote a new score. This is a deft eighteenth-century pastiche about a heroine who in the end marries the wig-maker she loves rather than the apothecary her father has chosen for her. In her big number, 'Une fillette ingénue', there is a theme which resembles the minuet in Massenet's later *Manon*. Or would it be truer to say that both composers unwittingly used the same traditional sources?

Much less true to period was the chaconne he wrote for *Monsieur et Madame Denis*. 'Chacun sa chaconne' is the playful cue that leads in to this sprightly dance number which resembles not at all the dignified measure Bach knew or even the versions Lully and Rameau composed. The operetta also includes a marching chorus of some harmonic ingenuity for the soldiers of the night-watch and a luscious waltz theme, one of the most attractive Offenbach ever wrote, although for some reason he did not bother to develop it. None of these bon-bons much took the fancy of audiences, although *Monsieur et Madame Denis* fared a little better than its immediate predecessor *Le Roman comique*, an adaptation of Scarron's novel which fell still-born from the composer's pen. It concerned the adventures, still amusing to read today, of a seventeenth-century travelling actors' company. (Scarron was a cripple whose flow of wit and good humour went uncurbed by physical suffering. His widow later became governess to the children of Louis XIV, took the name of Madame de Maintenon, and married the King in secret.)

These half-successes, or half-failures – an optimist would say the theatre was half full, a pessimist that it was half empty – persuaded Offenbach to give up management for the time being. He could no longer even pay his singers and orchestra, nor was it often, these days, that rheumatic pain left him alone, and this, combined with financial worry, hastened the decision.

On 26 January 1862, three weeks or so after the first night of *Monsieur et Madame Denis*, he wrote to the duc de Morny: 'Urgent reasons of health alone force me to give up my duties, in the exercise of which I have always received from your Excellency such benevolent attention.' His liabilities, according to an estimate made by the comedian Bache, amounted to over two thousand francs. He was succeeded as impresario at the Bouffes-Parisiens by Pierre Varney, who had until then been conductor of the orchestra. Varney has his place in history as composer of a patriotic song, words by Rouget de Lisle who also wrote the *Marseillaise*, which figured in the 1848 revolution. His son, Louis Varney, wrote many operettas which outshone his father's stage works. And the elder Varney was soon to find that the optimism with which he took over the Bouffes had little justification. The year developed badly. That summer in Étretat the family was sitting in the drawing-room after dinner when the children's German governess appeared at the door.

'Matame,' she grated, 'there's a fire . . .'

Everyone laughed. They thought it another joke by Offenbach. Stolidly, the governess repeated her message. Clouds of smoke began to sweep through the door. Everyone jumped up in alarm. Somebody had left a candle burning in a cupboard. Clothes caught fire and the blaze swiftly spread. Madame Offenbach rushed to save the children. Her husband thought of his piano. It must not burn! So many memories clung to this modest piece of furniture, the gift of his publisher on the occasion of *Orphée*, the keyboard where he had tried out so many of his tunes, the instrument at which he accompanied the 'Alcazar d'Étretat' revues and the riotous farandoles when guests danced madly through the house and out into the garden . . .

While flames billowed near at hand the piano was hoisted up and balanced on a window-sill. For a moment it quavered. Then it fell, with an unmelodious crash, onto the lawn below. The pedals snapped. Strings twanged in alarm and keys spattered all round. Water from hoses drenched the case. It never played again, but Offenbach kept it, out of affection, and stored the battered remains in a cellar.

That night he watched in tears as the Villa Orphée sparked and flamed. He determined to rebuild it. At the time he was working with his librettist Jules Moinaux on a new revue entitled *Le Voyage de Messieurs Dunanan père et fils*. Moinaux received a telegram: 'Orphée burned. Dunanan saved. Both well.' Depression gave way to buoyancy. Though it took him several years, he succeeded eventually in restoring the Villa Orphée. As late as 1864, when negotiating a sale of music to publishers, he accepted cash on extended terms. 'It's all the same to me,' he said, 'as I still have instalments to pay on my villa.'

Later on in that same year compensation arrived for all his disappointments so far. The birth of a son transported him with delight. After four daughters he had ceased to hope for such luck. Letters flew out to all his friends: 'I want to be the first to tell you that I have a wonderful son. Congratulate me . . .' Nothing was too good for this new idol. The duc de Morny himself agreed to act as godfather. It was he who held the child at the font. Alas, the honour had to be paid for. Among the baptismal names the baby received was Morny's own: Auguste. It was a name the boy grew to loathe, and as soon as possible after his father's death he dropped it and preferred to be known as Jacques.

Offenbach doted on his son, the child who was to perpetuate his name. What was more, Auguste-Jacques gave early promise of musical talent. His favourites among visitors to the house were Delibes and Bizet. On Sundays in the church of Étretat, that inviting blend of Gothic and Roman, he played the organ at mass, one of his greatest pleasures. The music he performed always emerged at a decently reverent pace, but it was not impossible to detect, at the elevation of the Host for example, an echo from one of his father's quadrilles or the theme, appropriately solemnised, of the bacchanale in *Orphée*.

Although pleased by these musical gifts Offenbach hoped that his son would not become a professional. He disliked the thought of his own child undergoing the bitter struggles he had experienced himself, but in the meantime he tactfully avoided repressing August's ambition. The happy father envisaged an important career for him and took pains to see that he received the best education. His love for the boy had no limit.

That year of 1862, which had seen Offenbach's temporary withdrawal from theatre management and the birth of his son, ended with a new production called *Jacqueline* which flopped. He shrugged his shoulders and went to Ems. For some time now that agreeable spa had been one of his favourite places. Each year it was his habit to spend a month or so there taking the waters and nursing his rheumatism.

Usually, too, since he could never stop working, he would write and produce an operetta during his stay in Ems. This time it was *Les Bavards*. 'I must confess that I have a very special liking for Ems,' he wrote. 'I derive health and inspiration from it at the same time. It was in Ems that I wrote part of *Orphée*, a little of *Fortunio* and a great deal of *Les Bavards*: you can see I have reasons for being fond of this charming place. I also enjoy Ems because of the simplicity that still reigns there. Ems is to Baden-Baden and Wiesbaden a little of what Étretat is to Trouville, Dieppe and Cabourg . . .'

Les Bavards was so successful at Ems that Offenbach expanded it into a two-act version for Paris. The gossips of the title are the hero Roland, a debtor-haunted poet of Segovia, and Béatrix, mother of the girl he wants to marry, whose chattering drives her husband mad. Roland, to the husband's delight, vanquishes Béatrix in a gossiping match – and as a reward for his achievement is granted the daughter's hand. The libretto, based on an old Cervantes play, came from Charles Nuitter. The pseudonym was an anagram of his real name Truinet. He had been a lawyer who gradually drifted into the theatre and provided libretti for Offenbach, Lalo and Lecocq. As well, he devised ballet scenarios for Delibes. Later he was archivist at the Paris Opéra and organised the rich collections there, often adding to them at his own expense. His influence still hovers in the Opéra library, which must be the most elegant and urbane of all research centres in Paris.

Once launched on its Paris career, *Les Bavards* soon found other worlds to conquer. It travelled throughout Europe, went to England, and even penetrated Russia and the USA. The success of the operetta endeared Ems to Offenbach even more. It was there that he had conceived most of it, and there that he introduced it. He loved the bright atmosphere, the smart uniforms of the princes and noblemen who followed Prussian King William's example and filled the hotels, the dashing equipages of rich holiday-makers, the fashionable dresses of the women and the company of Parisian celebrities who added their own touch of brilliance to the resort. The manager of the Kursaal was also a Parisian, an impresario with the entrancing name of Briguibouille who, in Offenbach's phrase, 'holds the sceptre of pleasures. Balls, concerts, entertainments, there's everything here ...' It was no surprise that Monsieur Briguibouille should welcome Offenbach as guest composer to his theatre.

With Herminie and the children safely installed in Étretat Offenbach was free to enjoy himself. Besides the pleasures already listed there were others equally enjoyable. He could never resist the gaming tables in the casino and roulette was his delight, swallowing many of the royalties he drew from his music. 'I have two – no, three – passions,' he once confided to an acquaintance. 'Cigars, women, and gambling as well.' And as he spoke the word 'women' his eyes rolled expressively.

One evening among convivial friends there was talk of the speed at which Offenbach worked. Someone bet that he could not write, orchestrate and produce an operetta in a week. Instantly he accepted the challenge. The result was *Lieschen et Fritzchen* which he duly put on at Ems within the given period.

Like the Auvergnat accent, that of the native of Alsace has a comic ring to the sophisticated Parisian ear. This 'Alsatian conversation' in one act features a hero and a heroine who speak

with the Teutonic burr. He, a servant, has been dismissed.
Asked by his master to fetch a *pierre*, a jewel, and place it before
a lady as a surprise at dinner, he had brought in a *biére*, a beer.
The heroine, a seller of brushes, can find no buyers for her
wares. Affliction draws them close together. She sings a 'Fable'
based on the La Fontaine story of the town rat and the country
rat. The two innocents fall in love. The act ends with a repeat of
an earlier duet in which, mixing German with French, they
decide to marry.

This duet, soon to become deservedly popular, had the catchy
refrain:

> '*Je suis alsacienne, Je suis alsacien,*
> *Quand une alsacienne, Trouve un alsacien,*
> *La main dans la sienne, Chantant leur lien,*
> *Top! dit l'alsacienne, Top! dit l'alsacien.*'

It is set to a winning tune. However, Offenbach did cheat a little
to win his bet. The melody is exactly the same, and in the same
key, as a song in *Les Bavards* of a few months previously. In all
the excitement no one seems to have noticed this and Offenbach
would scarcely have drawn attention to the self-plagiarism. Or
perhaps he honestly did not realise it, because he wrote so much
and so fast that it would have been easy to do such a thing.

The rôle of Lischen was played in Ems and Paris by Zulma
Bouffar. Offenbach had seen her one night at the theatre in Bad
Homburg. Struck by her unusual charm he went backstage and
congratulated her. She was not, contemporaries report, beautiful.
Her nose was small and awkwardly shaped, while her face
looked rather flattened and the curves of her figure were a little
too pronounced; the lips were over-full and the chin turned up
saucily. Yet she had talent and a fresh quality of voice. Her
gestures were delightful and she knew how to please an
audience. Although she came from the south of France she had
fair hair and uncommonly blue eyes. Offenbach found her
irresistible.

As they talked in her dressing room she told him her story.
She had spent her life on tour with her father who was a strolling
musician, and who taught her singing. When she was twelve she
was engaged by a German troupe and taken to Cologne.
Cologne! Offenbach started. He heard how she had even

appeared at one of the restaurants where he himself had performed as a child prodigy. She had sung rather naughty songs there in French while her father, at a nearby table, led the applause. Afterwards when she went round to make a collection the plate soon filled up.

Offenbach's own days in Cologne came back to his memory. He thought of his father, of his early poverty, of Zimmer and that mysterious waltz. However melancholy the scenes of childhood, however unhappy they may have been, an adult cannot help revisiting them in the mind, with a blend of nostalgia and, at the same time, relief that they are over. He contemplates them with the morbid fascination of an ex-prisoner looking at the gaol from which he has been released. Zulma's reminiscences evoked a curious feeling.

After Cologne she had toured other parts of Europe. Her father died and she played a long engagement in Brussels. Then she came to Bad Homburg where Offenbach discovered her at twenty years old. He was on holiday and ready for adventure.

He admired her talent and the way she dominated a stage with her quick personality and she was somehow different from his other conquests. The link with Cologne gave a special flavour to their relationship, and although there were many actresses far prettier than Zulma, none could rival, at the moment, her unique combination of sexuality and sentiment. He was perhaps her first lover.

The affair lasted some time, probably a dozen years or more, which was an unusually long period for Offenbach. Zulma Bouffar established herself as a star in Paris where her odd name – the first hinting of Oriental mystery, the second with its incongruous echo of the slang verb *bouffer*, to guzzle – intrigued the public. A few years later she was on tour in Prague with the composer. Herminie, obviously, did not know, and he was anxious to keep her in ignorance. He wrote confidentially to his librettist Nuitter asking him if he would arrange with a friendly editor to insert a news item in his paper. It was to report that several artistes from the Bouffes-Parisiens, among them Mademoiselle Z. Bouffar, were performing in Nantes. The newspaper in question, Offenbach added, 'is read in my home and those few words will come at absolutely the right moment. I ask for the greatest discretion from you and our friend de Pêne [the editor].'

As late as 1875 Jacques and his Zulma were together. In that year they stayed at Aix-les-Bains. Of course there were other distractions in Offenbach's life during this extended liaison, but none of them seem to have had the staying power of Zulma's attractions with the associated memory of Cologne. She appeared in many of Offenbach's later productions, but her star began to wane as the years passed. An attempt to retrieve her lost fortunes in theatrical management failed and she ended her days in a home for old actors and actresses.

From Ems in the summer of 1863 Offenbach went on to Vienna where he met Johann Strauss, the composer of a *Morgenblätter* waltz written as a friendly answer to the *Abendblätter* which Offenbach had recently composed for a carnival ball. 'You ought,' said Offenbach helpfully, 'to write operettas. You could do it.' Did he, years later when his own operettas were being shouldered aside, ever remember and regret this friendly remark?

Vienna made much of him. The director of the Opera House attended with a flattering commission and once again the will o' the wisp of grand opera danced temptingly before Offenbach's eyes. Into *Rheinnixen*, or *Les Fées du Rhin*, he poured everything he could think of. It would be the incarnation of romanticism, this opera about the water sprites of the Rhine, stuffed with pixies, elves, ruined castles by moonlight, soldiers, village maidens and dreamy landscapes. He added to it the waltz from *Papillon* and, as a thoughtful piece of insurance, the patriotic ditty he wrote during his Cologne exile in 1848. But the score was not wholly bad. It included a goblin's song which later emerged as the famous barcarolle in the *Contes d'Hoffmann*.

For months the febrile silhouette flitted about Vienna. The composer wrote to Halévy: 'Here the war cry is: Offenbach for ever!' The Emperor granted him an audience. The Imperial court in all its glory attended the first night of *Rheinnixen*. Magnificent settings and clever lighting effects provided a triumph of stagecraft. The music was another matter. After eight performances the fairy epic had to be withdrawn. The only person to be pleased at Offenbach's failure was doubtless his old enemy Wagner, who, having been rejected by the Vienna opera, had had the unspeakable annoyance of seeing the Parisian mountebank welcomed into the fold.

Though Vienna did not take to *Rheinnixen*, Offenbach's operettas were always more than welcome there. So popular did they become that for a long time pirated versions were staged to meet an ever-growing demand. Then Offenbach came to Vienna himself and, using his original orchestration and supervising his productions, he reached the peak of celebrity. His influence on the development of German operetta was profound.

In the summer of 1864 he was again at Ems, his other German headquarters. A letter he wrote to Herminie described his daily routine. He rose at half-past six in the morning and took the waters; then at nine o'clock he rehearsed two actors in his latest operetta; an hour later there was a dress rehearsal of another work in the theatre. He stopped for lunch at eleven, after which he supervised a rehearsal of yet another piece. At half-past two he paid a social call on the French Ambassador, and at four he took baths for his gout. At five o'clock he wrote letters, with dinner following at six. The rest of the evening vanished away in still more rehearsals at his hotel for two of the operettas he had already run through earlier.

Despite these absorbing activities and the nervy zest with which he wrote, composed, rehearsed, conducted, entertained and amused himself and everyone else, the failure of *Rheinnixen* had been a sad disappointment. Was he, after all, to be known merely as the composer of works like *Il Signor Fagotto* which had preceded it, a skit on Berlioz in which Offenbach utilised his drawing-room trick of imitating animals in music? Would he go down to a footnote in history as only the creator of *Les Géorgiennes*, which followed his unsuccessful grand opera? It told how the girls in a harem rose up against the pasha and, in a chorus entitled 'Down with men!', sang a women's *Marseillaise* demanding their rights. (Since the action took place over a century before 20th century feminine militancy, it is not surprising that the women return at the end to their original submissive state and the men once more take over.) 'There are some nice things in the music.' Halévy wrote. 'Madame Zulma Bouffar with her tiny little voice had her usual success. She's certainly the gem of the theatre.' But, he recorded, the piece was not a triumph. At the same time a music paper asked to be spared from 'M. Offenbach, his music and his absurd pretensions.'

If he could not rival Meyerbeer and Halévy, if he could not

even succeed with the trifles expected of him, what was he to do?
A grotesque incident which occurred about this time seemed to
emphasise his ambiguous position. While travelling down the
Rhine to Ems his boat drew in at a port decorated with flags and
bunting. A band played the quadrille from *Orphée aux enfers*
and a joyous crowd rushed forward cheering. Such a reception
was like balm to Offenbach's wounded feelings. He beamed with
delight and graciously acknowledged the applause as he came
ashore. Surrounded by a procession of townsfolk and dignitaries
he made his way along the high street. Decorations fluttered
gaily in the wind and bells pealed forth. The brass band
thumped and blared, a salute was fired and maids of honour, all
clad in white, surrounded the distinguished visitor.

Outside the town hall the procession came to a halt. Much
moved, Offenbach said a few words of thanks for the splendid
welcome he had received. The mayor started on an oration.
Offenbach listened with flattered attention to some orotund
remarks on the progress of humanity. Then, as the discourse
proceeded, his blandness gave way to perplexity and a distant
unease. The mayor had now launched into an eloquent plea for
gas lighting to be installed and was begging His Excellency the
Governor of the province to see what could be done about it.
Gas lighting? His Excellency? A horrible feeling invaded
Offenbach. The Governor had obviously been detained elsewhere on his tour and the composer, involuntarily, had deputised
for him. His vanity shattered, his innocent pleasure destroyed,
the unwilling imposter crept away as soon as he could while the
hungry citizens made off to a banquet.

PART IV

KING OF THE BOULEVARD

16

La Belle Hélène

In 1860 Ludovic Halévy was commissioned to write a play for the Théâtre des Variétés. Being topical it was needed urgently and as often happened, his collaborator proved unreliable. Scenes were left incomplete, appointments were missed. Halévy was a man of precision and regular habit, as one would expect of a civil servant, and behaviour of this sort infuriated him. It was impossible to work with such an unreliable man. While mounting the steps of the Théâtre des Variétés on his way to inform the manager of his decision, he came across an old schoolfriend.

As a boy he had been a classmate of Henri Meilhac. The latter, since then, had worked in a bookshop, contributed humorous articles and sketches to Paris newspapers and had written several farces. Halévy invited him to help with the unfinished play. Meilhac agreed – to such effect that his name alone appeared on the printed copy as author.

This was the birth of a partnership that supplied the nineteenth-century French theatre with some of its best-known titles. For Offenbach alone, Meilhac and Halévy were to write *La Belle Hélène, La Vie Parisienne, La Grande-Duchesse de Gèrolstein* and *La Périchole*, to mention only the most famous of the dozen or so libretti they singly or in collaboration gave him. They also wrote *Carmen* for Bizet and inspired Johann Strauss with the plot of *Die Fledermaus*.

They sensed an immediate mutual affinity: Meilhac was the architect, the engineer who constructed the broad outline of the piece and Halévy provided the verse for musical numbers. Together they blocked out the dialogues. Meilhac would have an idea and Halévy would bring it to life by transforming the inspiration into words. The two men had a perfect understanding. Their friendship, both personal and professional, was unclouded by argument. If a notion did not work they quietly dropped it and waited for another to turn up. The harmony between them was complete. Many years later, after Meilhac and Offenbach had died, there was an important revival of *La Belle Hélène* which Halévy attended in rehearsal, wearing his thick blue petersham overcoat, a white scarf draped untidily round his neck, a stick in his trembling hand. Problems arose that called for rewriting.

'No, no,' cried the old man, 'I can't do it any more. You're very kind, but I'm quite incapable of writing the lines you want from me. Naturally I'd enjoy it, but alas! I've lost the habit, the knack. And without Meilhac . . .'

One of their earliest ventures together was a play called *Le Brésilien*. It contained a song which Halévy asked Offenbach to set to music. The latter did so on condition that he remained anonymous: 'It goes without saying that my name won't be mentioned in connection with this bit of nonsense, nor put on the poster tomorrow . . .' He was just doing an old friend a good turn.

The three men had more ambitious projects ahead of them. They set their sights on the Opéra-Comique and drafted a two-act piece variously entitled *La Baguette* and *Fédia*. There were problems: the finale wouldn't work out, the second act proved impossible to get right and Offenbach foresaw casting difficulties. In the end they decided to leave it.

The composer badly needed a spectacle that would bring his name into prominence and draw the crowds once again. What about a sequel to *Orphée aux enfers*? He proposed the capture of Troy as a subject, the title to be *La prise de Troie*. Since English newspapers had introduced the custom of sending out war correspondents, why not link together the various scenes by featuring Homer as correspondent to *The Times*?

Ideas flew back and forth. Meilhac and Halévy set to work on the legend of beautiful Helen. She was, in Greek mythology, a daughter of the god Zeus who had turned himself into a swan when he conceived her with Leda. Menelaus, king of Sparta, became her husband. Later she was seduced by Paris and whisked off to Troy, whereupon Menelaus attacked the city, regained his wife and took her back to Sparta.

These were the details that Meilhac and Halévy proceeded to fill out. There was to be no Trojan War in their operetta: the action ended with the successful abduction of Helen. Among the cast were Ajax, Achilles (inconvenienced by a sore heel) and

Agamemnon. Having already adjudicated a beauty contest between the goddesses Juno, Minerva and Venus, the handsome Paris, disguised as a shepherd, announces a competition in which the prize is Helen. Naturally he wins, for Venus has promised him the prize in return for awarding her his vote in the beauty contest.

La Belle Hélène, as it was eventually called, had the same flavour and approach as *Orphée*. Helen is discontented with her lot. 'I'd like to have been a quiet middle-class woman, the wife of some worthy businessman in Mitylene,' she confides, instead of being the queen of Menelaus, whom, try as she may, she cannot love. In any case, how can she help being a flirt since she is the daughter of a bird?

There are the usual amusing gags. A dove flies in bearing a letter from Venus and lands beside the addressee. It flaps its wings. 'What's the matter with it?' 'It's asking if there's any reply,' answers Paris. 'No, there's none,' he tells the dove, which nods and flies off. Then Helen asks Paris: 'What time do you make it by the sun?' He looks upwards: 'Twenty-five past three.' She peers in another direction: 'Already! I make it twenty to two.' 'You're slow,' he replies.

The competition for Helen's favour involves a charade, a pun and a rhyming game. The solution to the charade is 'locomotive' – and Paris exclaims: 'How brilliant to have hit on that one 4,000 years before the invention of railways!' During the scene of the competition, which mocks *Tannhaüser* a little, there is a fanfare, harsh and raucous. 'That's nice,' says Agamemnon. 'Is it yours?' 'No,' responds Menelaus, 'it's German music I commissioned for the ceremony.' Finally the theme of the operetta is summed up by Helen in person: 'What causes scandal isn't cheating but being found out.'

Before working on *La Belle Hélène*, Offenbach drew up a mock contract. 'Desirous of always being on the best of terms with Messieurs Henri Meilhac and Ludovic Halévy, the under-signed, Jacques Offenbach, residing in the rue Laffitte, Paris, asks forgiveness in advance of his collaborators should he at any time offend them. Messieurs Meilhac and Halévy may take this declaration as definitive without, however, drawing profit or material advantage from it; it is made only for the purpose of offering exclusively personal and preliminary apologies.'

This was something more than a joke. Offenbach knew that he had found the ideal collaborators. He also knew that in the heat of composition he was easily carried away by fits of irritability and even rage when the words were delivered too slowly to keep up with his pen. Impatience is the chief mood of the letters that hurtled from Ems, Brussels and Vienna during the summer of 1864. Where was the finale to the first act? At the start of September he was 'burning' with anxiety for the second. A flood of suggestions and new ideas and second thoughts swept in through Halévy's letterbox. Even 'dear Ludo's' promotion to Chevalier in the *Légion d'honneur* was not allowed to hold up work: 'I'm doubly happy at this honour, as collaborator and friend. In all your happiness, don't forget either our operetta or your old J. Offenbach.'

He was never in better mood than when writing under pressure. If that pressure relaxed he would tauten it up again on his own initiative. Halévy remembered him working on *La Belle Hélène*, 'orchestrating at the little desk in his study in the rue Laffitte. He wrote, wrote, wrote – with what speed! – then, from time to time, in search of a harmony, he would strike a few chords on the piano with his left hand while his right hand still flew writing across the paper. His children came and went around him, shouting, playing, laughing and singing. Friends and collaborators arrived . . . Entirely at ease, Offenbach chatted, talked, joked . . . and his right hand travelled on and on and on . . .'

La Belle Hélène was not to appear at the Bouffes-Parisiens. Varney had soon given up the struggle there and been succeeded by another manager. A court action arose between him and Offenbach in which the latter had the expert advice of his sometime librettist Charles Nuitter, the ex-lawyer. Helen, therefore, would make her début at the Théâtre des Variétés, which in any case was twice as large. But who would play her part?

Offenbach's first and only thought was for Hortense Schneider. She at that moment had reached a difficult point in her life. Her ducal lover was so obviously ill that the end could not be far away. She lacked money desperately and the recent sale of her jewellery had brought in nothing like its true value. She took a bitter decision. The theatre must do without her. She would leave Paris, return to Bordeaux and live with her mother. Her furniture went up for auction, her bags were packed and her servants travelled ahead to prepare for the move.

Alone in her apartment she heard the bell ring. She ignored it and it rang again. A third time the shrill buzz was heard. She put on a dressing gown and went up to the closed door. 'Who's there? Who's disturbing me?

'Us – Offenbach and Halévy.'

'I can't let you in. I'm in my petticoat.'

'All the more reason to open the door!'

Offenbach pleaded through the keyhole. 'I'm bringing you an operetta. You'll be able to show off those lovely shoulders of yours.' Very reluctantly she admitted her callers. Without further argument Offenbach made for the piano. Humming, singing softly, he played '*Amour divin*', Helen's bittersweet aria where she deplores the colourless age she lives in and begs for the gift of love. Then he played the invocation to Venus, a beguiling yet plaintive tune: 'Tell me, Venus, why do you find such pleasure in making virtue crumble like this?' While Hortense listened in silence he strummed out '*Un mari sage est en voyage*', that sly celebration of the classic incident when a husband returns home at the unexpected and inevitably wrong moment – or at least so far as his wife is concerned.

Each of these songs was guaranteed to stop the show and Hortense knew it. 'What's your piece called?'

'*La Belle Hélène*. What a part, darling, what a part!'

So stubborn, however, was she, that, despite her eagerness, she determined to go ahead with her original plan. Coyly rearranging the folds of her gown, she gave Offenbach her address in Bordeaux. A few days later, in her home town, a telegram arrived: 'Operetta accepted for the Théâtre des Variétés. Want you for the part. Terms agreed in advance.'

She telegraphed back: 'I want 2,000 francs a month.' It was an immense sum, nearly half what she had been earning in a year. Three hours later the reply arrived: 'Agreed. Come immediately.'

Schneider realised that she was all-powerful, that Offenbach and his colleagues wanted her and no one else. She gave full rein to her every whim, she argued every trifle, she questioned every line of every song. The men in the cast, anxious for a quiet life, easily gave way. Her most redoubtable enemy was a woman, the inaptly named (to English ears) Léa Silly who acted the part of Orestes. She was tough and beautiful with a reputation gained in *pièces à femmes*, plays which relied on the physical attractions of the women rather than on acting ability. As Orestes in *La Belle Hélène* she made a very graceful boy, alert, witty, impudent. Schneider loathed her, not only for the publicity she engineered – it was her custom to promenade the boulevard dressed as a man – but for her luxurious carriage, her dazzling turn-out, her 100,000 francs' worth of jewellery.

They quarrelled interminably. They upstaged each other. They waged a permanent and ruthless battle. La Silly won on points. She caught the interest of a very rich pasha who came to know her well. One day, as she was enjoying the hospitality of his mansion, a butler presented a visiting-card. She took it from the silver salver, noted the name, and remarked blandly: 'Tell Mademoiselle Schneider that *we* are not at home.'

Rehearsals went on in the usual atmosphere of uproar and disorder against a background of vicious interplay between Schneider and Silly. Offenbach contended with them dauntlessly, as he did with an inferior orchestra, dull-witted stage-hands and interruptions by the censor. Wrapped in a fur coat that he never left off, clutching in rheumatic agony at his music stand, his flying hair shiny with sweat, he kept his humour and his good spirits. He would limp onto the stage and hobble among the cast beating time with his stick, directing the chorus, manoeuvring the principal players into new positions, tapping out the rhythms with his feet. Then he would sink exhausted into a chair, a scarcely concealed flicker of pain on his visage. He watched intently. The scene went on too long. '*Une bedide goupure!*' The red pencil slashed out whole pages. Or the scene didn't work. He rewrote it completely there and then, doing in an hour or so what would have taken another composer a week. The players started again. The familiar refrain arose. 'Very good, my dears! Charming!' Pause. 'But do it once more – *that's not what's wanted at all!*'

His face suddenly took on the expression of a goat afflicted by some deep and irremediable grievance. 'Why,' he cried to Hortense, 'are you singing "*Il nous faut de l'amour*," when I've written the music as "*Il nous faut d'l'a-amour?*"' She pointed out that it sounded badly the way he'd written it. He bridled. Then he examined the score again. 'Oh well,' he sighed, 'she's right. She knows versification better than I do. Let her get on with it.'

Suddenly a noise from the auditorium distracted him. 'There's someone there!' he shouted. He never allowed strangers at rehearsals. 'I'll have nobody here.'

'Nobody?' said Meilhac. 'Not even the duc de Morny?'

'Ah, that's quite another matter,' Offenbach replied hastily. The minister had contributed a few lines which were diplomatically inserted into *La Belle Hélène*. He was also to help out when the censor became troublesome.

It was all like something out of Emile Zola's *Nana*. The large, empty, echoing theatre, its seats shrouded in covers, was dark except for a single gaslight at the front of the stage. In its pale wavering gleam the actors moved about trailed by grotesque shadows. Zola's novel describes the rise of Nana, the beautiful daughter of a laundress, who goes on the stage and becomes a notorious courtesan. She makes her name in an operetta called *La Blonde Vénus*, a satire on the old Greek gods and goddesses in which Jupiter quarrels with Juno over the housekeeping accounts. It is obvious that Zola's model for *La Blonde Vénus* was *La Belle Hélène* and that Nana was to a great extent inspired by Hortense Schneider.[1]

When Nana/Hortense makes her appearance a murmur of surprise runs through the audience. The men swallow hard and watch her in breathless silence. Beneath the transparent gauze of her brief tunic she is naked. The filmy material clings to the voluptuous lines of her body like white foam. She walks the stage with insolent self-confidence, aware that every man in the theatre is lusting after her, the victim of her powerful sexuality.

Nana is not the only memorable character. Another is Bosc, the reliable veteran of hundreds of plays. He is a composite portrait of all those senior comic actors who formed the mainstay of the regular troupe Offenbach gathered around him. Immediately he exits off-stage he makes for his shabby dressing-room, a thick coat slung over his gold-spangled costume, and grasps the bottle with a hand trembling slightly from incipient alcoholism. He throws aside his cardboard crown and wraps

---

[1] In fact, when Zola was gathering material for his book, Halévy took him behind the scenes, introduced him to theatrical people and generally helped him to document himself on Hortense's world.

himself up against his draughts. From the distant stage comes a muffled buzz. Yet, although the words and music are indistinguishable, like an old war-horse he knows without being told when the cue for his next entry is coming up, and deliberately, without haste, he marches towards the footlights on unsteady legs. The smell of sweat, make-up, gas and stale scent hovers behind the flats, their reverse panels buried under a thick crust of old posters. The lighting engineer studies his complicated switchboard of gas taps. A fireman peers round an angle to see what's happening out front. Higher up, a stage-hand is poised to ring down the curtain, oblivious to everything except the bell that warns him when to release the rope.

The impresario is a crude and cynical debauchee. When people congratulate him on his smart theatre, he sarcastically interrupts them: 'My brothel, you mean!' and never refers to it by any other word. As for Nana, he refuses to admit that she can sing. She can't act, he goes on, and she doesn't even know what to do with her hands and feet. But, he asks, does a pretty woman need talent for acting and singing? Nana doesn't: all she has to do is show off her lovely thighs and beautiful skin and his theatre is packed. 'She'll go far, by God yes, she'll go far.'

Unlike Nana, however, Schneider did have something beside her attractiveness. Her timing was exquisite and her acting included fine shades of comedy. While Zola's heroine met early death from a horrible disease, Schneider lived on for many years into a long and wealthy retirement. The days of her great fame began on 17 December 1864, when *La Belle Hélène* established her as queen of the boulevard theatre.

Of course, at the dress rehearsal nearly everything went wrong. The air describing the beauty contest among the three goddesses – '*Au mont Ida trois déesses*' – was received by the invited audience with icy dislike. That night Offenbach wrote three new versions of it. He played them to the singer involved. Both decided on the first one. An easy, nonchalant, ambling tune, it became one of the most popular melodies in the operetta.

The first night was a thorough success. Although many critics brought out the familiar objections to sacrilege and irreverence, the public was delighted. Bookings at the Théâtre des Variétés ran for months ahead. Hortense was saluted as 'the greatest star in the world'. Dukes and generals came to the theatre simply to feast their eyes on her. Even the eighty-year-old Auber, composer of many a serious work, admitted that he went to hear her whenever he wanted to 'fill my ears with delight'. The music was played everywhere, in restaurants, taverns, dance halls and at military parades where ranks of soldiers marched to the jaunty strains of the chorus introducing the kings of Greece: '*Ces rois remplis de vaillance, plis de vaillance, plis de vaillance,*' and Ajax himself: '*Ce roi barbu qui s'avance, bu qui s'avance, bu qui s'avance . . .,*' while in ball-rooms throughout Paris, and then throughout France, the langorous sweep of Helen's waltz could be heard.

La Belle Hélène put into circulation a flood of new slang words and catch-phrases. '*Bu qui s'avance, bu qui s'avance,*' chortled those who liked to think they were up to date. They were met with knowing laughter from others who belonged to the freemasonry of fashion. Remarks such as the Gallic equivalent of 'Take a peep at my ticker,' or 'I haven't a bean in my treasury,' knew a long and widespread vogue.

Life was a great big joke, announced *La Belle Hélène*. The most important thing was to enjoy yourself. Pleasure represented the supreme purpose of life. '*Je suis gai, soyez gai, il le faut, je le veux,*' Paris commands the people of Greece. Orestes spends all the family money on women, but what does it matter? The country will pay. To a certain extent the operetta reflected a social mood which regarded pleasure and the pursuit of a good time as the only worthwhile aim. Yet an ominous undercurrent flows beneath the frenzied merriment. There are hints that disaster may not be far off. 'You know,' says Agamemnon, 'it can't last much longer.'

The team made up by Offenbach, Schneider, Meilhac and Halévy became in effect the accredited entertainers of the Second Empire in its concluding phase. They were the favourites of the class that ruled, of a world people by big businessmen, financiers, leading politicians, fashionable personalities and the group that had as its centre the court of Louis-Napoléon. Offenbach had reached the highest point of his career. He sold the publication rights of *La Belle Hélène* for an excellent price: 2,000 francs on signing the contract, 1,000 at the fiftieth performance, 1,000 at the eightieth and a final 1,000 at the 120th. He did not have long to wait. And in any case, performing rights brought him an income of steady and handsome proportions.

17

Bluebeard and *La Vie Parisienne*

What next? In the following year Offenbach's most important production was the marriage of his eldest daughter Berthe. She was just nineteen years old. Her bridegroom was Charles Comte, son of the man from whom Offenbach had bought the original Bouffes-Parisiens, and later his business manager. The ceremony gave the composer an opportunity to organise one of the most spectacular events he ever staged at his seaside home in Étretat.

On 10 August 1865 a long convoy of cabs and vehicles wound its way through the town picking up large numbers of guests from Paris. Early in the morning a mobile kitchen had already distributed among the various lodging places a supply of hot chocolate and coffee for breakfast. A procession led by two violinists set off for the church. A solemn mass composed by Offenbach himself accompanied the Catholic rite. (Fragments of the manuscript still survive.) Then followed a ceremony in the Anglican church, for Comte had Swiss Protestant origins.

Having triply bound the links of matrimony – with a civil ceremony in the town hall on the day before and two religious functions afterwards – the wedding party, eighty-six in all, sat down to a vast banquet spread over three substantial tables. The meal, noisy and tumultuous, went on until five o'clock, when the newly married couple took their leave. And Offenbach started trying to think of an excuse for his next elaborate celebration at Étretat. His silver wedding, perhaps? But that was four years away now and he couldn't wait. Never mind: he still had three daughters and a son left, and family birthdays alone would be enough to keep the 'Alcazar d'Étretat' supplied with reasons for festival.

It was a quiet year in the theatre for him. At Ems in the summer he put on *Coscoletto*. It never reached Paris and remains unpublished. Autumn brought *Les Refrains des Bouffes*, a selection of items from past successes which played to good houses though it offered nothing new. His biggest work of the period was a three-act operetta called *Les Bergers*. As with *Les Contes d'Hoffmann*, each act told a different story. There was a flavour of Watteau about this presentation. Offenbach felt notably pleased with it: 'I have never written a score with greater love,' he declared. The stage effects were ingenious. They included a live ox which lumbered on to the boards to enhance the pastoral atmosphere. A large balloon filled with gas was intended as a halo for one of the cherubs. At the dress rehearsal, just as the chorus of shepherds was about to pay respects to Eros, the balloon exploded with a terrifying bang. The first performance had to be postponed. Some months later, so great was the fright she received, a lady in the cast died of the after-effect to her nervous system.

This was not the only misfortune that awaited *Les Bergers*. The principal comedian, in the part of a modern shepherd, had to leap on a cask and remark: 'I speak to you in the name of the principles of 1789.' As he did so, the cask fell to pieces. Unable to resist an impromptu gag, he covered up by saying: 'As you see, my cask is like the principles of 1789: it's not very sound.' Some of the opposition newspapers took up the incident and attacked this show of disrespect for the sacred principles of the Revolution which, even under an Imperial régime, they agreed, should not be disdained. The government, anxious to avoid trouble, made soothing noises.

In this case, publicity did not help. Nobody wanted to see *Les Bergers* and it quietly faded from view together with the balloon and the ox. A happier occasion was the 500th performance of *Orphée aux enfers*. An audience of dukes and princes assembled to applaud Cora Pearl in the rôle of Cupid. With them sat the best-known courtesans in Paris, curious perhaps to see how their fellow-worker in the sphere of high-class prostitution would perform under conditions rather more public than those to which she was normally used. She, born Emma Crouch, draped in diamonds from head to foot, sang in a quavering voice and a strong English accent: '*Je souis Kioupidonn!*' The novelty of the situation carried her through. But at a later performance, students from the Latin Quarter demonstrated noisily over the outrage to morals. She replied by cocking a snook at them. After a dozen nights she had to withdraw.

The revival of past triumphs was, for Offenbach, only a financial tactic, a means of recouping his fortunes when business was bad or of filling the theatre until the next piece was ready. His true delight lay in novelty. That is why impatience with his collaborators' apparent sloth sometimes drove him mad with frustration and his own frantic zeal for work made him dictatorial. 'My dear Ludo,' he wrote to Halévy at the beginning of 1866, 'I'm astonished and frightened at receiving nothing from you. Not a single line? And we're at the end of February, it's unforgivable. Are you ill? Is Meilhac in love for the hundredth time? I'm very distressed by the way you go on. Really, how do you expect to succeed? . . . It's not nice of you both. We have the Opéra-Comique, the Variétés, the Palais-Royal, there's a fortune ready for the taking, and you don't want it. I expect, by return of post, a word from you and Meilhac which will explain your strange conduct, not to use a harsher phrase . . . words, words, words, in the name of God Almighty . . . or I shall be very angry indeed . . .'

Often he enlisted members of his family in the pursuit of dilatory writers. Herminie would take up her pen: 'Jacques has written to me several times asking me to remind you and Tréfeu about the two-act piece for Ems . . . I write to ask whether you would kindly think of him and work for him.' Occasionally the situation turned desperate, and, without tempering her remarks, she wrote: 'Do you know, Sir, that Jacques has urgent need of your three acts?' As the children grew up they too acted as lieutenants in the constant battle to ensure the flow of words for Offenbach to set. 'Papa is here with an attack of gout,' wrote his daughter Marie to the librettist Charles Nuitter, 'he very much wants to see you as soon as possible to talk about important matters, I expect, because he's been asking for you these past two days.'

His incessant badgering of Meilhac and Halévy at last produced the libretto of *Barbe-Bleue* which was given in February 1866. Basing themselves on one of Charles Perrault's more sinister fairy tales, which in turn was inspired by the abominable fifteenth-century child murderer Gilles de Retz, they made it into a parody of the Middle Ages. The villainous Bluebeard comes out as a figure of fun. 'I am Bluebeard,' he sings sparkishly. 'Oh never was there a jollier widower.' As soon as he tires of a wife he hands her over to his court chemist Popolani to be disposed of by poisoning. Popolani, however, is a tender-hearted official. He prefers live beauties to dead ones and thus, over a perod of time, has been able to assemble at no expense to himself a convenient harem of six complaisant young women. In the third act Bluebeard learns with surprise of the deception. What shall be done with these charming but no longer needed ladies? A neat solution offers itself. The Queen of Brittany happens to have half a dozen ex-lovers of whom she has wearied. So Bluebeard obliges her by marrying off his discarded wives to them.

Many years later, with the aid of Maeterlinck's exquisite libretto, Paul Dukas was to compose his own very beautiful opera *Ariane et Barbe-Bleue* on the same subject. He drew from it much poetry. But for Offenbach the old tale was only an excuse for buffoonery and topsy-turvydom. A woman is murdered only to pop up again a few minutes later as bright and breezy as ever. Evil and horror are laughed at. The heroine Boulotte, an uneducated but shrewd peasant girl, mocks court life and the pomp of power. One of the best numbers in the score is '*Un bon courtisan s'incline*'. To a mincing tune suggestive of the courtier bowing with smooth deference, we are told that his trade is a difficult one: just when he thinks he is doing the right thing he finds he has committed an appalling blunder. Whatever his master says, he must swoon with delight. If he wants to succeed, 'a good courtier must bow, bow, bow, and bend his spine, spine, spine, as far as it'll go, go, go.'

None but Hortense Schneider would do for Boulotte. Having thoughtfully quoted the high salaries other theatres were offering her, she contrived to squeeze out 300 francs a night from the agonised management, but she gave value for money. As Boulotte she had a lot to do with the success of the piece and was called by one overjoyed critic 'the Malibran of musical comedy.' The size of her fee was rivalled by the lavishness of the production and many thousands of francs were spent on costumes and scenery which for months dazzled full houses with their splendour.

By now, with another hit on his hands, Offenbach could drive a hard bargain. Never again, as he did in the early days with *Orphée aux enfers*, would he let one of his scores go for such a derisory sum. A typical letter to a publisher would run: 'It's a charming operetta, both words and music. Very seriously I think it a *very good piece of business*. It's crammed with tunes – enough to set the whole country dancing, with quadrilles, waltzes, polkas, etc. . . . If you like, I'll let you have it for 1,200 francs, and *that's because you're you*.'

Sometimes he would do a package deal. Having lured a publisher into accepting an operetta he then offered him one more as well. He would mention other successful pieces which the publisher had let slip in the past and would tempt him with the promise of future triumphs. Why not, for only a little extra, take the additional work Offenbach threw in? There followed a complicated timetable by which instalments of the price were to be paid. The dates when the publisher's notes of hand fell due were carefully specified. German rights were reserved since Offenbach always sold in advance to his Viennese publisher. Yet, ingenious as he was in conducting negotiations, no sooner had the money come in than he spent it. He was only half a businessman.

While *Barbe-Bleue* was still playing at the Théâtre des Variétés he launched, at the Palais-Royal, an operetta destined for ever to outshine it. But at the start very few people, except as usual the composer himself, expected much of *La Vie Parisienne*.

Even members of the cast were pessimistic. One of the ladies did not bother to order a new dress, so convinced was she that the production would never succeed. Others only went through the motions of learning their words since they thought it unlikely that on the opening night *La Vie Parisienne* would survive until the third act. They were not, in any case, a very suitable cast. The manager of the Palais-Royal, an impresario with the uncompromising name of Plunkett, insisted that Offenbach write for the troupe he had assembled over the years at his theatre, although musicality was not among their strong points. As a concession, Offenbach had been allowed to engage his current mistress Zulma Bouffar among the singers. Nonetheless, as preparations went forward, Halévy noted gloomily: 'I have very, very little confidence in *La Vie Parisienne*.' A few days before the first night he wrote: 'Rehearsals for *La Vie Parisienne* are driving me mad.'

Soon after the curtain rose on the night of 31 October 1866, all these fears were dissipated in the thunder of applause and cheers which at frequent intervals drowned the voices of the singers and held up the action until the audience had expressed its enthusiasm in full measure. At one point, on the other side of the footlights, Hortense Schneider noticed that Princess Metternich clapped so vigorously in a neighbouring box that she split her gloves. At midnight the theatre still resounded to cheers and laughter.

Within a few months yet another great exhibition was to open, the Exposition Universelle of 1867, which was the main reason why Plunkett had commissioned the new operetta. *La Vie Parisienne* could not have appeared at a better moment: the timing was perfect. While the Exposition demonstrated with brilliant showmanship the prosperity and strength of France, *La Vie Parisienne* depicted its capital city as the queen of pleasure and fashion. Had not a wealthy Turkish potentate summed up the views of many visiting foreigners when, gazing out on the boulevards, he murmured: 'It seems to me that the whole of Paris is my mistress?'

The opening scene takes place at one of the main-line railway stations where the platforms are crowded with arriving tourists, fortune hunters, guides and touts of every description. For the chorus of porters Meilhac and Halévy ingeniously rhyme place-names in the railway timetable: Conflans and Vernon, Nointot and Yvetot, Guingamp and Fécamp. The Swedish Baron de Gondremarck bursts out from his carriage eager for the delights of Paris. He wants to go to the theatres – not the ones where you're bored but the ones where you see pretty actresses displaying their charms. For his wife Paris is the town where she will hear great singers who are all the rage.

Just as keen is the wealthy Brazilian. In a breathless patter song, '*Je suis Brésilien et j'ai de l'or*', he explains that this is his second visit. On his first he arrived with a luggage-load of gold and diamonds which bought him six months of rapture, two hundred friends and four or five mistresses. Having spent it all he went back to Brazil and made another fortune. Now he has returned so that Paris can in turn steal from him all the riches he's stolen from his native land. What I want from you, Paris, he exclaims, is your women: not the respectable middle-class ones nor great ladies, but the others, 'Do I make myself understood?'

Those, he means, who, queening it in theatres and restaurants, have a flirtatious but ice-cold eye that can instantly pick out the richest man in a crowd.

The same message, but in a gentler fashion, emerges from Métella's famous letter song. The courtesan reads a letter from one of her past lovers, the baron de Frascata, a foreigner she can now only dimly remember. '*Vous souvient-il, ma belle?*' he writes from a distant land, eaten up with nostalgia for his brief six weeks of love in Paris. 'If only you knew how rare a thing pleasure is in our chilly country.' Though he lacks the happy cynicism of the Brazilian, Paris for him is no less the centre of light and warmth and life. It is noticeable how the operatic convention of the letter song seems to inspire a composer. Here, as in the later *Périchole*, Offenbach creates a marvellously bittersweet tenderness – and he does it with great simplicity.

La Vie Parisienne is, among other things, a vivacious portrait gallery of types. Here are the naïf tourist, the world-weary courtesan, the young man on the make, the confidence trickster, the flashy adventurer, and the aptly named Urbain, the discreet head waiter who knows all his customers' weaknesses and caters for them with impeccable diplomacy. Another is Gabrielle, a merry widow. 'I'm the widow of a colonel who died in the war,' she sings lugubriously. 'I keep his helmet under a glass case. Now I live in such a way that up there in heaven, his last dwelling place, he's content.' The solemn march abruptly changes to a livelier rhythm: 'My colonel's happy ... or at least ... at least I hope he is.' Later on Gabrielle has a quick-fire number describing the Parisian woman dressing up to conquer, and arming herself at all points for the battle of sex: '*Sa robe fait frou frou frou frou, Ses petits pieds font toc toc toc.*' It is obvious that she is justified in wondering if her dear dead colonel was ... entirely happy.

The atmosphere of this rush for pleasure attains a climax in the dizzying chorus '*Tout tourne, tout danse*'. Everything whirls round in an explosion of giddy effervescence. The Brazilian, as he wished, has plunged head-first into the fun. Baron de Gondremarck has marvelled at the splendours of a high society reception. (The fact that it is a hoax and that the hero of the evening is an Admiral in the Swiss Navy shows that the librettists had a philosophical turn of mind.) Excitement has reached its highest, most neurotic pitch.

La Vie Parisienne must have been one of the earliest contributors to that durable legend of 'gay Paree'. Carefully cherished by Frenchmen over the years, the legend has created valuable propaganda for the tourist industry. Even today, when the centre of 'naughtiness' has moved elsewhere and gaiety is confined to the melancholy routine of 'Paris by Night' coach trips, the tattered myth lingers on. In Offenbach's time there was no doubt that Paris had an irresistible lure for pleasure seekers all over the world and the audiences who saw *La Vie Parisienne* witnessed a tribute to what was then an undoubted phenomenon.

It is doubtful, though, if all the spectators at the Palais-Royal appreciated the more satirical implications of the operetta. At one point, such are the demands of the plot, servants are obliged to dress up as fashionable ladies and gentlemen and to act as if they were members of high society. Butlers and cooks masquerade as princes and duchesses. Louis-Napoléon had just introduced belated measures to liberalise a régime up to then noted for its repressiveness. *La Vie Parisienne* is aware of this and dares to hint that the socially inferior classes are perhaps not entirely without merit or intelligence.

The contemporary setting of *La Vie Parisienne* enabled the authors to speak out more clearly than in *Orphée aux enfers* or in *La Belle Hélène*. Though words and music have a typically Parisian lightness, they also have a quality which forms the other side of boulevardier wit, a sort of resigned disenchantment, like the feeling which inspired Beaumarchais to say that if he laughed at everything it was only to avoid weeping. If life is a hoax and if everything ends in disillusionment, the only thing for a wise man to do is to shrug his shoulders.

The last act of the operetta has a magnificent waltz, the best Offenbach ever wrote. The form and inspiration are similar to the waltz in *La Belle Hélène*, although they are even richer and lovelier. Again, the theme floats up from Offenbach's favourite 'cellos with support from clarinets and rhythmic pizzicati from the double bass. Métella pictures the scene where young men not yet of age throw away the money their fathers have earned and squander the future dowries of their sisters. It is midnight – time for the revels to start. Expensive carriages draw up. Smart women, blondes, brunettes, redheads, the pick of the bunch, get out, attended by handsome escorts of every nationality. In this preliminary 'adagio of the bacchanal' smiles begin to appear, the atmosphere warms up, the rustle of silk dresses is heard vanishing along corridors.

Then laughter breaks out and champagne corks pop. A tinny piano grinds out popular tunes: the noise increases and becomes a storm of sound. Joyous youth sings at the top of its voice. Is this pleasure or madness? The climax is reached. When exhaustion sets in peace falls and gaiety departs. Some have gone to sleep standing up, others are on the floor, while morning comes and the bleak dawn puts a full stop to enjoyment. The revellers wake up with a hangover. At last they stagger out into the daylight, haggard, pale-faced, still drunk with the fumes of champagne and imitation love. The street sweeper watches them pass by, ill and uncertain of step. And the tune sung by Métella, at first soft and alluring, has become now strident and full of despair. The party's over.

18

The Grand Duchess

In the last year of Ludovic Halévy's life – he was then in his early seventies – a journalist friend brought him a copy of the score of *La Grande-Duchesse de Gérolstein* and asked him to autograph it.

The old man paused. Then, with emotion, he wrote: '*La Grande-Duchesse!* . . . 1867 . . . That's forty-one years ago!

'I can still see Bismarck walking through the Passage des Panoramas during an interval in *La Grande-Duchesse*.

'I can still see Hortense Schneider's dressing-room on another evening . . . It was Couder's birthday, the man who played General Boum. He was treating his comrades to champagne.

'The Prince of Wales arrived in Schneider's dressing-room and I was introduced to him by the Grande Duchesse, and he drank a glass of General Boum's champagne.'

In that distant year of 1867, when Paris had become, according to one chronicler, 'the cabaret of the world', the massive buildings of the Exposition dominated the Champ de Mars with its heavy iron and glass. A mixture of pagodas and Egyptian temples sprawled next to an Inca village. There were 42,000 exhibitors from nearly every country. In the vast park all around sprouted cupolas, domes, minarets and sideshows. You could choose from Austrian beer, Turkish coffee, Chinese tea, English ale and French wine. One of the most impressive exhibits was a large cannon said to be the biggest in the world. It was presented by Herr Krupp.

Like everyone else in the entertainment business, the manager of the Théâtre des Variétés was anxious to put on a special attraction for Exhibition year. He signed a contract with Offenbach who, after much prodding of Meilhac and Halévy, elicited from them the words of *La Grande-Duchesse de Gérolstein*. The composer as usual played no small part in the writing of the libretto. Indeed, to judge from his correspondence at the time he deserves to have his name coupled as librettist

Offenbach with a grandchild

The patriarch and family

with those of 'Meil' and 'Hal'. The latter received from him page after page of detailed criticisms and suggestions. He redrafted whole scenes, changed the shape of the narrative and brought in entirely new ideas, after which he apologised affectionately to his collaborators: 'I ask your forgiveness, my dears, for having spoken to you with the bluntness of an old soldier, but it's a duty; aren't we all in it together so far as work is concerned? On the other hand, I give you permission to tear my music to pieces!'

The name part was tailored for Schneider. Her fee spiralled accordingly to 4,500 francs a night. At rehearsals she was more difficult than ever before. When she sang '*Dites-lui*', one of the best songs in the whole work, Halévy broke in to say that the words were only temporary and that he would be writing others.

'Why?' she snapped. 'I think they're very suitable. Write others if you wish. *I* shall sing *these*.'

Again and again she threatened to give up the part. And Offenbach, weary of argument, stamped out of the theatre swearing never to return. She did not in the end withdraw, and the composer always came back.

She was one of several thorns in his flesh. The government censor's office went through the script line by line and demanded changes. The original title of *La Grande-Duchesse* must be altered. (The Grand Duchy of Luxemburg was represented at the Exposition.) So, remembering one of Eugène Sue's popular novels where the name occurs, the authors gave their grand duchess the fictional kingdom of Gérolstein to rule.

Then Hortense, who created for herself a most elaborate costume – a coat trimmed with gold and a crown sparkling with diamonds – also invented a splendid decoration to be worn over her bosom, but again the censorship intervened. Such a decoration, though imaginary, might be considered an insult to reigning sovereigns. The decision arrived just before the curtain rose on the first night and Hortense flew into a terrible passion. 'I shan't go on!' she screamed.

As time passed the audience began to wonder what had happened. Orchestra and chorus looked at each other in surprise. Backstage were heard the sharp tones of Hortense and the croaking pleas of Offenbach. Still she refused to go on. He took a risk and ordered the conductor to start. Whereat she, at the sound of the music, instantly changed her mind. She brushed away her tears and, in her own words, 'like a circus horse when it hears the music to which it must perform in the ring,' prepared to make her entry, and when she appeared on stage her face bore a radiant smile.

It was a Friday evening, 12 April 1867. The performance began at half-past eight. 'I can tell you,' wrote Halévy, 'that at a moment like this a fine old shiver runs right through you from head to foot. How impatiently you wait for the first effect to come off! The great thing is to break the ice. Once the audience is in the mood everything's all right, but how difficult it is to tear out of them the first roar of laughter, the first murmer of approval, the first applause, and how delightful it is to hear it! ... Our torture didn't last long ... At the first words and thanks, it must be said, to the incredible verve of Couder [as General Boum], the audience caught fire and only died down towards the middle of the second act. What a beginning!'

The third act did not go so well. Offenbach took out his blue pencil and ruthlessly cut the offending sections. Within two hours the collaborators had produced a satisfactory alternative. Thanks to these 'bedides goupures', La Grande-Duchesse de Gérolstein now embarked on what proved to be a very long run indeed and gave Schneider her biggest success in the theatre.

The fears of the censorship were understandable. Offenbach's latest work, far more than La Vie Parisienne, was open satire. It laughed at the military, at war as a political instrument, and at absolute rule. Yet it did so in such broad and amusing terms that no one could take offence. Louis-Napoléon himself attended soon after the première and was observed to smile enigmatically. He enjoyed it so much that he returned for a second hearing a few days later. His example was followed by all the kings and queens who had visited Paris for the Exposition. Often La Grande-Duchesse de Gérolstein played to stalls and boxes peopled with the reigning monarchs of Europe and beyond.

War is personified in the explosive General Boum (Boom). His high-boots are so grand and so large that he walks bandy-legged, and at the slightest noise he whirls round: 'Where's the enemy? Where's the enemy?' When offered a pinch of snuff he rejects it contemptuously and fires his pistol in the air. Lovingly he savours the smell of the powder: it is the only snuff he likes to take.

He is commander-in-chief of the Grand Duchess' army. It includes the humble Fritz, a common private as handsome as Adonis and as dim as the sword he carries. The Grand Duchess likes the look of him and promotes him to corporal. When she hears he has a sweetheart she makes him a lieutenant. A few minutes later she has put him up to captain. By the end of Act I he has become a general, a baron, and, to Boum's disgust, commander-in-chief because the Grand Duchess plans war on a neighbouring state and seeks new ideas. The war council that follows is a sharp parody of what goes on behind closed doors. She asks Fritz about his plan of campaign.

'Oh, it's very simple,' he replies. 'We all gather together, we go out to face the enemy, we meet them and we bash them with all our strength.'

'And you win the battle?'

'Or lose it as anyone else might.'

She gives him the sabre that her father had worn. It was, as she points out, the custom of her 'august mother' to hand it to him each time he went into battle. He buckles it on and sets off to war, returning victorious four days later. (Originally he won in eighteen days – but that was the length of time it took the Prussian army to beat the Austrians at Sadowa, and censorship changed the figure.) How did he achieve this miraculous feat? He outlines his strategy. Three hundred thousand bottles of wine and liqueur were temptingly laid out for the enemy. Next day a hundred thousand soldiers staggered drunk on the '*champ de bouteilles*' ('bottle-field'). They surrendered without a struggle. He now returns her father's venerable sword, bent and battered – though not from fighting but from the onslaught of a jealous husband.

The Grand Duchess promotes Fritz to the highest command. But she has now fallen in love with him. Some appearance must, however, be preserved, and she pretends that a lady-in-waiting has given her a message for him. 'Tell him he's been noticed and picked out. Tell him he's been found attractive. Tell him that, if he so wished, Heaven knows what this lady might be capable of . . .' Her feelings become too strong for her to keep up the pretence: 'Tell him that the moment I saw him I liked him, that I'm losing my head over him, that the rascal so fills my mind that I'm quite bereft of sense.' Although the situation is comic – and is made even more so by the wooden Fritz's inability to understand the lady's subtle approach – the music is delicate, touching, a 'jewel' as Halévy rightly called it. In a moment of unusual tenderness the barnstorming heroine reveals immortal longings: 'Tell him that I love him and that I'm beautiful . . .'

Her bird-brained favourite does not respond and makes matters worse by preparing to marry his peasant sweetheart. As speedily as she had raised him to the heights, the infuriated Grand Duchess reduces him to a private again. She even joins in a conspiracy led by the disgruntled General Boum to assassinate him on the eve of his wedding. As the conspirators sharpen their knives they sing a clever jingle:

> O poignard assez pointu
> On va te rendre si pointu
> Que vraiment on n'aurait point eu
> De poignard à ce point pointu

Boum and his friends, though, are checkmated, and the Grand Duchess, for once heeding the advice of her counsellors, makes a political marriage with Prince Paul of Stein-Stein-Steis-Laper-Bottmoll-Schorstenburg. Even in the names of their characters Meilhac and Halévy satirised those warring little duchies who made nineteenth-century European history so complicated.

The score of *La Grande-Duchesse de Gérolstein* brims over with marches, polkas, waltzes and galopades. One of the numbers that stopped the show was *'Ah! que j'aime les militaires'*, where Schneider explained how easily she was bowled over by soldiers, their uniforms, their moustaches, their conquering manner. Another was the song of the regiment, an inspiriting 'rub-a-dub-dub' march in which she led the chorus. Offenbach strewed his gems with a prodigal hand. *'Dites-lui'* has already been mentioned. Just as simple and refined is the *'Chronique de la Gazette de Hollande'*.

As in *Barbe-Bleue*, court life is the target. So is the widespread custom of favouritism by which men are catapulted into jobs entirely unsuitable for them. Dynastic marriage and jingoism come in for laughter as well. The legend of the military commander who plans every detail with cool mastery is also deflated: we are reminded that he is as much at the mercy of events as the humblest soldier, and that his conquests are more often due to luck than to anything else. Even history is a joke. In a little duetto the Grand Duchess and Boum exclaim: 'How great are the lessons of the past! History's just one big circle.' The ancestor commits his crime and the descendant does it all over again. And all this so that two hundred years later the guide at the historic monument can earn a nice little income by retelling the scene – just as his grandchildren themselves in time will turn an honest penny by enthralling tourists with the account.

For ever afterwards Hortense Schneider enjoyed, besides the nickname of the *'Passage des Princes'*, that of 'Grand Duchess'. The first of these had even become out of date: her conquests now were kings, not mere princelings. Her dressing-room, glowing with a soft pink decor, filled with huge bouquets of roses and irradiated by a huge looking-glass, served as the place where she gave audience to her royal admirers in a heady atmosphere of scent and stage make-up. When the Prince of Wales came to pay tribute she was overwhelmed. Her conversation was heavily larded with 'your Royal Highness' and 'My Lord'. Soon she recovered from the novelty and was treating majesties as equals. How could she do otherwise when both the Tsar of Russia and his son quarrelled over her?

This hob-nobbing with royalty and her own skill as an actress often combined to make her believe she really was a Grand Duchess. One day she drove up the avenue Bourdonnais to the ornamental gate reserved for ruling families on their visits to the Exposition.

'Open up!' she commanded.

The astonished gate-keepers explained that they could only open for an Emperor or his Empress, a King or his Queen.

'But I'm the Grand Duchess of Gérolstein,' she retorted.

They opened up.

19

From Peru to the last Rose of Summer

At performances of *La Grande-Duchesse de Gérolstein* Bismarck
choked with laughter and exclaimed: 'That's it! That's absolutely
how it is!' His suspicion of French military incompetence was
confirmed.

With a post in the administration Halévy was near the centre
of government. He knew, more than most people, the way things
were going. Sombrely he wrote in his journal: 'Bismarck is
helping to double our takings. This time it's war we're laughing
at, and war is at our gates.'

As for Offenbach, he took little interest in politics or in
European affairs except as an excuse for plots. So long as he
could find a theatre to stage his operettas, an orchestra to play
them and a cast to sing them, he was happy. The spring of 1867
produced *La Grande Duchesse*. His 'summer holidays' consisted
of two one-acters at Ems: *La Leçon de chant* and *La Permission
de dix heures*. The second of these, a brief excursion into the
eighteenth century, features a heroine in love with a soldier.
'The ten o'clock pass is a good idea,' she sings, 'because it's
always dark by then and no one can see your blushes.'

With the autumn came *Robinson Crusoé*. It was a production to
which Offenbach attached great value. He still cherished the
longing to be accepted as a serious composer, and when the
Opéra-Comique accepted *Robinson Crusoé* he felt that he had
made a step in the right direction. He was also eager to atone for
the fiasco there of *Barkouf* some years previously. Away from
the boulevard, on the stage of a national theatre, he would show
his critics that they were wrong to disdain operetta.

Instead of isolated songs linked by stretches of spoken
dialogue, Offenbach gave his audience elaborate arias and
recitative with only short passages of speech. His *Robinson
Crusoé* aspired to the condition of grand opera. Yet for all these
refinements he could not subdue his natural gaiety. A menacing
chorus of hungry cannibals dissolves into a waltz-song. Man

Friday is, in effect, Woman Friday, since the part is written for a mezzo-soprano. (It was sung by Célestine Galli-Marié who later became the first Carmen.) The connection with Daniel Defoe's original is often tenuous and much of the book's interest lies in Crusoe's psychological reaction to loneliness and his grappling with the problems of solitude. An opera audience could not be expected to sit through an interminable monologue until the overdue arrival of Man Friday. The whole of the first act, therefore, takes place in Bristol, where Crusoe is shown with his family and his betrothed. Only in Act II does he reach his desert island.

Offenbach suffered more than usual from gout at this period. He was seen being carried through the doors of the Opéra-Comique to rehearsals, a thin, weary figure crouched in a chair and shrouded from top to toe in furs. His hopes for *Robinson Crusoé* were not entirely disappointed. It had an easier passage than *Barkouf* and won a respectable number of performances.

Next year he came back to the Palais-Royal and his old collaborators Meilhac and Halévy with *Le Château à Toto*. This was a skit on the old nobility and featured the Baron de Crécy-Crécy, an aristocrat down on his luck. By the third act he has acquired a job as a country postman and in a splendid patter song reveals the tribulations of his lot. Which is to be preferred: long legs or short ones? At first it seems better to have long ones since you can take long strides and not so many of them. Short legs mean shorter strides – but more of them. So it all comes down to the same thing in the end. Would the newly-invented penny-farthing be a solution? It's difficult to get up on it, though, and once you're on, it's difficult to get off . . . The postman's ditty and a whistling song are among the brighter things in a rambling score which even the talent of Zulma Bouffar could not always keep afloat.

Audiences preferred the one-act piece that followed it, a broad buffoonery about the absent-minded King of Tulipatan who was never quite sure whether he had two sons, or two daughters, and who, to solve the matter once and for all, tried to strike an average.

Then in October, Offenbach returned to better form with *La Périchole*. Meilhac and Halévy took the idea from a play by that graceful writer Prosper Mérimée, author of *Carmen* which they were later to plunder as well. *Le Carrosse du Saint-Sacrement* is an ironical venture in the author's most polished style. He based it on an episode said to have involved an eighteenth-century cocotte and the Viceroy of Peru. The woman, known as La Périchole, which is the French version of her nickname 'native bitch', ensnares the pompous Viceroy. The comedy of the piece flows from the encounter of this shrewd and calculating hussy with the drivelling old fool who loves her. The dialogue is enchanting and shows a subtle appreciation of character and the nature of jealousy.

Le Carrosse du Saint-Sacrement, though it inspired an amusing opera by Lord Berners and a good Jean Renoir film, was not a success when staged. Mérimée's language was perhaps too subtle. Naturally 'Meil' and 'Hal' found that a lot of carpentering was necessary to transform the play into a three-act operetta. They seized it, expanded it, and grafted on an entirely new plot. The result was a showpiece designed to exhibit the fiery genius of Hortense Schneider.

As usual she livened up rehearsals with her storms of temperament. She even criticised what was to emerge as the loveliest number in the score, La Périchole's song where she writes to her impoverished lover explaining why, for harsh material reasons, she has had to accept the advances of the rich Viceroy.

'I can't sing that phrase,' Hortense would shriek.

'Very well,' replied Offenbach amiably, 'I'll give it to one of the bit-players.' It was his favourite threat. According to well-established practice that had grown up at rehearsals, he then dodged back smartly to avoid the score she hurled at him across the orchestra.

'Tomorrow I leave for Italy!' she stormed as she slammed the door behind her.

Next day, as everyone expected, she was back, only too well aware of the superb opportunities Offenbach had given her and unable to resist the lovely music he had written for her. She would, indeed, have been mad to forgo the letter song. The idea is taken from the note written by Manon, the heroine of the eighteenth-century novel by Abbé Prévost. (Some years afterwards Meilhac and Philippe Gille turned the book into a libretto for Massenet. Auber's version to Scribe's libretto had already appeared in 1856 at the Opéra-Comique.)'*O mon cher amant, je te jure,*' says la Périchole, that she loves him with all her heart. But when you lack for bread how can you enjoy the raptures of love? And when you're dying of hunger, what chance is there for tenderness?

Oddly enough, this exquisite number gained little attention on the first night from an audience more intent on comedy. Hortense Schneider remembered that it went unnoticed by the stalls and that only the gallery saluted it with the applause it deserved. The theme, a slow waltz, is delicious, a melting tune scored with lucid but expressive economy.

Another small masterpiece is the arietta sung by la Périchole after the Viceroy has entertained her at a lavish dinner: 'I'm just a little bit drunk, but ssh! We mustn't say so!' The melody wavers, trembles on the edge of collapse, but never quite tumbles over as la Périchole, by a miracle, preserves her dignity and her stance.

'Above all,' Offenbach warned Hortense, 'don't overdo it. One gesture too much and the thing's ruined.' When she sang this difficult song for the first time, where the balance between delicacy and grossness rests on a hairline, she was shaking with nerves. But she succeeded. Offenbach, overjoyed, kissed her.

'Not an accent out of place, darling. It's perfect like that.'[1]

For the rest, there are boleros, seguidillas and galops to colour the exotic picture of eighteenth-century Peru. The finale to Act I, a blend of sweetness and vigour held together by the invincible pulse of a swinging march, has a joyous vitality which makes it difficult to credit that Offenbach when he wrote it was tortured by insistent pain. Neither did his agonies damp down the comic genius that enabled him to match his colleagues' word-juggling. In the rondo about recalcitrant husbands, which uses the trick that produced '*Les rois barbus qui s'avance*' in *Ophée aux enfers*, he created an excellent effect on plucked strings for:

> '... *Aux maris ré*
> *Aux maris cal*
> *Aux maris ci*
> *Aux maris trants*
> *Aux maris récalcitrants.*'

[1] It is interesting that the opening bars foreshadow the tune Sullivan used for 'A Policeman's lot is not a happy one'!

La Périchole was Schneider's last undoubted triumph. She still, of course, had many years and many new productions ahead of her before she retired, an ancient monument who lingered on well into the twentieth century, a formidable ghost to be approached with respect by young men nostalgic for the gaieties of a dead age. Yet after *La Périchole* she never again achieved the magic that Offenbach had put within her reach by starring her as Helen, as Boulotte, as the Grand Duchess, as the 'native bitch'. It would not be malice to suggest that as la Périchole she expressed her own private character most fully and in so doing painted a vivid self-portrait. Impulsive yet cunning, passionate yet cool, Hortense put all her own know-ledge of life into that world-weary song: 'Good Heavens, how stupid men are!'

Probably Offenbach realised that Schneider portrayed herself when playing la Périchole, for the following year he took the idea to its logical conclusion by writing an operetta which, in suitably dramatic form, told the story of her rise to fame. *La Diva*, with its promise of revelations about a famous personality and glimpses at romance back-stage, should have attracted a wide public, and the auspices were good, which encouraged Offenbach to recruit his trusted 'Meil' and 'Hal' and engage his old theatre, the Bouffes-Parisiens. The score is by no means inferior. An account of dinner with the rakish Prince Rococoff ('The service was Chocnosoff') has all the composer's usual neat wit. The heroine's love affairs are touched on with affectionate grace, there is an appealing duet about provincials touring the sights of Paris, and an old Alsatian melody is skilfully used as the basis of a Tyrolean number. Yet the public stayed away. They were not, it seemed, interested in drama behind the scenes. *La Diva* flopped resoundingly. 'There are days of bad luck,' observed a kindly critic, 'when nothing goes right.'

Only a week or so before, Offenbach had opened at the Opéra-Comique with *Vert-Vert*. Here he had better luck. The piece was remotely based on a humorous poem by the eighteenth century writer Louis Gresset whose work enjoys the unusual distinction of having made Napoleon laugh. It had already been the subject of two operas by earlier composers and it lightly recounted the misadventures of a favourite parrot bred in a boarding school for young persons. As the third musician to dramatise this blameless epic, Offenbach enriched it with a delightfully serio-comic funeral march for the parrot Vert-Vert and with an attractive chorus for dragoons. The dancing lesson in Act III may well have inspired Lecocq to a similar passage in his *Le Petit Duc*. Offenbach was rewarded with a longer run than *Robinson Crusoé* had achieved, though again there were criticisms about his mingling of the boulevard spirit with opéra-comique.

At the end of the year he was directing rehearsals of three new operettas at the same time. They had their first performances one after another on 7, 10 and 11 December respectively. For a man who had spent the summer desperately nursing his gout at the Villa Orphée – and writing hundreds of pages of orchestration – such activity is awe-inspiring.

La Princesse de Trébizonde had as its central character a travelling showman who wins a castle, an estate and a baron's title in a lottery. With his fellow workers, clowns, tumblers, tight-rope walkers, he arrives to take over his property. Among the wax figures in his booth is one of the Princess of Trebizond. The nose is broken, so the showman's daughter puts on the figure's costume and takes its place. A Prince's son falls in love with her and, after the statutory complications, wins her hand.

The work is pure fantasy. 'Ah, those were the days!' sigh the juggler and his friends when, installed in their grand new quarters, they look back on their time as wandering performers. Where are the barkers, the knockabout turns, where are the snows of yesteryear? The old showman tries to spin a plate. It had been one of his most successful tricks, but now he finds that his hand has lost its cunning. After the 'plate' quintet the mood becomes yet more dolorous with a 'toothache' song. But this is the world of operetta, and everything ends with a grand galop.

Les Brigands, which opened three days later, had a more acrid tang. Meilhac and Halévy joined forces with the composer again to create a piece which, although laced with comic absurdity, peppered the world of finance with some shrewd hits. Besides which, Offenbach had adopted a rather different style from his previous works. The public, he told Halévy, 'is tired of little tunes, and so am I.' He asked his librettists to take care over the building up of situations rather than to strive for amusing cross-talk. His music followed the procedures of comic opera. The obvious model was Auber's *Fra Diavolo*. He wanted to create properly worked out scenes, thought right through, instead of songs and concerted numbers loosely inserted within the dialogue.

The score, as a result, is more homogeneous than usual. Even so, the new direction they had taken did not curb the wit of Meilhac and Halévy. 'Once upon a time,' says the bandit's deputy, 'there was a great financier.' 'And what comes next?' asks one of the other characters. 'That's all,' is the cynical response. Another of the bandits has this thoughtful remark to make: 'You should always steal according to the position you hold in society.'

Les Brigands was composed in the summer of 1869 while Offenbach was travelling from Nice by way of Genoa to take the waters at Baden-Baden. At every hotel he anxiously awaited the parcels of manuscript which Meilhac and Halévy were, after their custom, too slow to deliver. At last he put the finishing touches to his score in Étretat.

The best-known number is the policemen's chorus. It expresses some of the Frenchman's traditional distrust, and contempt for, members of a service which is, in France, not particularly noted either for its gentle treatment of civilians or its impartiality. Falsacappa, the bandit chief, hears the tramp of boots and quickly spirits his men to a safe hiding place. The guardians of law and order arrive and announce themselves: 'We are the carabineers, the guarantee of people's safety. Yet through an unfortunate chance we always arrive too late to help the citizen in need.' For English ears this has a familiar ring. The London adaptation was made by W. S. Gilbert. When he came to write *The Pirates of Penzance* with Sullivan he remembered *Les Brigands* in several of his jokes and particularly in the choruses where the British bobby is mocked with gentle fun.

There was also a British link in Offenbach's final production of 1869, *La Romance de la Rose*, which had as its theme song 'The Last Rose of Summer', already known to Europe from Flotow's opera *Martha*. This one-acter is a typical mixture that reaches back in style to Offenbach's earlier trifles: it has for heroine an American widow, a French artist as hero, and an Irish tune as the leading motif. 'Oh! what is sweet love in miou-sic!' exclaims the widow in Americo-French.

There was something appropriate about the melancholy of 'The Last Rose of Summer'. It marks the concluding Offenbach production of the doomed Second Empire. For the next two years his name was absent from theatre posters. Indeed, there were few theatres open at all during that period, because within months France had declared war on Germany.

Yet when, later on, he looked back at 1869, it was not with regret but rather with affection. That year brought the annivers-ary of his silver wedding and at the celebrations in Étretat he excelled himself. On 14 August there was a huge dinner party followed by a masked ball with a march played by forty reed pipes. Jacques and Herminie dressed up as a village wedding couple and guests were summoned to a 'Grand Nautical, Aquatic and Rustic Marriage' at which Herminie was to espouse, 'after twenty-five years as supporting player, the most illustrious, the most excellent, the most fantastic

MAESTRO
JACOBUS OFFENBACHUS
MAGNUS

author of many celebrated works including *Berthe* the vivacious; *Mimi* the devoted; *Pépita* the majestic; *Jacqueline* the sympa-thetic and incomparable; *Auguste* known as Delight to the eyes, Nectar of the heart. These five works were produced in collaboration.'

At the ball, according to the programme, time would be allowed for 'mutual admiration, compliments on the originality of the costumes.' An uncle was to perform his party pieces which included the dance of the tottering toad and the dance of the grasshopper that had missed its train. At half-past eleven an 'Exhibition of the Offenbach family' was scheduled. It comprised 'a description of each member, enumeration of virtues, aptitudes and little talents, and confession of vices and hidden faults.'

After feasting and fireworks came the bedding of the bride. 'The fire brigade at Vattetot-sur-mer have spontaneously despatched a deputation with the task of assisting the bride in her supreme moment,' added a note. At Herminie's request a strip of paper obliterated this section. It bore the words: 'Cut by the censor.'

The family came down on Étretat in droves. There were uncles and aunts, nephews and cousins, nieces and in-laws, and a torrent of friends and acquaintances. Although for Offenbach it was child's play to hatch the most involved stage plots and to elaborate them further with a whole mesh of subsidiary incident if necessary, he found himself incapable of sorting out his relationship with Herminie's vast family. There were ramifications he could never grasp. No sooner had he tracked down the links of second cousins once removed, than he was confronted with the daunting problem of a third cousin by marriage. Often, over the dinner-table at Étretat, kindly attempts were made to enlighten him. He would take crumbs of bread and lay them out in front of him, each one representing a member of the monstrously distended clan. Then, when he believed that at last he had seized the pattern of kinship, with a flick of the finger he sent the bits of bread flying.

'Well, that's that,' he exclaimed. 'We shan't need to talk about *that* again.'

The next moment he had forgotten it all anew.

But if the structure of his wife's family escaped him entirely, he was clear in his own mind about what Herminie meant to him. Though often mean over the housekeeping, though frequently unfaithful, he always regarded her as the centre of his life. One of the revues he staged in Étretat contained the following verse, sung to the tune which accompanies the goddesses in *Orphée aux enfers* when they laugh at Jupiter and his naughty exploits:

> Offenbach est insupportable,
> Il est toujours plein de manies
> Et lorsqu'il est un peu aimable,
> C'est qu'il pense à Herminie . . .
> Ah! ah! ah! . . .

Offenbach is unbearable, says this self-portrait, he's always full of fads. Yet when he's pleasanter than usual it's because he's thinking of Herminie. In the months to come he was to need her more than ever.

PART V

MISFORTUNATE IMPRESARIO

20

The Man who lost the War

Offenbach reached his fiftieth birthday in 1870. He was now the unrivalled master of French operetta. There were at least four theatres in Paris featuring either a new operetta by him or revivals of earlier works. If, of late, his touch had occasionally seemed unsure, if the formulas he adopted struck some of his hearers as a little out of keeping with the times, his music remained for the general public the most tuneful and the most agreeable of all.

Though Halévy foresaw the dark days that lay ahead, Offenbach did not really anticipate them. For him, the political manoeuvres of warring states were scenario material. The feints and ploys of bellicose politicians were good for satire. But when General Boum materialised into real life and, as diplomatist and soldier, outwitted the sick and failing Emperor Louis-Napoléon, there was no convenient stage trick available to ensure a happy ending for the last act.

On 19 July France was tempted into declaring war on Bismarck's Germany. Crowds marched the streets of Paris roaring '*Á Berlin!*' A wave of patriotism swamped the customary nonchalance of the boulevards. Offenbach's distress was increased when he called on his dear 'Hal' before going to Étretat. A close friend of Halévy's had just committed suicide on hearing of the declaration of war. And in Étretat Herminie greeted Offenbach with tears: her brother had been called up.

The atmosphere clouded even more because of a vicious newspaper campaign directed against Offenbach. Every successful man attracts malice and envy as surely as a magnet draws filings. Offenbach had his full complement of spiteful rivals and failed competitors. In those hysterical days articles appeared accusing him of being 'a Prussian at heart'. At the same time, as if to preserve the balance of denigration, German newspapers attacked him with ferocity. He could do no right.

Although he was trying to work on a new operetta, his

thoughts were distracted by the hurtful calumnies. He limped disconsolately through the garden in Étretat, shoulders bowed, mouth drooping. He wrote, a little shrilly, to his friend Villemessant at the *Figaro*: 'I have, in Germany, a family and friends who are dear to me; it is for their sake that I ask you to print this:

'Since the age of fourteen I have lived in France;

'I have received full naturalisation papers;

'I have been appointed Chevalier in the Légion d'honneur;

'I owe everything to France and I would not think myself worthy of the name of Frenchman, which I have obtained through my work and my honourable standing, if I had made myself guilty of cowardice towards my first country.'

Most wounding of all were accusations that he was a renegade, an outsider. He felt himself to be wholly French. Yet, for all that, was it his fault that he had been born in Germany?

Even his accent was a subject of reproach. In the old days he had joked about it. Now it was no longer funny.

He was startled and saddened by the violence of feeling against him. Soon after the war began his name came up for promotion to the next grade in the Légion d'honneur. The Empress Eugénie herself struck it off the list.

As August went out the French army capitulated at Sedan and Louis-Napoléon was taken prisoner. In Étretat that month Offenbach decided to move his family out of the country. They went over the border into Spain and rented a house at San Sebastian. 'Ah, my dear friend,' Offenbach wrote to one of his librettists, 'whoever would have thought that those horrible Prussians, those so-called civilised people, would bring ruin to our poor dear France?'

After a long and exhausting siege Paris gave way to the enemy. An armistice was signed and in March German troops came down the Champs-Elysées. 'I hope,' Offenbach told one of his friends, 'that Guillaume Krupp and his horrible Bismarck will pay for all this. Ah! what horrible people these Prussians are and what a grief for me to think that I was born on the banks of the Rhine and am linked in any way with those horrible savages! Ah! my poor France, how I thank her for having adopted me among her children!' In his agitation he misspelt words and repeated phrases. Then a little of the old irony returned. '. . . I am sorry for those dear colleagues who hope, because I've had a lot of success, to harm me by saying that I'm German, when they know very well that I'm French to the very marrow of my bones! . . . Write to me at the Goldene Lamme, Vienna, Austria (not Germany); I'll never set bloody foot again in that cursed country.'

The declaration of a Republic did not put an end to France's torment. In Paris the revolutionary Commune established itself while the elected government, under the good grey lawyer Monsieur Thiers, retreated to Versailles. Weeks of atrocity and massacre followed. At the end of May the government reasserted itself. By then 25,000 Frenchmen had died at the hands of their fellow-countrymen.

Offenbach meanwhile journeyed on business throughout Europe. If all French theatres were closed to him, that was no reason to ignore other opportunities. 'Jacques is in Milan on a trip through Italy,' Herminie wrote to Charles Nuitter. 'He'll be back within a fortnight at Étretat, where I plan to go very soon. He's been very deeply upset by this awful war. His health has been very seriously affected by it and in three months he hasn't had a single good week.'

For once in his life he did not feel like writing operettas. He composed a *Dieu sauve la France* and a symphonic piece which included a setting of patriotic lines by Victor Hugo. Inspired by the terrible events of 1871, it was to be called either *Symphonie Solennelle* or *In Memoriam*. It remained unfinished.

There were no finales to be tightened up, no singers to be tyrannised, no theatre managers to be engaged in battles. He did not know what to do with himself. He had time to think about things in the aimless void that now engulfed him and it was an uncomfortable sensation. Without the drug of ceaseless work he felt lost, afloat, bereft of purpose.

The memoirs of Berlioz had just been published and Offenbach read them with an absorption that verged on the masochistic. Offenbach had had many critics and for the most part he ignored them. In any case their carping was buried as soon as the next issue of the newspaper appeared. The only critic he respected was the public, which, by paying to hear his operettas or by staying away from them, delivered a judgement to which there could be no answer. Berlioz, however, had long been a source of discomfort.

He was like no other journalist. He had the gift of the vivid phrase, the cutting epigram, the memorable sally. He wrote with ease and brilliance. His ridicule was precise and lethal and more than a century later his ferocious wit still shines. Offenbach had been his victim on several occasions. Each time the poisoned dart struck home.

During those months of desolate idleness Offenbach read Berlioz' memoirs line by line. In bed at night, sleepless from rheumatic pain, he turned the pages with a bony finger. From time to time his indignation caused him to scribble outraged comments in the margin. He finished the book quivering with anger. Scores of pencilled annotations revealed his boiling hatred for the composer. 'The musician Berlioz never accepted a criticism,' he scrawled on one of the pages, 'yet as a critic himself he was pitiless often and malicious always.'

What made his irritation strangely unbearable was the respect he could not deny to Berlioz as a composer. He admired wholeheartedly the creator of the *Damnation de Faust* and in particular the *Enfance du Christ*. This 'manly, exalted, skilful talent,' he decided, had only one deficiency in his struggle for recognition: that of being French.

The sincerest compliment he paid was in his use of Berlioz' *Traité de l'instrumentation*. There were certain technical problems he could never solve on his own, and he found the treatise invaluable. Writing for horns and trumpets sometimes gave him difficulty. What was their range? How would they sound in a given combination? He turned for salvation to Berlioz, but in secret and always borrowing a copy from a discreet publisher.

The Paris to which he returned in the summer of 1871 had more urgent matters to think about than the quarrel between two composers. Houses lay smoking in ruins. Everywhere in the streets lay rubble and smashed paving stones. The palace of the Tuileries was reduced to a series of blackened walls and few public buildings had escaped damage or plunder. Those which the shells of the Prussians failed to destroy had not always been lucky enough to avoid the fury of the Communards. It was a long time before they were restored.

Gradually Parisians drifted back from the countryside to

which they had fled. The ruins were tidied up and life began all over again. In June the army paraded before Thiers, the president of the new Third Republic. At its head rode Marshal Mac-Mahon who two years later was to succeed him. Despite the ravages of war and insurrection, the Paris created by Louis-Napoléon and his architect Haussmann remained. War had not altered the grand design of broad boulevards and airy vistas.

Yet the city was quite different from the one Offenbach first knew as a boy. A million people then lived in it. Now it was the home of twice that number. No longer did the aristocracy and the upper classes set the tone and manage public affairs. They had been followed by a new and vigorous middle class which prospered to the rhythm of fast-growing industry and commerce. Without an Imperial Court to mould fashion and sponsor grand events, social life took on a quieter tone. The atmosphere of *La Vie Parisienne* was out of date.

For a time the musical mode favoured patriotic songs. This meant stirring appeals for the lost provinces of Alsace and Lorraine, and sentimental verses about prisoners of war returning home. Then satire and comedy replaced patriotism as the main theme of popular song.

Offenbach found himself a little out of place in all this. The attacks against him continued. In the random recriminations that engaged a country fresh from its material and psychological defeat, he served as a convenient scapegoat, a symbol of the frivolity which, so the theory went, had sapped the morale of the nation and led to its downfall. He had played a large part, said his enemies, in encouraging the buffoonery, the irreverence and the careless materialism which had dragged France to its ruin. Those who saw him as the arch-corruptor even hinted that the humiliation of Sedan might as well be laid at his door.

The puzzled musician retired to Étretat. The house was untouched, the sea glittered in the summer sunshine, and, best of all, Herminie and the family were there to comfort him with laughter and affection. Paris newspapers continued to revile him, now accusing him of cowardice because he had left the country at the outbreak of war. His detractors neglected to explain how Offenbach could have stemmed, single-handed, the Prussian advance. He found the climate of the new régime distinctly uncomfortable. In public he said little, but in private he expressed his opinion with discretion, as the manuscript sub-title of a waltz that he wrote a few years later demonstrates: '. . . composed by chance and by Jacques Offenbach . . . in the third year of grace of the new and, alas! neither good nor beautiful Republic.'

As usual he found his remedy in work. He had struck up a friendship with the playwright Victorien Sardou. Though later to be ridiculed by Bernard Shaw as the prince of 'Sardoodledom', this fertile craftsman wrote plays which can still hold the stage today, musty though their idiom may be. He excelled at the well-turned climax and the neatly tailored dénouement. By the 1870s he had established himself as one of the most successful theatrical figures of the time, with a flair for what the public wanted which he provided with a generous hand.

For Sarah Bernhardt he wrote some of her most extravagant triumphs: melodramas about Greek courtesans, Egyptian queens and Spanish heroines. For Réjane he concocted the famous *Madame Sans-Gêne* which a long line of actresses including even Mistinguett have been performing ever since. His char-acters are wooden, his dialogue is paltry, but he had the supreme gift of theatre which enabled him to create scenes that any leading lady worth her salt would burn to play. The opera Puccini based on *La Tosca* is only one example of the crude but effective blood-boltered epics he knew how to serve up.

Sardou was a genial man, affable to all and accepting people on their merits. He did not bore his dinner guests with talk about literature, but instead with chat about figures, takings, receipts at theatres, and which play in Paris at that moment was doing the best business. When he cracked a joke his thin lips and clean-shaven face screwed up into an actor's grimace.

Here was a man after Offenbach's own heart. He was, moreover, a Bonapartist and loathed the Republic. Together they worked on an operetta called *Le Roi Carotte*. It was an allegory in which King Fridolin (Louis-Napoléon) is dethroned by an ungrateful country in favour of Carotte (the Republican opposition). But under the rule of Carotte life becomes far worse, and after another revolution Fridolin is offered the crown again. He returns amid rejoicing.

Offenbach enjoyed working on *Le Roi Carotte*. Although satirical in nature it was different from his pre-war operettas and the form was that of a pantomime. The characters included a witch, a sorcerer and a necromancer. Spells were cast, a magic powder transformed public opinion, and vegetables turned into human beings. The combined stagecraft of Sardou and his musical friend engineered a handsome spectacle of eighteen scenes which included the last days of Pompeii (Offenbach's idea) and a ballet of insects.

Zulma Bouffar, who still had a relationship with Offenbach, played a leading rôle. *Le Roi Carotte* also featured a new discovery of his called Anna Judic. She was the daughter of the box-office cashier at the Théâtre du Gymnase and had grown up backstage. Having married the actor Judic (whose real name was Israël), she won immediate success at the Eldorado, a famous café-concert which was to see many other distinguished beginnings, among them those of Maurice Chevalier and Mistinguett. After the war she turned to operetta. Offenbach was one of the first to appreciate her plump charms.

The collaboration with Sardou went smoothly. Alert, quick, always in motion, Sardou valued Offenbach's knowledge of the stage which was as great as his own. The two veterans treated each other's craft with respect. If Sardou, as a man of letters, was occasionally fearful that his words might be lost in the music, Offenbach did his best to accommodate him. As with Meilhac and Halévy, he kept up a vigorous correspondence, though the tone of his letters this time was more discreet.

Le Roi Carotte had a successful run. Its satirical implications were cheered by some and booed by others, but receipts were excellent. In all it had 149 performances and would have passed the 150 mark, but that was the figure at which, under their contract, the authors were to receive an extra payment. The management decided to take the profits and go.

Three days after the première of *Le Roi Carotte* in January 1872, the Opéra-Comique gave Offenbach's three-act version of *Fantasio* based on the Musset play. Overburdened with a poor libretto it scarcely survived a fortnight. Messager was to have greater luck with the subject in 1907. This was the last Offenbach work to appear there during his lifetime. A similar venture with the disastrous *Barkouf*, now re-vamped and entitled *Boule-de-neige*, collapsed almost as quickly. The snowball melted with alarming speed.

Paris was not, in those days immediately after the war, a congenial place for Offenbach. She seemed to have withdrawn her favours from the man she once covered with success. Had the master's touch deserted him? Audiences at *Le Roi Carotte* were attracted more by the spectacle than by his music. But perhaps Vienna would remain faithful to him.

There he went in the autumn of 1872. In his baggage was the score of a new piece called *Le Corsaire noir*. This curious black pirate had a libretto supposedly by the composer himself. On the strength of rehearsals Offenbach had high hopes. It would, he wrote, 'have an *immense* success ... The first act comes off well ... The second is charming ... The finale has a *very, very great* effect. As for the third act, I've not been mistaken for a moment, it's a terrific laugh from start to finish ...'

Alas he was wrong again. The Viennese did not share his opinion. The failure of *Le Corsaire noir* was not the only disquieting event to occur on this Austrian visit. Returning to his hotel one day he saw an old man sprawled in the gutter and stopped to ask if he could be of help. The man's name, they told him, was Zimmer, Rudolph Zimmer. He had collapsed from hunger and exhaustion.

Zimmer!

Immediately the tune of Zimmer's waltz ran through his mind, the tune so close to his childhood and his early struggles that it was a very part of him. He summoned a doctor, had the aged musician taken home and left him some money.

A fortnight later Zimmer called to thank him. He was astonished at the warmth of the greeting he received. Somebody still remembered him, and that somebody was the famous Offenbach! The composer begged him to play his waltz. Still rather puzzled, Zimmer sat down at the piano. He played the first eight bars and stopped, then began again. Yet still he could not remember what came after. Offenbach seethed with disappointment.

Some weeks afterward when Offenbach returned to Vienna, a packet was handed to him. It contained a sapphire ring, an old envelope, a sheet of music and a letter from Zimmer. The musician had died in the meantime, but before his aged body drew its last breath he had delivered up the key to the mystery.

The ring had been intended for his fiancée, but her sudden

death prevented their marriage. Since then Zimmer had lost all appetite for life, wandering sadly from place to place and earning a bare subsistence as an itinerant musician. The old envelope contained a lock of hair belonging to his fiancée. He asked Offenbach to burn it and to keep the ring.

The sheet of music bore the complete waltz that Zimmer, with a supreme effort of memory, had at last managed to write out. Offenbach did as he was asked. He burned the envelope and preserved the ring. Then he played Zimmer's waltz in full. And as he did so all the old images returned with a haunting melancholy: his father's house in Cologne, the noise of music coming from all over the home, the attic in the rue des Martyrs, those lonely first days in Paris...It was a tale from Hoffmann.

He came back to Paris in a thoughtful mood. Nostalgic, weighted down with bittersweet memories, he suddenly felt very tired. Rheumatism pincered the muscle of his leg and sent waves of red-hot pain down his back. He shivered and, although it was the middle of August, huddled more deeply into his cumbersome fur overcoat.

That summer *Les Brigands* was revived at the Théâtre des Variétés. Here he returned to the arena of his old triumphs, the theatre where *La Belle Hélène* and *La Grande-Duchesse de Gérolstein* had first seen the footlights. The musty, rambling place had been turned into a makeshift hospital during the war. Now demobilised, the shadowy auditorium lay waiting for the magician to fill it again with brightness and music.

When Offenbach arrived the chorus was rehearsing the finale to the last act. He climbed rheumatically onto the stage and watched them. Ludovic Halévy joined him and asked after his health. Oh, groaned Offenbach, he hadn't slept a wink that night. He was too tired to take any interest in the rehearsal.

Almost before he had finished his sentence he was on his feet, brandishing his walking-stick and screaming at the chorus: 'What's all this you've been singing, ladies? Start again, start the whole finale again!'

He went up to the piano beside the conductor and took charge of the rehearsal. The chorus, which until then had been merely ambling through the music for form's sake, looked at him in surprise. Offenbach warmed up, shouted at them, sang, mimed, danced about and flew from one part of the stage to another as he gradually brought a somnolent chorus to life. A moment ago he had been shivering, but now the sweat poured in rivulets down his face. He ripped off his coat and sent it flying and beat time so vigorously with his stick that it snapped in two. He swore, threw the pieces to the ground and, without ceasing to mark out the rhythm, snatched a violin bow from the hands of the startled conductor.

The singers were galvanised. Their voices rang out clear and vigorous while the finale gathered pace and exploded into a flash of gaiety. After the last note ended everyone clapped Offenbach, who fell into his chair.

'I've broken my stick but I've got my finale back!' he cried. Offenbach was himself again.

21

Bankruptcy – and the Shadow of Lecocq

He was never seen to walk on the boulevards. He travelled everywhere in a carriage that took him from door to door. One day he arrived at a café, descended from the vehicle and went to meet a colleague. For some time now he had been awaiting the words of a number for his latest operetta. At last they were ready. He sat at table with his librettist and scanned the verse that was offered him. Music started to form in his mind. Afraid that he might forget the tune, he seized a plate, drew on it the regulation five lines and added the notes. His inspiration preserved, he resumed the interrupted meal and went on talking.

The new work that preoccupied him was called *Les Braconniers*. It was produced at 'his' Théâtre des Variétés where he gathered round him Zulma Bouffar and familiar faces from the company that had made its reputation there in pre-war days. He gave an important rôle to the youthful Marie Heilbronn who was later to be Massenet's first *Manon*. His eye for new talent had lost none of its keenness.

This comedy about poachers did not last long. Audiences found it too reminiscent of *Les Brigands*. There were also dramatic quarrels between Offenbach and the manager of the Variétés. Although these arguments often reached a titanic fury, by the next day, as usually happens in the theatre, the opponents were on the most affectionate terms. Nevertheless Offenbach began to think it was time he ran his own theatre. He had done it before with the Bouffes-Parisiens. Why should he not do it again?

The temptation to be his own master was irresistible. He had new ideas and experiments in mind. His programmes would alternate between the lavish production and the more modest light opera that recent developments had shown to be gaining in vogue. In between, or if times became difficult, he could always keep the pot boiling with a revival of one of his own past successes. The Theatre de la Gaîté, which he planned to take over, would be the grandest house in Paris.

He had reckoned without the Société des auteurs, the French equivalent of the Performing Rights Society which existed to protect the interests of writers and composers. One of their statutes forbade theatre managers to produce their own works. It was an obvious precaution. The Society, under the chairmanship of Alexandre Dumas, called Offenbach to appear before them.

One afternoon, on the stage of the Théâtre des Variétés, in the eerie twilit atmosphere of an auditorium where no play is being acted, Offenbach pleaded his cause. For more than eighteen years, he said, he had been a man of the theatre. During that time he had written more than eighty operettas. The Society should not forget that if he were to be prevented from producing any more, so also would be the librettists with whom he worked. Was that just? Was it right to smash his career?

The Society, in its fear and distrust of theatre managers, thought it was. A vote was taken and showed a large majority against him. His reaction to the dilemma was swift and simple. He took the Théâtre de la Gaîté, as arranged, on 1 June 1873, and resigned from the Société des auteurs.

The plans he had in mind were grandiose. He engaged two companies of actors, one for operetta and the other for plays. Having spent over 380,000 francs to acquire his lease, he then laid out half as much again on redecorating the barn-like interior of his theatre. New seats were installed, carpets and hangings of the richest quality were ordered. Equipment and machinery backstage were taken out and replaced with up-to-date models. It was like those heroic days when Offenbach had set up the Théâtre des Bouffes-Parisiens. Only this time he was launching his career as a great impresario. Or so he proudly believed.

His partners were Etienne Tréfeu and Albert Vizentini. Tréfeu he had known since the early years, an easy-going writer who had worked on half a dozen libretti for him. Vizentini came of an old Italian family, established in France and long associated with the theatre, who had begun by playing the violin at the Bouffes-Parisiens and who eventually conducted orchestras at other playhouses. His travels led him to England, Ireland and

St Petersburg, at which last he managed a theatre. Besides composing several operettas he wrote much journalism, and this diversity of talent, allied with his southern blood, made him a lively and exigent partner. Where Tréfeu was slow-moving and anxious to avoid making decisions, Vizentini was impulsive and given to zany notions. The three men were, perhaps, the most unlikely trio ever to embark on large-scale theatre management.

While Offenbach was away conducting in Vienna and taking the waters at Aix-les-Bains, he deluged his friends in Paris with instructions about every aspect of the work in hand. To Vizentini he wrote: 'Since my departure you've received thirty-odd letters and 245 telegrams, and you complain!' Had Offenbach lived in the age of the telephone his collaborators would have had still greater cause for self-pity.

That summer he was full of energy, thrilled with his projects and happy to be wrapped up in a venture that challenged his imagination. It was in this mood that he wrote a new operetta for another of his discoveries, the nineteen-year-old Louise Théo. He heard her at a café-concert singing things like 'Don't you tickle me' and 'I'm a greedy one'. Her voice was poor, a mere thread of sound, but it had an attractive huskiness, an inviting accent that was delectable. She was a child-like, mischievous blonde, ideal for the leading rôle of *Pomme d'api,* or 'lady-apple'. Like that fruit, which in French owes its name to Appius who first cultivated it, Louise was glossy, firm and well sugared.

Offenbach took her and the cast down to Étretat for a performance of *Pomme d'api.* The old diversions had started up again at the Villa Orphée. Throughout the summer 'the actors in ordinary to Madame Offenbach' played skits on Wagner and galas 'in honour of the presence of the President of the Republic in Trouville'.

It is easy to see Louise Théo as *Pomme d'api,* the maid who introduces herself in spirited couplets as being able to cook, wash the laundry, post letters, run errands, and give her employer 'everything that an honest girl can give for thirty francs a month.' She also has a crackling rondeau where she declares herself ready to take on soldiers and civilians, MPs and lawyers, farmers and men of letters, big men and little men, fat ones and thin ones, blacks and whites, baritones and tenors. In fact, anyone who can show he loves her.

Pomme d'api enjoyed as warm a welcome in Paris as it had at
the Villa Orphée, but two days before on 2 September, the
Théâtre de la Gaîté had opened in all its renovated splendour
with a play called *Le Gascon*, which turned out to be the most
notorious failure of the season. Offenbach had chosen unwisely.
It was a black moment. While he looked around desperately for
something to fill the breach, he had two new full-length
operettas to supervise elsewhere.

Madame l'Archiduc came out at the end of October, a comedy
about an Italian prince who, attracted by a tavern waitress,
decides to abdicate and hand over power to her. There was
nothing here of the satire contained in *La Grande-Duchesse de
Gérolstein*. It was an opportunity for Anna Judic as Madame
Archduke to review her troops and express comic surprise that
they were led by 'a little chap no bigger than *that!*' With a
dramatis personae that included characters named Andantino
and Tutti-frutti, an 'English spoken here' quartet was inevitable:
'Oh! yes splendid l'Italie, London y préfer, Oh! yes moi comme
vous y préfer Birmingham and Manchester. Oh! Venise elle est
jolie, Very beautiful, y préfer Dublin oh! Liverpool! Very nice
Liverpool . . . Oh! d'houdou you dou.'

'Very Nice Liverpool.' More subtle was the 'alphabet' sextet.
Then came an effective number for the Archduke:

> '*Original! original! Combien je suis original!*
> '*Non rien n'est plus original Qu'un Archiduc original!*'[1]

No scandal here in my fine house, he pleads, when the dragoons
arrive and carry out an arrest to the rhythm of a polka. One
occasionally feels that Offenbach and his writers were Surrealists
fifty years ahead of their time.

A month later it was the turn of *La Jolie Parfumeuse*, a three-
act piece which, like *Pomme d'api*, Offenbach agreed to write
for the Théâtre de la Renaissance, a large theatre opened in the
previous year and already badly in need of a strong draw. The
plot deals with the love affairs of the pretty perfume seller and
her friend, a dancer at the Opéra. Offenbach wrote it in seven

---

[1] Well in the tradition of Maurice Chevalier's '*Quand un vicomte rencontre
un autre vicomte, qu'est-ce qu'on se raconte? Des histoires de vicomte!*'

weeks. The music included a blind beggars' chorus, (*'Chacun d'nous souffle et beugle, Oui beugle comme un aveugle Dedans son instrument'*), which is sung by the crafty mendicants as they prepare to set off on a day's fleecing of Parisians. This reminder of the much earlier *Les Deux Aveugles* has a sharp humour parallelled by the 'Letter' rondeau in which a naïf suitor requests the hand of their daughter from her disapproving parents. It was not vintage Offenbach and owed its run chiefly to Louise Théo, for whose abilities it had been carefully made to measure. The only other point of interest about *La Jolie Parfumeuse*, at least for an English reader, lay in the name of the actress who played the part of Madelon. Whether or not her birth certificate would have confirmed it, she called herself Jane Eyre.

Meanwhile there was the problem of the Théâtre de la Gaîté. Offenbach simply could not afford another disaster there. Putting aside his ambitious idea of producing *A Midsummer Night's Dream* with Mendelssohn's music and Beethoven's *Ruins of Athens*, he fell back instead on *Orphée aux enfers*. It had been his first success. It was part of his legend. It would not let him down. Yet he could not help feeling a little shamefaced about the revival. He dearly wanted to gain laurels with a new work. But this time he had no alternative. He covered up with mock braggadocio in a letter to his partners describing himself as 'the greatest manager, the greatest composer, the wittiest man that ever *creator* created . . .'

An orchestra of sixty was engaged, a brass band forty-strong, 120 singers, and a ballet troupe of sixty dancers. The modest production of 1858 was expanded into a four-act pantomime and swamped in a blaze of special effects. Olympus emerged in gorgeous perspective and the Theban countryside shone in the warm glow of a brilliant lighting system. Paris loved it. Fathers who as young men had seen the original performance took their children to the Théâtre de la Gaîté. Now two generations had come to know the charm of Offenbach.

At the hundredth performance the composer himself conducted. Edging along by clinging for support to the rails around the orchestra pit, he entered to a storm of applause. From a box the whole Offenbach family waved at him. Once on the rostrum he led the music with all his old energy. The years dropped

away, gout and rheumatism were forgotten in the furious pace
he set as he goaded players and singers into the delirious
measures of the breathless Offenbachiade. When it was over,
surrounded by the family and troops of friends, he went back
home for a triumphal supper.

By the end of 1874 the revised version of *Orphée* had taken
over two million francs at the box-office. The lesson was obvious.
Offenbach went ahead and freshened up *La Périchole*, added a
third act and, wonder of wonders, persuaded Hortense Schneider
to sing the rôle she had created. It was an emotional evening.
She appeared in a dress covered with diamonds that winked and
flashed into every corner of the auditorium. 'She must have
discovered a diamond mine,' said a first-nighter. 'A mine...and
miners!' replied his companion.

Not all Offenbach's activity was confined to revivals. At the
request of his son-in-law Charles Comte, still manager of the
Bouffes-Parisiens and anxious for help, he wrote the little
Bagatelle. It helped him assuage his artistic conscience, though
at a cost to his aching body. He composed it in bed, scarcely able
to struggle out and try an occasional chord at the piano. From
time to time a ring at the doorbell presaged the arrival of a
messenger to collect the freshly written manuscript for rehearsals
that evening. Despite these handicaps he managed to endow
Bagatelle with a graceful setting that involved a 'friendship'
rondo for Judic and an ingeniously comic 'snoring' trio.

When *Orphée* at long last ended its run he had to find
something else for his Théâtre de la Gaîté. He decided to stage
La Haine by his friend Sardou. It was time he gave work to the
company of actors who, while *Orphée* occupied the stage, had
been standing by in salaried idleness for many months. 'I gladly
guarantee you a hundred performances plus twelve per cent of
the takings,' he wrote with enthusiasm to Sardou when he
accepted what he called 'your masterpiece'. Immediately he
spent close on 350,000 francs to give it the production he
thought it deserved. Much of this went on bales of silk and velvet
and specially made armour that was never used. Over a hundred
extras were enlisted to act out battle scenes which Offenbach
directed with such care for realism that after each rehearsal the
place looked like a hospital ward. Even Sardou trembled at his
prodigality.

Melodic line of a song

Offenbach's maniacal absorption in his theatre may have been a reaction against the intense physical pain he now suffered continuously. The medical treatment he was receiving increased, rather than cured, the devastating agony that had implanted itself in his right arm. A month before the première of *La Haine* he wrote to Tréfeu and Vizentini: 'When I've a moment's respite I start working. Yes, but I'm extremely anxious about it all . . . Ah! if I didn't have you I'd blow my brains out. It's true I wouldn't have taken over the Gaîté. I'd be less happy but more tranquil, I'd die in a corner like a dog and no more would be heard of me. Thanks be to Heaven I've got you! If my arms are sick, I know I've four of yours I can count on. That's my consolation in distress.'

La Haine opened on a chilly December night in 1874. The audience, as Sardou had feared, was so impressed by Offenbach's luxurious production that it tended to overlook the words. This was no great disadvantage, for the play itself had more than the usual share of improbability. Next day snow fell heavily on Paris and discouraged potential theatregoers. Offenbach was astonished, disappointed. His eye scanned row upon row of empty seats. He decided to 'paper' the house with a vengeance. 'This evening the theatre must be crammed with people,' he wrote to Vizentini, 'so give away tickets, give them away. It's better to refuse 1,000 francs than have a theatre half-full; leave a box with three seats and two stalls in an envelope with the concierge for M. Fochet. Also a few stalls, four, and half a dozen in the upper gallery for Choudens. Send two stalls in the circle to Madame Jenny Lind. Have them taken immediately to this address: 49, rue de Lafayette, Hôtel du Monde. If you and Tréfeu have reliable friends, give them tickets for the circle and orchestra; fill up, fill up. I don't want a single empty seat in the place. I'll be with you in the theatre at twelve to talk about things.'

The tide refused to turn. *La Haine* bombinated nightly to an ever dwindling audience. Offenbach, who in person counted the takings at the box-office, totted up a figure that shrank as each day went by. 'I'm heart-broken, unhappier than even you are to see that your piece, your *masterpiece*, in spite of my efforts, isn't making all the money it ought to,' he told Sardou. 'It's a terrible shame: why didn't we shove in a few nude women or some cute tricks or lions or something or other. I blush in thinking it . . . I don't know what to do. Will you come to see me tomorrow morning? Everything's against us at the moment. What weather! Let's hope the end of December will send up the takings again. Come to me, come, I'm very unhappy, especially because of you . . .'

Sardou responded by striking a noble attitude. Despite the grave situation he enjoyed the chance to make a gesture, particularly as all the money sunk in *La Haine* was not his but Offenbach's. Speaking like one of his own characters faced with a second-act crisis, he declared: 'If we had been told that a play written with so much care, love and conviction, welcomed by its interpreters with such enthusiasms, produced by you with so much art and taste, applauded at its first night with the rare honours of a curtain call for the company at the end of each act, and encouraged next day by the almost unanimous approval of the whole press, that this play at its twenty-fifth performance would not take enough to cover its expenses, we'd neither of us have believed it. And yet that is what happens.'

One senses the throb in the voice, the hand raised towards the distant gallery. 'I have too much pride in my work to allow it to stagnate in takings unworthy of it. And I'm too fond of you to associate you any longer with its unjust fate. I ask you as a favour to cancel performances of *La Haine* and to assure theatregoers who do not find this tragedy in prose *amusing enough* by promising them that for my part I shall not write another.' Wrapping his toga proudly round him, Lear-like in his defiance of the fates, the playwright concluded this mellifluous blend of commercialism and exalted feeling by signing himself 'Your affectionate Sardou'.

Through Villemessant's good graces Offenbach published this letter in *Le Figaro* together with his own reply, one of sorrowful agreement. An unexpected result was that the publicity stimulated interest. Towards the end of the month, three weeks after the first performance, receipts had mounted to over 8,000 francs a night and *La Haine* could have survived.

But it was too late. Offenbach had already arranged yet another revival of *Orphée aux enfers*, which took the stage in the dying days of 1874. *Orphée*, ever dependable, enabled him to pay off some of his worst debts. With the suits of armour and other trappings left over from *La Haine* he also put on *Geneviève de*

Brabant again. Many hundreds of thousands of francs were laid out to mount a ballet and a transformation scene dazzling with coloured lights. He still could not attract the public.

From London came a brighter piece of news which helped to lift his spirits a trifle. *Whittington et son chat,* played originally at the Alhambra as 'Dick Whittington and His Cat', earned him, to the great surprise of his collaborators Nuitter and Tréfeu when he shared it with them, the sum of 60,000 francs. Based on the old legend, it featured a roast-beef type of quartet, 'Every good citizen of England', which Offenbach deemed suitable for the occasion. Londoners seemed to think so too. A more Gallic flavour peeped out of the duet 'Now tell me, what is a lady cat . . .?'

The fiasco of *La Haine* had not spoilt Offenbach's friendship with Sardou. It served, on the contrary, to bring them closer together. They dined frequently in each other's homes and even talked of further collaboration. Sardou had plans to dramatise *Don Quixote*. The two men spent pleasant hours talking of the wonderful scenes they would stage: a bull fight with live animals, a thunderstorm, beautiful lighting effects to represent sunrise and the passing of clouds over the sky . . .

Reality broke in with the disgruntled clamour of those to whom Offenbach owed huge sums. He could no longer stave off the reckoning. In May 1875, even Offenbach the eternal optimist, the dreamer of dreams, had to admit that he must give up the Théâtre de la Gaîté. His ambition of dominating the Paris stage as a great impresario, just as he had once dominated it as composer, vanished into a blur of I.O.U.s, notices of distraint and threats of legal action.

Friends offered to help him out with loans. He proudly refused them. At the theatre he summoned the members of his company, the actors, the singers, the orchestral players, and told them: 'My children, you'll be paid down to the last centime; I've not been very wise, perhaps, but I insist on remaining honour itself . . .'

On 15 May 1875, he sold the Théâtre de la Gaîté to his former partner Vizentini, who, as events turned out, was to make no greater a success of it than Offenbach had. After three years of ambitious productions during which he mounted one of Saint-Saëns' operas, Vizentini went under. The Théâtre de la Gaîté once more came on the market.

The deal with Vizentini included a million francs' worth of equipment and stage properties. This alone was not enough to rescue Offenbach. His own savings were thrown into the yawning gulf of debt. Royalties on works past and present were impounded and those on works to come were mortgaged for years ahead to his creditors. Nothing was left of his adventure in management. He was ruined.

The Villa d'Orphée in Étretat was let as an economy measure and Offenbach decided to stay at a hotel there. As the train from Paris drew into the station he saw a line of halberdiers on the platform. Dressed in armour improvised from unimaginable sources, they came to attention and saluted him. Their leader waved the tricolour flag of the Étretat Casino from astride a donkey. Fireworks stood ready to blaze a salvo in his honour. As he climbed out of the train he was offered on a ceremonial tray (electroplated) the key to his hotel room.

The friends who organised this little joke congratulated themselves on the way it had gone. But Offenbach, more emotional than ever as a result of his late disasters, more naïf than he usually was, could only mutter in a tear-choked voice: 'It's too much, too much . . .'

Herminie and the children did what they could to protect him from the outside world. They still had their little family jokes, the celebrations, the Friday evenings when old acquaintances called and the hours vanished in laughter. The parodies and amateur dramatics continued. Offenbach watched the fun from his armchair, a dressing-gown wrapped over his shrunken limbs. It did not seem possible that a human body could be as thin as his. At the end of the evening the revellers would lift him up in his chair while the rest danced a jig around him.

In theory he obeyed his doctor that July by taking a cure at Aix-les-Bains. In reality he worked as hard as ever, for the year of 1875 saw no less than five new works of his on the Paris stage in addition to a revue made up of his most popular music from earlier operettas. One reason was that he urgently needed money to pay off the mountain of debt. But even without that spur he would have been just as active. The demon that drove him was inexorable.

While in Aix-les-Bains he wrote three operettas simultaneously. They were *La Boulangère a des écus, La Créole* and *Le Voyage dans la lune.* A letter to one of his daughters shows him in a customary breathless mood with a sentence of unending, Proustian dimension:

'My dear Mimi, what can I tell you? That I'm working, that the weather's started being fine again, that I'm very well although my right foot is hurting me a bit, the effect of the waters, that yesterday my right hand played me up, today I'm not bothered with it, that I'm sleeping well, that my appetite keeps up, that I don't know which way to turn with my three operettas all at the same time, that I jump from one to the other, fortunately I don't need my feet for that, that I've had a letter from Comte [his son-in-law, manager of the Théâtre des Bouffes-Parisiens] asking me to write to him but not giving me his address (kindly tell him), that I had this morning a letter from Pépita, that I think about you all a lot, that I'd like to see you split in two (shocking), that a solo by you would please me and that a duet would delight me still more, that I talk with many people but see no one, that I play whist in the evening, that I take my baths with pleasure, my showers with happiness; as you see, none of this is very interesting, and I'd have done better not to have sent you it all; tell your Mama that I kiss her and that I am absolutely determined to start a new lease of thirty-one years' constant happiness; when you've embraced that dreadful nice and worthy husband, all my dear children, it will only remain for you to hug yourself good and strong, this from your father filled with joy and rheumatism.'

Later that year he was in Vienna. To another daughter, this time Pépita, he wrote:

'Vienna is a sad spot, money is scarce there and bankruptcies are frequent. If my ears are saddened by the melancholy gossip here, my eyes, on the other hand, are *delighted*. The desk at which I write is a true, charming little museum in itself. I have *aufgestelt* [put] in front of me your four portraits, my Jacqueline first, then Auguste, you and finally, though your natural mother, your *beautiful* mother: my eyes *egotzen* [delight in] looking at your adorable faces . . .
'Farewell, my dear Pépita, and tenderly kiss: your mother,

your sisters, your brother, your aunts, your uncles, your nephews, *your niece Herminie*, your brothers-in-law, your chambermaid, your cook, your coachman, your concierge.

'I kiss you on your two pretty cheeks.'

From which it will be seen that the Offenbach family, for ever contracting new alliances and sprouting grandchildren in all directions, had now attained the state of a numerous tribe. If the composer found it hard to grasp all the relationships on Herminie's side, the ones for which he himself was responsible were beginning to rival them in complexity.

Business detained him at Vienna well into the new year. On 20 January he wrote in a letter to Ludovic Halévy: 'At the Opera-house I saw *Carmen* by our poor Bizet. It's admirably done and gives a great deal of pleasure. Ah! what adorable music, what orchestration, how he knew and understood it all, poor, poor Bizet. The third entr'acte brought tears to my eyes. What a talent lost for ever.'

Bizet had died the previous June, already in poor health, worn out and disappointed by the tepid reception that at first greeted *Carmen*. Ever since Offenbach had given a hearing to his early opera *Le Docteur Miracle*, Bizet had been a frequent guest at his home and a leading entertainer at parties there.

The other musician who had vied with Bizet in the competition that resulted in *Le Docteur Miracle* was certainly not as friendly to Offenbach. For years afterwards Charles Lecocq (1832-1918) nourished an obsessive dislike towards him. The poverty of his childhood and the bullying he suffered on account of his crippled leg had early on made him very sensitive, ready to detect insult in a careless remark and yet determined, whatever suffering it cost him, to become famous in the theatre.

In 1868, the year of *La Périchole*, Lecocq's ninth operetta gained him initial celebrity. It was called *Fleur de Thé* and had a Chinese setting with a mandarin's daughter as the heroine. The libretto, though unremarkable, offered Lecocq a chance to write music that was fresh and discreetly spiced with exoticism. *Fleur de Thé* ran for a long time and gave Offenbach food for thought.

Lecocq had Massenet's habit of using his manuscripts as diaries on which to note down passing thoughts and events of the day. His score of *Le Docteur Miracle* has a long account of

Charles Lecocq

the circumstances in which it was produced. He speaks of the delays in putting it on and of other annoying incidents. 'In this respect I had differences with Offenbach, whose behaviour towards me was very unpleasant. To begin with, he wanted me to change part of the music, something to which I would not agree. From that moment I was on bad terms with him and our quarrel lasted several years. I did not suspect at the time that one day I would be able to take my revenge. It only came eleven years later with *Fleur de Thé*, my first success in the theatre.'

His contentment leaps out from the faded ink. On the reverse pages of his score of *Fleur de Thé* he notes, wryly, that a lady who heard it exclaimed: 'Oh! that Offenbach, he's the only one who can write music like that!' Lecocq goes on to say: 'In those days Offenbach's music flaunted itself in all the theatres; and many people had never heard anything else for years. I would add that since my differences with the maestro he had become my pet aversion. As a result of which, very far from imitating him, as I was sometimes advised to do, I have always given a wide berth to those old, Alsatian-type rhythms of his which so many of my other colleagues have used to their profit.'

His *Les Cent Vierges* in 1872 confirmed the new direction French operetta was taking. Despite the ribald implication of the title – the plot concerns the misadventures of a hundred maidens who are dispatched by the British admiralty to help re-populate a desert island – it enchanted the middle-class audiences who now, successors to the moneyed and fashionable arbiters of the Second Empire, laid down the rules of success.[1]

Lecocq took his fullest and most telling revenge on Offenbach with *La Fille de Madame Angot* in 1873. This agreeable mixture of anecdote, popular history and easy emotion achieved over four hundred performances, many provincial and foreign tours, and frequent revivals ever after. A sensation like this had not been known in the theatre since the day of *Orphée aux enfers* and *La Belle Hélène*. At the first night in Paris the audience was so absorbed by the rhythm of the second-act waltz that it did not notice a fire which broke out among the draperies at the back of the stage. Spellbound by the hypnotic rhythms, no one paid attention to the resourceful members of the chorus who quickly

---

[1] Victorian London preferred to call it *The Island of Bachelors*, under which title it knew popularity at the Gaiety Theatre.

doused the flaming curtains. Individual items were encored many times over.

Lecocq brought something new and much more to the taste of postwar audiences than Offenbach gave them in those uncertain years after 1871. *La Fille de Madame Angot* had its setting in the period of the Directoire immediately after the Revolution. Madame Angot was based on a person who had really existed, as was another character, the popular songwriter Ange Pitou about whom Alexandre Dumas wrote a novel. Lecocq's music had a genuine feeling for the period. In many ways it lived up to Offenbach's own declared aim when he opened the Théâtre des Bouffes-Parisiens: that of returning to the genuine spirit of opéra-comique and its peculiarly French gaiety.

The vogue for parody and burlesque so enjoyed by Second Empire audiences was over. *La Fille de Madame Angot* indicates a rebirth of French light music. It is said that Bismarck once attended a performance incognito. At the end, wrinkling his forehead, he remarked: 'I hate that little trifle we've just heard because its "terribly French": these people have been beaten, they're not conquered.' Whether or not the story is true, Lecocq's work signals both a national recovery and a new age in operetta.

Although he never reached the heights that Offenbach did, Lecocq was technically a better musician. He had no need to consult reference books when faced with a tricky point of orchestration. The harmonies he found were often subtler than Offenbach's. An instinctive elegance preserved him from the crudities which the exuberant genius of his rival tended to produce. If, inevitably, inspiration ran thin during the fifty or so operettas that he wrote, he could usually rely on a smooth technique to carry him through. Lecocq took time over composing his music and liked to polish and revise. As a poet in his spare time he had a just appreciation of words, their values and their accents, whereas by comparison Offenbach wrought much violence on the French language.

Lecocq aimed to charm and did not ridicule or satirise. A gentle irony flavoured his approach while the humour was quiet and unforced. Very rarely did he and his authors touch on political subjects, one exception being the famous quatrain in *La Fille de Madame Angot*, which at the first night caused a brief protest:

'Voilà comment cela se mène
C' n'était pas la peine, c' n'était pas la peine
Non pas la peine assurément
De changer de gouvernement!'[1]

The structure of Lecocq's operettas was tighter and more symmetrical than Offenbach's. In *La Fille de Madame Angot* he introduced the idea of repeating the main themes in the finale as a summing up. Where Offenbach, in *Les Brigande* for example, had tried not very successfully to emulate the form of opéra-comique, it was Lecocq who initiated the merger.

The number of times the word 'little' appears in his titles is significant – *Le Petit Duc, La Petite Mariée, La Petite Mademoiselle*. He set his sights within a prescribed range and, as often as fate allowed, he hit the target. His style was familiar and intimate rather than showy and expansive. It was characteristic of this sensitive musician that towards the end of his life he occupied himself with preparing a new edition of Rameau's opera *Castor et Pollux*. Curiously enough, when he heard the early work of André Messager, born in 1853, he remarked: 'It's original. It's interesting. It lacks imagination!' Yet Messager, who conducted the first performance of Debussy's *Pelléas et Mélisande* in 1902 at the Opéra-Comique and of Poulenc's *Les Biches* in 1923, was a subtle craftsman. In the perspective of history he may be seen as not only very French and very accomplished, but as responsible for the finest flowering of the plant which Offenbach and Lecocq had tended.

Despite the rivalry that divided Lecocq and Offenbach there were striking personal similarities between them. With his bristling moustache, neat pince-nez and sober business suit, Lecocq appeared at first sight, as did Offenbach, not at all a man for the gaieties of operetta. They had both known poverty when young and both had been forced to work and fight hard. Neither man ever enjoyed perfect health: the rheumatic pain that tortured Offenbach started early in life, while Lecocq was afflicted from birth with his mangled hip.

Lecocq by 1875 was a dominant figure in the Parisian light

[1] 'That's how things go on – no, it wasn't worth the trouble, it certainly wasn't worth the trouble to change governments.'

theatre. Close behind him came Johann Strauss with *Die Fledermaus* (first given in Paris in 1877) and other Viennese operettas, one of them starring Offenbach's former protégée Zulma Bouffar. Offenbach and Hervé, two embattled veterans with many a scar, struggled on. During the war Hervé found new opportunities in London. From then onwards he shuttled back and forth between the English capital and Paris, acting and producing in the one and mounting new productions in the other. The English connection may have inspired his latest frolic, *Le Trone d'Ecosse.* It featured a descendent of Robert Bruce, and a Queen Jane in search of a husband. Hervé's lunatic invention remained unimpaired. 'I wish I were the polish on your boots so that I could spend my life at your feet,' declares the amorous Flora to a character named Buckingham.

Offenbach's outlet was Vienna, but it did not serve him as well as London did Hervé. In Paris he battled with Lecocq on their home ground. The opening skirmish took the form of *Les Hannetons*, a revue made up largely of Offenbach's popular songs. A special drop-curtain was plastered with advertisements which turned out to be mock puffs for Offenbach as the inventor of chemist's products, Offenbach as the inventor of a famous paste, Offenbach as the builder of a railway line . . . This declaration of versatility did not guarantee success.

More serious competition with Lecocq was provided by *La Boulangére a des écus.* For this, Offenbach after much argument managed to cajole Meilhac and Halévy into writing a libretto. In later years composer and librettists had drifted apart. This was not Offenbach's fault. Rather, it arose from the writers' disloyal but realistic view that Offenbach had lost his touch and was out of date. On this occasion they allowed themselves to be persuaded and his joy was complete when Hortense Schneider agreed to appear in the new work. The old team was together again and he foresaw a triumphant come-back.

Schneider was on the verge of retirement. Her figure had plumped out so much that even she realised the absurdity of wearing costumes that once displayed the beauties of a handsome shape but now revealed how cruelly it had gone to seed. Yet she could not resist a final appearance in an operetta by the men who had, more than anyone else, helped her to stardom. She arrived for rehearsals full of temperament. When something annoyed her she stamped out in a fury. When she returned next day she could not believe her eyes. The manager of the theatre had taken her at her word and replaced her with his mistress, the youthful Mademoiselle Aimée. Hortense brought an action against him and won it. When she tried to get a seat at the opening night and found the house solidly booked out, she made a witty pun that even her opponent enjoyed. He would be forgiven, she joked, '*parce qu'il a Aimée.*'

Her longing to strut once more behind the footlights was not to be denied. She accepted the leading rôle in a new operetta by Hervé and entered upon a stimulating battle with the manager of the theatre. One of her disputes involved the costume she was to wear. The colour, she demanded, should be cardinal velvet. The manager preserved, with an effort, his good temper and asked what shade was desired.

'The shade of Bordeaux wine, naturally,' she answered in a reference to her birthplace.

His self-control vanished. 'And what year?' he bellowed.

She wanted, too, a dressing room on a level with the stage.

'There isn't one,' he replied, 'the only room level with the stage is my office.'

'Never mind! I'll take that then.'

Out of respect for her past fame audiences dutifully clapped her. But she knew, and they knew, that things had changed. The saucy dialogue and frivolous capers imposed by her new rôle did not suit the statuesque matron she had become. One critic even described her as an 'ageing Mum'. Hortense, unlike many other actresses, decided to retire while memories of her as a star remained untarnished. Her house in the avenue du Bois de Boulogne went up for sale. She auctioned off most of her jewellery and art objects. From a modest home in the avenue de Versailles she inaugurated a life as sober and dignified as her stage career had been free and easy. Though she did not go quite so far as some of her contemporaries and enter a convent, she devoted herself to charitable works and patronised orphanages. Each morning at half-past five she woke up and read a book until the newspapers arrived. After a well-wined lunch she would go on a tour of the shops. The rest of the day was spent in visiting the poor and administering charities. Until the 1920s, when she died, well over the age of eighty, she led the quiet life of a wealthy bourgeoise.

As seen by a
Viennese cartoonist

Although she rarely went to theatres she kept in close touch with everything that was happening throughout the domain she had ruled for six glorious years. Friends and the newspapers told her how Offenbach's latest productions were faring. She did not grudge him the success of *La Boulangère a des écus* in which her own impetuousness had lost her the main part. Her memories of him were too full, too rich for that.

La Boulangère a des écus did something to polish Offenbach's fading reputation. The influence of Lecocq was obvious. The action took place in the eighteenth century, an excuse for pretty costumes and display, and instead of topical satire there was a plot that called on historical fact to eke out the story of the newly-rich lady baker of the title.

But something was absent. Halévy wrote: 'Offenbach, Meilhac and I can't do it any longer, and that's the truth. We've written too much. We've run out of choruses, entries and exits, marches, leave-takings, songs for ladies in waiting, rondos for pages . . . And besides, we aren't twenty years old any more, nor even forty. Daring and fantasy vanish with youth, and operetta is a form that demands them more than any other. By now, I think, we know our craft very well. And that's not without inconvenience. It makes us timid, prudent. We no longer have the bravery of inexperience, we no longer dive head-first into the water without worrying about the depth. We look for a ladder to climb down. We try out the ground. Is there a footing? Yes . . . it's safe. So we go ahead and we write *La Boulangerère a des écus*, a flat and commonplace work that could neither succeed nor fail, which is what has happened.'

La Boulangère was the last operetta to be created by the famous trio. Soon Meilhac and Halévy were to provide the words for some of Lecocq's best-known operettas. Halévy's misgivings can only have related to Offenbach, whose approach, as he saw it, had been overtaken by new fashions.

The composer had neither the time nor the inclination for self-questioning. Doggedly, a week after *La Boulangère*, he staged *Le Voyage dans la lune* which his friend Vizentini put on as a kindly gesture at the Théâtre de la Gaîté. This trip to the moon was inspired by Jules Verne whose novels were proving at the time a useful source for dramatists. Vizentini built a model of the planet, craters and all, and displayed it by floodlight outside the theatre. Inside, there were still more wonders: a huge gun that shot the adventurers to the moon, a snow ballet, and an exciting volcanic eruption that filled the theatre with angry red flames.

The week that followed brought *La Créole*. From the pantomime of *Le Voyage dans la lune* Offenbach turned to another venture in the style of Lecocq. His Creole heroine (Anna Judic browned up with liquorice), belonged to the time of Louis XVI and sang a declaration of love in charming patois. There were flashes of the old gaiety in a chorus of Bordeaux women as they waited for sailors to land from the boats just entering harbour. Yet *La Créole* failed to hold the stage of the Bouffes-Parisiens for long. Not until 1934, nearly sixty years later, was it revived, and then as a show-case for the indomitable Joséphine Baker, who did without liquorice to stain her cheeks, and who loaded the part with that husky seductiveness which was her own inimitable charm.

Having produced three full-length operettas in three successive weeks, Offenbach danced a final pirouette by throwing in a one-acter as well. *Tarte à la crème*, described as a 'waltz in one act', did not have his name attached to it. Perhaps he felt it unseemly for one man to dominate all the theatre posters.

This frenetic burst of activity, as 1875 drew to its end, had no great material results. Although *La Boulangère a des écus* did fairly well and achieved, in fact, a revival the following year, the composer still wanted money desperately. Mortgaged, bankrupted, he had even been forced to hand over all the foreign rights in his works and so to do without the bonus they represented.

Yet somehow he still managed to play the dandy, to frequent the best eating-houses in Paris and to enjoy a life of conspicuous luxury. He had formed the habit of staying with his family in the Pavillon Henri IV at Saint Germain, a section of the former royal palace now converted into a fashionable and expensive hotel. His bust may today be seen in the garden there, a tribute, one imagines, from a grateful management to a free-spending guest. How did he do it? The secret of how to live in splendour without visible means of support was one he shared with other theatrical people and with many financiers whose empires have crashed.

PART VI
SWANSONG

22

Orpheus in New York

There is a play by Sacha Guitry in which a husband, anxious to get away to his mistress, invents on the spur of the moment an improbable appointment with the most unlikely character that springs to mind. He conceives of a South American with whom he has pressing business that will deprive him of the pleasure of his wife's company for a while. 'You never know the truth about South Americans,' he improvises. 'You never know whether they're Brazilians, Chileans, Argentinians . . . or anything else. When they've said "South American", they've said it all. Anyway, they don't know themselves. Brazilians usually have their relations in Chile, their home in Argentina and their money in Guatemala . . . how can you expect them to know what's going on? They're very intelligent people, moreover.'

It was just such an ambiguous personage who gave Offenbach the chance of restoring his lost fortunes. On a spring morning in 1875 at the Pavillon Henri IV Offenbach was playing in the garden with one of his children. He had given strict instructions that no one in any way associated with the theatre was to be admitted. A servant announced that Madame Hortense Schneider had called to see him. Ah! Hortense! That was different.

For some time they chatted nostalgically. Whenever the composer saw Hortense, he felt, it was as if he were watching all his successes parade by, for she, more than anyone else, embodied the past. They talked agreeably of battles they had fought together and of old acquaintance.

The servant entered again, this time with a card bearing a name unknown: Lino Bacquero. A moment afterwards the South American himself bounced in. He apologised with voluble charm and came to the point. Would Offenbach like to go to America?

'Monsieur,' laughed the composer, 'let me tell you that for a lot of money I wouldn't even go as far as Saint-Cloud today . . .'

Bacquero explained. The year 1876 marked the hundredth

anniversary of American independence. An international exhibition was to be held in Philadelphia and the government of France had donated the Statue of Liberty. Richard Wagner himself had been commissioned to write a march in honour of the occasion. Lino Bacquero told Offenbach that the American impresario Maurice Grau would pay him 30,000 dollars for thirty concerts. The cash, he added thoughtfully, would be deposited beforehand in the Bank of France.

Offenbach was so French by now that he had fully absorbed the Gallic insularity of mind. How could he leave his adoring family? How could he even dream of tearing himself away from the boulevards? Señor Bacquero argued with Brazilian, Chilean, even Argentinian eloquence. The figure of 30,000 dollars pleaded with even greater force. Offenbach loved his family. He loved Paris. But he needed funds in any currency.

On 21 April 1876, ushered by a cohort of sons-in-law and brothers-in-law – he had begged Herminie and his daughters to stay at home so that the parting might be less painful – and with only his son Auguste to represent the immediate family, he embarked at Le Havre on the *Canada*. The new luxury liner was bound on its maiden voyage to America. Since, Offenbach observed, he was a veteran of many a theatrical première, he had no fear of being present at its début. What about sea-sickness? enquired a reporter. 'Ah!' came the answer, 'don't worry. My health is so delicate I haven't even the strength to be ill.'

The ship put out to sea. The little group on the quayside dwindled. For a long time Offenbach could still make out the figure of Auguste whose buttons flashed in the sun. But the proud father needed no help to identify the son he idolised.

They ran into a dreadful storm. The captain, anxious to bolster Offenbach's failing spirit, urged him to go aloft and enjoy the sight of the ship proudly breasting the waves. The composer feebly replied that it must be interesting for a spectator to view the storm from afar, but that as an actor directly involved in the piece he had to admit that his enjoyment was restrained.

When the *Canada* sailed into New York harbour, a small fleet of boats came out to greet Offenbach. One of them carried a band playing musical honours. As the vessel bearing the players went further out to sea the waters became rougher. 'It was like Haydn's *Farewell* Symphony,' Offenbach wrote home, 'where the musicians put out the lights and disappear one after another. Only in this case our musicians had nothing to put out, and instead of pouring forth sounds, one after another they poured out . . . their souls into the sea.'

Journalists who travelled over to the *Canada* were hardier. They found him 'a pleasant-looking gentleman' with a face 'somewhat thinner and more deeply furrowed with wrinkles' than they had expected. 'He has a fresh, lively way of speaking and acting and his face is always lit up by a smile. He can understand English but is not able to use it in conversation.' Offenbach had conquered.

Across the balcony of his hotel stretched a huge poster lettered in immense capitals 'Welcome Offenbach'. A sixty-piece orchestra serenaded him with his own music. 'Vive Offenbach!' roared the crowd. The composer appeared on the balcony. 'Thank you, Sir,' he enunciated carefully.

There is usually a delay of some years before the art of one country penetrates to another. Books, plays, music, ideas, take time to cross frontiers. Offenbach was now declining in favour at home, but in America his vogue had only just reached its peak. There he enjoyed the sort of popularity he had known in France before the war and the time-lag proved to be an agreeable surprise. Everywhere he was fêted with banquets and receptions and had he eaten all that was put before him, he said, he would never have returned alive. The Americans, it appeared, stuffed their visitors with food the way Breton cooks stuffed the breasts of turkeys. Doubtless his New York visit did his reputation good – but it certainly deepened the roots of his gout.

The hall where he gave his first concert was known as Gilmore's Gardens and stood on the site now occupied by Madison Square Gardens. Tropical flowers and plants and grass flourished everywhere in the rainbow light shed by coloured window panes. There was room for some 8,000 people. Here, on 11 May, Offenbach conducted an orchestra of a hundred. The leader was the youthful John Philip Sousa.

The audience was a little disappointed. Vocal music did not feature on the programme and Offenbach himself only conducted four of the items. Damped by failure the star of the evening offered to cancel his contract, but his impresario Maurice Grau refused. Instead, he varied the programmes, engaged soloists

Offenbach in New York

and reduced ticket prices by half. These changes worked. The thirtieth and last concert on 9 June ended a series which brought large audiences and earned a profit. Anxious to make the most of a promising situation, Grau then took a theatre and put on *La Vie Parisienne* and *La Jolie Parfumeuse*. Offenbach conducted and the leading rôles were played by Marie Aimée – not the Aimée who had supplanted Schneider in *La Boulangère a des écus*, but a French-born singer who was very popular in America.

The visit to Philadelphia went off just as well. The concerts were given in yet another winter garden called the Alhambra and temporarily baptised 'Offenbach's Garden' for the occasion. Despite the sweltering heat thousands of people crowded together in the hothouse atmosphere. 'Their enthusiasm was great,' reported an observer. A week of opera followed with Offenbach and Aimée repeating their New York success.

Then Offenbach made a quick trip to Niagara Falls. Though he was impressed by the cataract, his scepticism went unchecked in observing the commercial exploitation, and having bought a number of the inevitable souvenirs, he reflected that he would be taking trinkets back to France which had doubtless come from the bankrupt sale of some Parisian department store.

The New World amused and entertained him. He was astonished at the vast quantities of food served in restaurants. The waiters, he found, had all the American qualities of independence and spirit. One evening he dined at Pétry's restaurant in Philadelphia and the waiter, consulted about the menu, made a face and advised against the soup. The vegetables were tough, he said. The salmon? Not really fresh. Steak? Not to be recommended – the cook did it badly. Strawberries? Spoiled. Cheese? 'I'll ask it up. I know it, it'll come up without any help. It can walk on its own.' A member of the party exploded: 'If I were Pétry I'd fire you.' The waiter bowed. 'Mr Pétry hasn't waited for your advice, I'm working out my last evening here.'

American advertising provided another source of delight for a man who was himself a clever publicist. Riding in a train he happened to see on a telegraph pole the slogan: 'Only cure for rheumatism.' Instantly, as a sufferer, he was intrigued. He looked out anxiously for the next telegraph pole. The message was repeated but still did not give the maker's name. This happened most of the way along the line until suddenly the required information flashed past. The American advertising man, Offenbach decided, played on the human mind as a musician plays the piano.

Naturally he went a lot to the New York theatres. At one of them, by an eerie coincidence, he saw and remarked on the skill of a 'Miss Josephine Baker'...(not of course the later star of the Folies Bergères) He took a keen interest in the ways of American impresarios. They had the right, it seemed, to at least four bankruptcies and the deeper they fell the higher they came up next time. One in particular, the hero of six or seven bankruptcies, was pointed out to him as a smart operator who would have a fine theatre company next winter again. Where did he get the money from? enquired Offenbach. From his debtors, he was told. They lent him still more money in the hope that a future success would retrieve what they'd already lost. The answer made Offenbach thoughtful.

By the end of his tour he had been elected an honorary member of the Association of New York Musicians, the powerful trade union which then controlled music in the city. A decorative scroll and a baton tipped with gold symbolised the affection he inspired from orchestral players who worked under him. His wit, his humour, his vivacity, endeared him to them all. An exception was the German-born violinist and conductor Theodore Thomas, who often included in his programmes a work by his namesake Ambroise Thomas, composer of the popular *Mignon*. Since Ambroise always appeared as 'Thomas' pure and simple, audiences forgiveably assumed that the conductor himself had written the piece and gave Theodore the credit. Such was his self-importance that he would never, so he said, degrade himself by conducting Offenbach's music. But Offenbach replied that he himself would not be so particular – he would, he added, be delighted to conduct a piece by Theodore Thomas when that gentleman attained the dignity of becoming a composer.

In America there was more than enough to please Offenbach's taste for novelty. Yet, as he wrote to his 'dear Ludo', despite the flattering reception, the money, the admiration that surrounded the guest of honour at banquet after banquet, he felt homesick. 'What a lovely town New York is, what lovely women, what lovely walks, what lovely mud when it rains, it's all quite superb, but . . . Ah! my pretty Paris, my dear boulevards, my adorable theatres, where are you?'

His letters home were still more emphatic. He longed for his wife and family and often complained that they did not write to him often enough. His favourite daughter Mimi, mother of the little girl called Herminie after his wife, sent him a family photograph and received a long reply. 'Nothing could give me greater pleasure than the dispatch of your dear faces, but why do you look so serious? Did dear little Herminie wee-wee on your lap, by chance? Didn't you dare move? Did dark thoughts preoccupy you in thinking of your naughty father's return? . . . Really, once again, I get enormous happiness from looking at all your dear faces; how very sweet my dear little Herminie looks. You must, I bet, I swear, have read all I've written to my darling Herminie (*my* Herminie), my anxiety, not fear, but my sorrow at thinking I'd never see you again; I've spent some very painful days and fearful nights . . .'

So deep was his need for tidings from the rue Laffitte that he wrote a comic letter to his granddaughter Herminie. Since she was barely one year old the message can be taken as a loving reproach to the Offenbach circle for not keeping in touch more closely. 'If I write to you it's because your naughty Mama doesn't spoil me with her letters. And so when you're grown up you'll do as she does, you'll forget you've a Mama, which will be a just punishment here below. You've been ill again, my poor darling, which is what comes from going out in society too much, dining here, there and everywhere . . . never being satisfied at your nurse's bosom. You drink and drink until the white liquor runs out of your pretty little mouth . . . Tell your father he's naughty not to have written to me. If he comes near you, give him a squirt of milk in his pretty face . . . Tell your brothers they're wicked not to give any sign of life. Obviously it runs in the family. A fine brood I've blessed you with. Don't give this letter to your mother. It will vex her, perhaps. Hide it carefully in your shawl. Goodbye, my dear adored little darling, try and read this, love me well, because I think about you a lot and I kiss your pretty little face and even, if you allow, your pretty little . . . rump.'

Replete with many dollars, joyful at the prospect of seeing his family again, the adoring grandfather set off for home. His jolly spirit made him indiscreet. On the way back he uttered some facetious comments about Republicans, which a left-wing French senator on board took amiss. The senator quivered with patriotic indignation and sharply drew Offenbach's attention to the ribbon of the Légion d'honneur he was wearing and to the fact that he was a naturalised Frenchman.

Financially, Offenbach had rescued his fortunes, but politically, he was now in trouble again. The outraged senator magnified his careless witticisms into a disgraceful attack on the homeland and republican newspapers took up the theme, reminding their readers that Offenbach was a 'man of the Empire'. They referred to him as 'Herr Offenbach' and called him *'le grand responsable'*. Responsible for what? Presumably for the catastrophe of 1870. It was disgusting, they claimed, that this Prussian should speak ill of the country whose defeat, it seemed, he had brought about single-handed.

Offenbach felt too distressed, too worn out for retaliation. The affair caused such a stir that a police enquiry was held which cleared him absolutely when all the witnesses testified that his remarks aboard the *Canada* had been blameless. At last he rallied his strength and published a letter defending himself. He suggested that an independent committee examine the persons concerned in the incident and that whoever was proved wrong should pay 25,000 francs to charity. The left-wing senator, usually so voluble for his country's honour, this time kept resolutely mum. An opposition newspaper observed that he had made the mistake of confusing the Republic with France.

The unhappy incident resonated for some time afterwards. A proposed revival of *La Grande-Duchesse de Gérolstein* had to be cancelled because the government felt that 'under present circumstances it would have a very bad effect.' In a climate of feeling where bellicose politicians were demanding with vehemence the return of Alsace and Lorraine, it was not considered decent to laugh at patriotic excess and to ridicule war. A confidential letter from the Minister of Education warned all Prefects throughout the country that the *Grand Duchess* was not to be heard and that they allowed performances at their own risk. The Republic had turned out to be less tolerant and more nervous of criticism than even the Second Empire. Offenbach was not surprised.

23

The Drum Major's Daughter to the Rescue

He went on composing. Aboard the *Canada* he had worked on a new full-length operetta intended for Charles Comte at the Théâtre des Bouffes-Parisiens. *La Boîte au lait* had an undistinguished libretto and drew the moral of La Fontaine's fable about spilt milk, and resignation was indeed necessary when the piece had to close after running for a little more than eight weeks. During rehearsals Offenbach had written a curtain-raiser, *Pierrette et Jacquot*, to show off a couple of young actresses he had discovered in Strasbourg. They, too, disappeared after their brief hour on the stage.

A surer proposition seemed to be Jules Verne. A dramatisation of his *Around the World in Eighty Days* was just then attracting the town at the immense Théâtre du Châtelet. Remembering the success of *Le Voyage dans la lune*, Offenbach seized on another Jules Verne story for *Le Docteur Ox*. In this fantasy a scientist doses the inhabitants of the town of Quiquendonne with a newly discovered gas. The good Dr Ox's assistant is called Ygène, whence the term *ox . . . ygène*.

Offenbach demanded many novel effects: he asked for syphons filled with compressed carbonic acid to make the sound of gas being released; a peal of bells, he declared, was also essential, and he wanted a full brass band for the work. Forgetting the pain of his gnarled and tortured joints he rushed about the stage, a whirlwind of reproof and command, as he marshalled the singers and scolded the orchestra. Then he dropped onto a chair and snuggled deep into his fur coat. Jules Verne watched in astonishment from the back of the theatre.

Le Docteur Ox was lavishly mounted and gorgeously costumed and had a colourful gypsy march and a romantic guitar serenade. As soon as he had set these luxuries in order, Offenbach drove away to the Théâtre des Folies-Dramatiques where, a fortnight later, he produced *La Foire Saint-Laurent*. Here he returned to the fairground atmosphere of *La Princesse*

As the evil eye

de Trébizonde. There was an effective 'ear' trio where the guardians of the peace warned a young suitor that the next time he misbehaved his two ears would be pinched and pulled and then cut off, 'la! oh! la la!' Another item was one of those 'cat' ensembles for which Offenbach had a fondness. The hero, surprised by an outraged husband, escapes by climbing over the roofs at night. The inmates of a girls' boarding school hear him scrabbling along the gutter and imagine that the culprit is their pet cat, the mischievous Barnabé. Yet a good cast failed to ensure long life for the new production.

Offenbach had done all he could. At rehearsals he amazed everyone with his vigour to the extent where, when singers wearied and the chorus began to lose heart, he jumped onto the stage and threw himself into a fandango with fingers snapping out the metallic rhythm of castanets as he spun round and round, hair flying and his glasses dangling at the end of their ribbon. At the end, company and stage-hands burst into applause.

The effort that this cost him was great, and at home, when not composing, he had to lie on a sofa without speaking so as to preserve his strength. He knew that the deserters Meilhac and Halévy were right, and that for the time being he had lost his touch, yet he still hoped that his next production would bring back the favour that had deserted him. Work was all he had left, the forcing of his crabbed, painful hand across sheet after sheet as his twisted fingers moved the pen in a frantic rush to capture the melodies that his brain was creating. 'I shall die with a tune at the end of my pen,' he used to say. Herminie watched and worried in silence.

They had moved from the rue Laffitte and now lived in an apartment on the third floor at No 8, boulevard des Capucines, just around the corner from the Opéra. Below them was the Sporting Club. On the upper floor lived a doctor and his pretty wife. The doctor was an amateur violinist and after dinner frequently had an invitation to step down with his wife to see the Offenbachs – but on condition he left his violin behind.

After so many years in another apartment it took Offenbach some time to find his way around the new building, so that one evening, returning late from the theatre, he took the lift, emerged, opened the door and made for the dressing-room, walking quietly so as to disturb no one. A light suddenly switched on and he glimpsed the doctor's wife undressing. Horrified at his mistake, he quickly made his exit.

'That's odd,' cried the lady, 'I'd have sworn Offenbach just came in.' Her husband, revolver in hand, searched the flat and assured her there was no intruder. The incident, not without a Pickwickian flavour, could have been the starting-point for an Offenbach piece, but life is not so ingenious, and next day the composer's apology left no room for the development of sub-plots.

Was it pure absent-mindedness that caused him to ignore routine things? In the old days, when he had forgotten to do up essential buttons, there was a secret code by which Herminie had reminded him of the oversight. They had agreed that the phrase: 'Jacques, Monsieur Durand . . .' would be the hidden warning, but at many a social occasion when she would hiss meaningly in his ear: 'Jacques, Monsieur Durand . . .,' he, blank-faced, would reply: 'Eh, what? Monsieur Durand? . . . what about him, my dear?'

He simply could not spare the time now for anything apart from his work. Every ounce of energy must be stored up for the operettas which he believed would reconquer the position he had once held. His predicament was cruelly summarised by Emile Zola. A man has grown old, said Zola. 'He has been blinded to his own worth by the incense of the crudest flattery and has dreamed the dream of a lasting reputation. Then one day everything collapses, glory crumbles into the dust, he is buried before he is dead. I can think of no more appalling old age.'

Offenbach as usual kept open house on Friday evening and the 'vendredis de Jacques' still brought hosts of friends to the apartment in the boulevard des Capucines. They acted charades and put on impromptu entertainments as before, but the pace lacked the old sparkle. The master of the house lay on a sofa heaped with furs and rugs from which he applauded jokes, laughed at the epigrams and contributed many of his own, but now there was irony in his smile and a fatal melancholy in his eyes.

In 1878 another great Exhibition was held in the French capital, this time to advertise the achievements of the Republic.

Offenbach in fur coat

Offenbach remembered that other exhibition in 1867, the year of *La Grande-Duchesse de Gérolstein.* Could he repeat this triumph? Schneider was no longer available, but Meilhac and Halévy were still in business and he appealed to them with hopes of a new collaboration. They did not respond. Their destinies were now inevitably bound to the rising star of Lecocq, and during that year they wrote for him one of his most notable successes, the operetta *Le Petit Duc.*

Offenbach put together a libretto of sorts and composed a great deal of his new work at Nice where, in January that year, the sun came out to warm his rheumatic bones. But *Maître Péronilla* failed and when the Exhibition opened his name was absent from theatre posters. He wrote to Halévy with news of *Maître Péronilla.* 'If I tell you all this,' he ended his letter, 'it's because I know all the interest you take in the works of your *friend.*' And with acid humour he signed himself : 'Charles Lecocq.'

Summer granted him a minor consolation. He decided to revive *Orphée aux enfers* yet again. One day he happened to meet his old rival Hervé on the boulevard and they talked and laughed together until Offenbach had a sudden idea: he asked Hervé to play the rôle of Jupiter. Hervé agreed, but 'on condition that you conduct the orchestra. The very least I expect, since I'm to be your interpreter, is for you to do me the honours of your score.' They went off arm in arm to sign the contract.

The conductor only had strength to guide the second act, but this was enough, combined with Hervé's inspired clowning, to give *Orphée* a brilliant new lease of life. At the end of the year, as if rejuvenated by this dip into the past, Offenbach produced *Madame Favart*, one of the better works of his last years.

His new operetta featured the eighteenth-century prima donna Marie Favart whose husband had belonged to a well-known theatrical family of the time. She had caught the eye of the Maréchal de Saxe, the victor of Fontenoy and other great battles. (Unlikely as it may seem, he was the ancestor of the novelist George Sand.) Since she loved her husband much diplomacy was needed to outflank the seasoned warrior, and upon this depends the action of the plot.

When Bernard Shaw attended a London production of

Madame Favart, he spoke of the true Offenbach spirit, 'the restless movement, the witty abandonment, the swift, light, wicked touch, the inimitable *élan* stealing into concerted pieces as light as puff paste . . .'. *Madame Favart*, he declared, had a 'grace, gaiety and intelligence' that even an English company unused to the style could not destroy.

The grace of *Madame Favart* lies in such items as the heroine's song recalling her escape from the convent where she had lived as a girl. It is present even more so in the minuet and rondeau of the second act. Here Madame Favart looks back on the various stages of her romantic life. By the age of forty, she reflects, autumn has come, and it is then, according to connoisseurs, that the tree gives its best flavoured fruit. The number begins as eighteenth-century pastiche, but by the end it has developed into something unique and original. It is an exquisite thing.

Madame Favart signalled a renewal, but unhappily, in the January of 1879, Offenbach's next work, *La Marocaine* was a disappointment. This exotic venture, written to help out his son-in-law at the Théâtre des Bouffes-Parisiens, had to be withdrawn after a dozen performances.

He would not acknowledge defeat. At the end of the year he came up with *La Fille du Tambour-Major*. It had all the ingredients Parisian theatregoers had lately been taught to expect: historical romance, lovely costume and appeals to patriotism. '*Je suis mam'zelle Monthabor, Ra ra ra fla, La fille du tambour-major*,' announces the boisterous heroine. Both she and the theme of the piece were echoes of Donizetti's *La Fille du régiment* given in Paris almost four decades before.

First-nighters were untroubled by parallels with the Donizetti opera. They admired handsome settings which reproduced Italy in the opening years of the nineteenth century at the time of Bonaparte's 'liberating' invasion. They were touched by the playfulness of a donkey song in which the *cantinière*, supported by lifelike hee-haws from the chorus, extolled the animal that pulled her ration cart: he had a good character ('there are few men on earth can say as much') and a heart undefiled ('there are few women on earth can say as much'). They were amused by a 'migraine' song – which must be the only one of its kind in operetta – though it emerges that the singer is afflicted only with a bad headache and not with the disabling malady which in French is *hémicranie*. They enjoyed a waltz that had the old Offenbach lilt. And, at the sensational finale, they rose to their feet in excitement when the brassy strains of the *Chant du départ* thundered out from the stage and Bonaparte entered Milan at the head of his troops. This patriotic song, for ever associated with Napoleonic victories and ceremonial parades, had deep emotional currents. The idea of using it was a master-stroke of showmanship.

That winter snow lay thick on the boulevards. The air was strict with frost. The thermometer sank fifteen degrees below zero. It was so cold that theatres shut their doors for lack of heating. Offenbach had taken the close-down as an excuse for extra rehearsals of *La Fille du Tambour-Major*. The first night was an occasion of arctic chill. Yet in the warmth engendered by their enthusiasm the audience forgot the weather. At last Offenbach won the whole-hearted success he had wanted for years. His operetta soon travelled abroad. He dragged himself to Brussels and conducted it 'in a rain of flowers'. It went to London and Vienna. In Paris there was a banquet to celebrate the hundredth performance and afterwards the band played quadrilles made up of his music. He could no longer recall from which operetta the different tunes were taken.

He needed success for material as well as artistic reasons. Although he had made economies after his disastrous venture into theatre management, he gradually slipped back into the luxury that had been his custom. One day he added up what he spent in a month and a groan of horror escaped him when he found that his total expenses for rent, hotel bills, travel, clothes and furnishings amounted to 10,020 francs. The family must cut down! They must take up thrift! He exclaimed in anguish to Herminie: 'They find it quite natural that their father shuts himself up on his own to slog away night and day. They've nothing to do but sing, go for walks, put on pretty dresses (I except Auguste who wears trousers).'

His reaction was to work even harder. *Belle Lurette* was a last fizzle of gaiety about the buxom washerwoman Belle and her three lovers. (The title is excellent. It comes from the expression *il y a belle lurette*, meaning 'it's a long time ago'.) He started also on *Moucheron*, an escapade set in that milieu beloved of nineteenth-century comic opera writers, a girls' boarding school. For it he wrote a primping march faintly reminiscent of 'Three Blind Mice'.[1] Though often ill he could not prevent the humour from bubbling up, often with a satirical and macabre tone. When Albert Vizentini called one afternoon, he showed him a notebook which he used to jot down musical ideas as they came to him. 'Look,' he said mischievously, 'take this...you can give it to Saint-Saëns after my death!'

---

[1] Both these little pieces were completed by Delibes and produced after Offenbach's death.

Offenbach composing Contes d'Hoffmann

24

Tales that Hoffmann told

Many years previously, when he was a struggling 'cellist in his early thirties, Offenbach saw a play entitled *Les Contes d'Hoffmann*. He thought it would make a good opera and went so far as to talk over the necessary alterations with Jules Barbier and Michel Carré who had written it. There already existed, it appears, a musical adaptation, and in 1878 extracts from a version of Hector Salomon were publicly performed. When Salomon learned that Offenbach had at last made up his mind to use the idea, he politely stepped aside.

The figure of E. T. A. Hoffmann sometimes resembled a character from one of his own bizarre stories. He was a composer as well as a writer and changed the last of his Christian names to Amadeus in tribute to Mozart. The operas and ballets he composed are as correct and proper in style as his writings are eccentric. He held various posts as conductor, as manager of an opera troupe and as legal administrator. In his poverty-stricken youth he took to drink and only when drunk could he find inspiration. It was then that his mind filled with the devils and monsters and water-sprites who peopled his stories. Alone in his room he often spoke to ghosts and goblins he thought he perceived, and his drunken hallucinations created a misty atmosphere of drama dissolving into comedy, of laughter abruptly succeeded by fear.

The libretto of the *Contes d'Hoffmann* was eventually written by Jules Barbier sometime before 1878. With his friend Michel Carré, who helped him on the original play, he had already supplied the words of Gounod's *Faust*. On his own, a fair-haired, blue-eyed hero of the drawing-room, he provided many libretti for Meyerbeer, Ambroise Thomas, Bizet and Saint-Saëns. For the new opera he chose three of Hoffmann's tales and linked them together by means of a character who was intended to be the author himself. Each episode gave an account of romantic passion leading to disaster. A prologue and an epilogue enclosed the narrative by setting the scene and drawing a moral.

In a tavern shrouded by the fumes of wine and pipe smoke Hoffmann quarrels with the rich councillor Lindorf. They are rivals for the beautiful singer Stella who is that night performing in *Don Giovanni* at the theatre next door. A friend calms them down. Hoffmann decides to tell the story of the three women he has loved. The first is Olympia, an automaton put together by Coppélius and Spallanzi. (This is the Hoffmann story which also inspired Delibes' *Coppélia*.) Hoffmann dances a frenetic waltz with her. But the mechanism is smashed by Coppélius and nothing remains of the lovely vision but springs and ratchet wheels. Hoffmann has loved something that never really existed, a clockwork imitation of life. The next act, which occurs in Venice, belongs to the courtesan Giulietta. At curtain-fall she deserts Hoffmann and moves away on the arm of her new lover who is none other than Lindorf. The final episode presents Antonia, a singer with a beautiful voice. But each time she sings she brings death nearer, for she is consumed by a wasting disease. The evil Dr Miracle orders her to sing and even conjures up the spirit of her dead mother to support his command. Antonia performs her swan song and dies.

Olympia, Giulietta and Antonia are, in fact, the same woman. They represent different aspects of that Stella who will eternally escape the narrator. He is in love with an illusion and is doomed never to capture it. The only reality is death, whereas all life, all love is a delusion. Hope will ever be disappointed.

Although the moral is clear enough, the narrative line tends to falter. For this reason, and the better to impose unity, the rôles of Olympia, Giulietta, Antonia and Stella should ideally all be played by the one soprano. Likewise the same baritone should personate Lindorf, Coppélius and Dr Miracle.

In the last resort the task of pulling the drama together falls to the music and it is doubtful whether Offenbach succeeded entirely in unifying three such different episodes. But he certainly tried hard. *Les Contes d'Hoffmann* had been in his mind for several years, and the man who normally dashed off a three-act operetta in a month or so laboured long and hard over what was to be his own swan song as much as Antonia's.

The libretto had poignant undertones for him. In 1878, when he finally began work on it, he sensed that death could not be far off. Like Antonia, he knew also that making music would only hasten his end, but an impulse that could not be denied forced him on. *Les Contes d'Hoffmann* was his own story and symbolised his own career. He had come to Paris full of youthful ambition. He had wanted his name to be famous, his music to be the talk of the town; he had wanted applause, the admiration of men and women, and he had wanted money and acclaim. All these wishes had been generously granted; few composers have known such quick rewards. And he had earned it all with his own effort and hard work.

Yet a man is never satisfied. He always has a lurking doubt that his talents have not quite been exercised to the full and that an extra little bit of good fortune still awaits him round the corner if only he had the power or the chance to run and meet it. Offenbach was no exception. His unluckier rivals who envied him the fame he appeared to garner so easily would have been astonished to hear that behind it all he was profoundly dissatisfied. A success in the theatre is so short-lived a thing, a brief illusion, forgotten in a matter of days. He felt this deeply. All he had desired as a poor and unknown immigrant had come his way, but he discovered that it meant little to him. In 1875, at the age of fifty-six, he wrote a preface to a volume of collected theatre reviews by a friend. 'The play or operetta that's brought to life throws into oblivion the one that dies,' he remarked. 'People don't compare the two, put them side by side or draw similarities between them. It's like a series of pictures that dissolves, as in a magic lantern, and once past, the greatest success weighs no more heavily on the spectator's mind than the most sensational failure.' He went on to exhort the chronicler of vanished time: 'Bring us to life again, my dear friend; revive the evenings we have lived so quickly; remind us that we were happy, or sad, or bored, or tired, or moved, on such a date and at such an hour. Bring back to a man of the theatre grown old the emotions of a successful premiére, what was said about him among the audience, what he looked like and what the colour of his hair was, if he had any; remind the forgotten actress of the bouquets that were thrown to her and the love letters she received.'

But he knew in his heart of hearts that nothing could recapture those precious emotions that were gone almost as soon as they had been experienced. The theatre was only a mirror of life's impermanence. Prematurely aged and ill with the stabbing pain that scarcely ever left him, he thought of an old ambition, one he had nurtured since the earliest days and the only one he had not yet brought to fruition. At the back of his mind he had always longed to be a composer as Mozart and Rossini had been composers, men whose work was respected and played long after their death. He wanted to be the composer of a real opera, of a work of art, and not merely the supplier of entertainments to pass an idle evening. Perhaps this last wish would not turn out to be an illusion as all the others had? *Les Contes d'Hoffmann* was to be his testament.

It so possessed his whole being that, unconsciously, he reached back into the past, towards his roots and the music of his native country. It was impossible for him to throw off entirely the French influence that had conditioned and moulded his work for more than thirty years. The finale of Act II, '*Voici les valseurs*', is the type of 'brilliant' waltz number whose pattern Gounod had elaborated into the set piece guaranteed to bring the house down – although Offenbach adds his signature with a characteristic tune played by his favourite 'cellos. Very Gounodian, too, is the last item in the opening scene of Act IV, 'Mon enfant! ma fille!' where the unseen presence of Antonia's mother joins with Dr Miracle in urging her daughter to sing. The cut of the melody and the situation itself recall irresistibly the finales of *Mireille* and *Faust* which also depend on off-stage heavenly voices. Bizet contributes another element that can be detected in *Les Contes d'Hoffmann*, the Bizet perhaps of *Les Pêcheurs de perles*. In a score where Offenbach resolutely avoided knockabout humour, the sole echo of his own former light-heartedness is the comic song given to the domestic Franz. '*Jour et nuit je me mets en quatre*,' he complains as he grumbles about the difficulty of singing in tune. Even so, this needs to be delicately handled. The effect, when performed by an insensitive actor like Bourvil, can easily topple over into broad clowning.

The main flavour of *Les Contes d'Hoffmann* is German. This emerges noticeably in the tavern scenes with their drinking choruses and in the pompous minuet. Here and elsewhere there is more than a touch of the Romantic composer Marschner, whose *Der Vampyr* and *Hans Heiling*, the latter based on a favourite Hoffmann theme, show that he could seldom resist a goblin. Offenbach's Legend of Kleinzach, where all the rhymes miraculously end in 'ac', is a typical piece of German Romanticism in its musical presentation of that eerie freak. Another example of atavism is Olympia's '*Les oiseaux dans la charmille*'. In this bravura piece the mechanical doll takes her first clockwork steps. Gradually her movements become more supple, her enamelled eyes light up and the pink bloom of humanity seems to spread over her painted face. She launches into flourishes and trills that might have come from the peasants' waltz in Weber's *Der Freischütz*. And this is not the only point where Weber's influence shows itself.

Offenbach is most original in numbers like '*C'est une chanson d'amour*', the duet between Hoffmann and Antonia. The tune, gentle and languorous, develops into a mood of light melancholy. It makes a welcome return in the finale of Act IV. Then there is Hoffmann's '*Ah! vivre deux*' which contains one of the loveliest modulations Offenbach ever wrote. However many times it is heard – and it is repeated later in the opera – it never fails to create the same little shock of delight, the same charming unexpectedness. As for the Barcarolle, one is grateful to Offenbach for salvaging it from the ill-fated *Rheinnixen*. It is so very well known that, as on a worn coin, the detail of the beautifully incised design is apt to be taken for granted. One must try to imagine the effect of hearing it for the first time: the long tremolo joined by a phrase that swirls up from the violas, the birth of the swaying melody, and, as it unfolds, the occasional dissonance which adds piquancy before this '*Belle nuit d'amour*' fades in the breeze among the cries of gondoliers and the splash of oars.

25

'Our Grandchildren will be rich...'

During the last years of his life Offenbach had a dog, a lumbering Russian deerhound which he called 'Kleinzach' from the legend in *Les Contes d'Hoffmann*. It was the successor to a pet he had christened 'Boum' after the fire-eating general in *La Grande-Duchesse de Gérolstein*. While he wrote his opera, Kleinzach dozed in the room beside him. Offenbach would stroke him absent-mindedly. 'My poor Kleinzach!' he murmured. 'I would give everything I have if only I could be present at the first night.'

Madame Favart, La Fille du Tambour-Major and the other pieces he had written to earn a living were interruptions, irrelevancies to the all-important task of completing *Hoffmann*. In the summer of 1878 his son-in-law revived *La Grande-Duchesse de Gérolstein*. Hortense Schneider honoured it with her presence and totally unnerved the actress who took the part she had made famous. 'Two duchesses together,' remarked someone at the first night. 'Don't be mistaken,' said his companion, 'one of them is an archduchess at least.'

But the *La Grande-Duchesse* was past history. It no longer interested Offenbach. All his hopes were set on *Les Contes d'Hoffmann*. The manuscript accompanied him everywhere. He who once had been unable to compose except when surrounded by noise and laughter now sought calm and quiet. In the spring of 1879 he moved to the hotel at Saint-Germain. 'My dear Herminie,' he wrote to his wife in Paris, 'it's eight o'clock in the evening. I'm alone. Completely alone . . . I've worked all day at my *Contes*. Barbier came to work part of the day with me. I played him various things from my score. He wept and kissed me. He was delighted.' Then, as usual, he reproached the family for not writing to him more often. 'I'm not a demanding father, but their indifference and thoughtlessness surely go too far. Too bad for them. If people think rarely of me I forget them completely. You've an excuse for not writing to me, *you've a bad*

Jacqueline Offenbach

Pépita Offenbach

Auguste Offenbach, the only son

foot. I've been unwell since yesterday. Which doesn't prevent me, while being ill, from working at the piano all day and still finding the means of writing you this evening to wish you a good night and send you my kisses.'

In May that year the score was so far advanced that he decided to arrange a private hearing of the completed numbers. 'I think you'll be very pleased,' he told Herminie, 'and I hope my son will be kind enough to approve my work . . .' On the 18th, at their apartment in the boulevard des Capucines, some 300 guests crowded into the drawing-room to hear it.

Albert Vizentini supervised a chorus made up of friends and the Offenbach daughters. Professional singers took the main rôles. Even bereft of scenery and costumes, and with only a piano as accompaniment, *Les Contes d'Hoffmann* impressed the audience with its strange beauty. They clapped, especially, the Barcarolle. That evening Offenbach was feeling better and, from time to time, was able to get up and direct the music makers with astonishing vigour.

Among the guests was Léon Carvalho, director of the Opéra-Comique, a flamboyant Mauritian who, like his wife the prima donna Marie Miolan-Carvalho, had an irresistible urge to revise and tamper with the operas he produced. Once a composer had seen his work accepted by Carvalho his initial delight quickly withered as he beheld, on the one hand, the zealous director introducing all sorts of hare-brained changes and, on the other, his fearsome spouse rewriting her part the better to show off her roulades. Gounod, Saint-Saëns, Berlioz and even Wagner had all suffered from the attentions of this meddling couple.

Carvalho's notorious habit was probably the result of a frustrated creative instinct. He had wanted to be a singer, had not been good enough, and so had turned to management. Yet despite the annoyance he caused, musicians could not help liking him. His early experience gave him an appreciation of music which composers found helpful. He immediately saw the merits of *Les Contes d'Hoffmann* and, to Offenbach's intense happiness, accepted it for the Opéra-Comique. Had Offenbach lived there would have been terrible battles between two such strong-willed characters. When Carvalho produced the work after the composer's death he remained true to form: with a negligent flourish he cut out the whole of the second act.

Having settled, as he thought, the future of his cherished opera, the composer returned with new enthusiasm to the score. From Étretat, where he had gone to recuperate from a virulent attack of rheumatism that lasted a fortnight, he wrote to Carvalho: 'Quite clearly, every year at the same time (the month of September) I have to have my little bit of gout. I plan to get up tomorrow and be in Paris by Wednesday at the latest. Should I send the first act beforehand or wait until I bring it to you? I hope we can read it on the 1 October . . .'

The time-table did not work. There was still a great deal to be done and, in spite of the phenomenal energy he squeezed out of his thin, racked body, even Offenbach could not make the progress he wanted. That summer he did not feel up to going with the family on their annual trip to Étretat and settled himself instead once again in the peace of Saint-Germain. 'I'm very sad but I mustn't come to Étretat,' he told his daughter Pépita, who had stayed in Paris and who called on him every day or so. 'I've talked about it with [Doctor] Lamarre who tells me I'd be very ill-advised to go to the sea-side; I can see the point: as a result of travelling to Paris for one day I've been ill, and the day before yesterday I had a temperature from four o'clock to five. This morning I'm better but I'm eating nothing: if I were to fall seriously ill at the moment it would be a disaster . . .' He thought of Olympia, the automaton built by Coppélius, and went on: 'The spring of the mechanical doll gets out of order now at the slightest tiredness. I have just one month in which to write the third act of *Belle Lurette*, orchestrate the three acts, write the finale and the whole fifth act of the *Contes d'Hoffmann* (I don't even mention the orchestration which will come later) and do the one-acter for the Théâtre des Variétés. Shall I succeed? . . . Let's hope so.'

At mealtimes he took a few unwilling mouthfuls and then lit a cigar, the biggest and strongest he could find. The smoke curled luxuriantly around him as he plunged again into *Hoffmann*. In that torrid, wilting July he kept every window firmly shut. The smallest suspicion of a draught terrified him. A huge wood fire burned in the grate and made the room stifling hot. Yet for Offenbach it was still not warm enough. He lay on a sofa and shivered continually despite the thick, fur-embroidered dressing-gown he wore.

The flesh had dropped away and revealed the bones of the face so that it looked like a skull. Only the eyes burned with a tenacious glitter. The skin stretched tightly over his hollow chest. The arms and legs, alive with pain, had the appearance of brittle sticks. 'It's awful,' said Dr Lamarre. 'There's nothing left of his body at all.'

By a pleasant chance Meilhac and Halévy were staying nearby. Offenbach had forgiven their desertion to Lecocq. Each evening, with another old friend, the journalist Albert Wolff, they looked in for a hand of whist and as a matter of form they would invite him out for a ride. But each time, sadly, he would have to refuse. 'What a splendid article Wolff will write about me when I'm dead,' he croaked in a wheezing voice.

Often he would ask Meilhac and Halévy for advice. There was a line that gave him trouble. He wanted a refrain, but the only available one was too long and he couldn't repeat it four times. Would they help him? They did, remembering the early days and their first triumphs together.

For long periods he would lie inert. Then, from his ground-floor room, they would hear the sound of the piano. The melodies broke off and a fearful bout of coughing took their place. Once recovered, still breathless and panting with exertion, he drove his claw-like fingers over the keyboard again. Sometimes he tried to relax with a book. His choice would fall on a biography of Mozart, old and worn with much reading. After he had scanned a few lines of the familiar story it slipped from his weary hands. 'Poor Mozart!' he whispered in a voice full of tears.

Every week, on a Sunday, Auguste would come over to Saint-Germain. Offenbach looked forward impatiently to his visits. He loved his daughters. He worshipped his son. Auguste was eighteen years old, handsome, dark, rather slim. The boy knew all his father's music and brought it to an acute sensitiveness. Offenbach would play his latest work, and anxiously await his approval. For if Auguste liked it, then it must be good.

'When I'm old, very old,' Auguste once wrote to him, 'I shall sing your tunes to my grandchildren, in a quavering voice, and they'll say, as in that Béranger song, speaking of the great Jacques: 'He knew our grandfather . . .' The note was jealously preserved. Offenbach kept it among his most precious belongings.

Apart from Auguste and Pépita, Offenbach was not entirely alone at Saint-Germain. Albert Wolff often kept him company and asked him to play what he had written. Offenbach always refused at first, but after a little persuasion he inevitably gave way. Wolff applauded. 'Yes,' said Offenbach, 'it's really good. In fact, it's admirable . . .'

His greatest fear was that he would die before he had finished the *Contes d'Hoffmann*. 'Hurry up and put on my opera,' he wrote to Carvalho. 'I've little time left . . .'

In September 1880, having found that it was costing him far too much to live at Saint-Germain, he moved back to Paris and the boulevard des Capucines. News from the Opéra-Comique was good. A cast had been assembled for *Les Contes d'Hoffmann*. The opera was to head the list of new productions that winter. Scenery, costumes and effects were, Carvalho intended, to be of the finest. Offenbach wrote him letter after letter. In his over-heated room he stroked Kleinzach and dreamed of theatrical glory to come.

On the 25th he was unable to get up. His legs would no longer carry him and his whole body was stiff with gout. He coughed interminably, and, surrounded by sheets of music paper scattered over the counterpane of his bed, he went on writing until he fell back exhausted on the pillow. A little brandy was all he would take by way of drink. Herminie watched at his side. He forbade her strictly to let anyone in Paris know how ill he was. 'No, things must certainly be bad,' said his coachman Mathurin. 'The Master hasn't called me a fool today.'

As she sat looking at his wasted face, the dank hair limply stuck to the pillow, the skin taut and pallid, he thought of the music he was leaving behind, of the success that *Les Contes d'Hoffmann* would assuredly win. 'Our grandchildren will be rich . . .' he whispered.

On 4 October he asked for the *Hoffmann* manuscript to be brought in. The last act needed a few amendments. Suddenly, at four in the afternoon, he choked and clutched his heart. 'I'm not well! I'm not well! It's here!' he moaned softly.

He looked around him at Herminie and the children, all there except for Berthe and her husband Charles Comte. A passing estrangement had kept them from his bedside.

'I think the end will come tonight,' he said.

He fell silent. 'You do recognise us, don't you?' asked Herminie. There was no reply.

Then he muttered: 'Drink! Drink!'

Sometimes his breathing seemed to have stopped. A Catholic priest administered the last rites to the son of Isaac. At two o'clock in the morning a second doctor opined that there was no hope. Just before half-past three, by the dim light of a lamp and two candles on his table, Offenbach moved his arm to touch his head and then his heart. He breathed heavily and for the last time. The gout that had tortured him for so long had finally and fatally attacked his heart. Herminie threw herself weeping on her knees. Then she cut off a lock of his hair to be sealed up in a ring which never afterwards left her finger.

Later that morning, when it was daylight, a quaint figure wearing a white tie and big dark glasses strolled along the boulevard des Capucines. It was Léonce, the comedian who as Pluto in *Orphée* had made audiences sick with laughter at his clowning. He went up to Number 8 and rang the bell.

'Monsieur Offenbach is dead,' sighed the concierge. 'He died very gently, without realising it.'

'Ah,' replied Léonce gravely. 'How annoyed he'll be when he finds out.'

POSTFACE

Postface

There was a lavish funeral. On 7 October streets were cordoned off and a hearse laden with flowers moved under a grey sky up the boulevard de la Madeleine. A great mass of people crowded round the church. The insignia of Offenbach's *Légion d'honneur* was borne on a cushion. A detachment of soldiers lined up to honour the composer of *La Grande-Duchesse de Gérolstein*. In London, where the Alhambra Theatre was playing *La Fille du Tambour-Major*, the singers appeared on stage wearing black armbands.

At the service the famous tenor Talazac sang extracts from *Hoffmann* adapted to the words of the Dies irae and the Agnus. A muted organ played Fortunio's song as the offertory. The funeral procession made a detour along the boulevards to pass Offenbach's 'own' theatres of the Bouffes and the Variétés. By the time Montmartre cemetery was reached, a fine searching rain had begun to drizzle over the mourners. It drenched the black veil Hortense Schneider was wearing as she stood on the yellow slippery mud beside the grave.

Next year, on 10 February, *Les Contes d'Hoffmann* had its première at the Opéra-Comique. To the usual difficulties associated with the launching of a new opera was added the problem of the score, because, although Offenbach had completed the work, he had not been able to orchestrate it. That task was handed to Ernest Guiraud, an affable man with a genial expanse of beard, who had been born in New Orleans where his father, also a musician, had chosen self-exile from a Paris that refused his operas a successful hearing. The son came to France, had more luck in writing for the stage, and taught harmony at the Conservatoire. More easy-going than his colleagues there, he took in his stride even the audacities of his young pupil Debussy and proved to be a helpful teacher. He is remembered today, not for his precocious opera *Le Roi David*, staged when he was fifteen years old, nor for his ballet *Gretna Green*, but for having acted as an obliging maid-of-all-work to better-known names. Besides orchestrating *Hoffmann* he added the recitatives to Bizet's *Carmen*. When he, in turn, died and left an unfinished opera, it was Saint-Saëns who rendered him the obliging service he had done to others.

The first night of *Hoffmann* was snowy, cold and wet. The Prime Minister himself had his box there, a sign perhaps that the Republic now forgave Offenbach his shameful link with Napoleon III. Herminie stayed at home, unable to face the emotion such an evening would arouse in her. A relay team of friends and daughters kept her informed of the work's progress. They told her how the Legend of Kleinzach had won cheers, how Olympia had received loud encores, and how, at the end, the audience stood up and applauded for an age. She knew that her husband's ambition was fulfilled. The critics who had been so patronising about his operettas now spoke of him with respect, and his name became firmly established at the Opéra-Comique, the goal he had always sought.

Now that Jacques was gone she relied entirely on Auguste who succeeded him as head of the family, 'My dearly loved son', 'My beloved treasure'. He helped her in the dreary business of clearing up the estate, in negotiating with publishers and theatre managers, in arranging for the completion of *Hoffmann*. When he fell ill she strained her resources, which were not large despite her husband's deathbed prophecy, by sending him to recuperate in the sunshine of the South. On 7 December 1883, he died at the age of twenty-one.

This was the final blow. He was all she had left that reminded her most directly of the Jacques she loved. For thirty-six years she had been the wife of a composer famous throughout Europe. Her Jacques was not handsome. But, like many other women, she loved him for his exuberant spirit, his airy confidence, his wit, his determination to succeed. He was like a force of nature, spontaneous, invincible, and gaiety and laughter surrounded him as his natural element. She could not live without him, and existed under a cloud of sorrow that time failed to dissipate. When she herself died in 1887, she was sixty-one, the age her husband had been at his death.

The poignant circumstances under which *Hoffmann* was written and the great personal importance the work had for

Offenbach invite the judgement that it was the culmination of his life's work. This is tempting but erroneous. *Les Contes d'Hoffmann* will always be an interesting but unequal achievement. It should be seen, rather, as his swan song. His most truly rounded genius should be discovered in *Orphée, La Belle Hélène, La Vie Parisienne, La Grande-Duchesse, La Périchole,* and in others where it may gleam intermittently but no less clearly.

He was primarily an entertainer, a man of the theatre whose immediate ambition was a full house. As such, in his time and ours, he has often been contemptuously dismissed. Yet his music survives, even hindered by libretti that are no longer topical. Where, today, are the grand operas of Meyerbeer, once deemed a 'serious' composer and a far greater one than Offenbach? Where are those works by Auber, Halévy and Ambroise Thomas which held the stage for so long and were judged superior to the inspirations of a mere entertainer? Only a small handful of isolated arias are left. Offenbach, on the other hand, can show half a dozen operettas continually being played throughout the world and frequent revivals of many others.

Saint-Saëns, who was not an indulgent critic, allowed him: 'Great fertility. The gift of melody. A harmony that is sometimes refined. Much wit and inventiveness. Extreme theatrical skill. Which is more than what was necessary to succeed. He succeeded.' Despite his occasional patchy orchestration, despite his often brutal handling of the French language, Offenbach on the whole evolved the exact style for saying what he wanted to say. And that is one of the secrets of art. He is unique. The mood of the Second Empire chanced to be one that was cynical, even fatalistic. Offenbach expressed it admirably. He depicted pleasure that was not happiness or contentment, and desire that fell a long way short of true love. We should not forget that such a mood is not restricted to any one period. Offenbach continues to appeal in every age.

His music has the traditional French merit of going straight to the heart of things. Ornamentation is there, but the embroidery is not allowed to obscure a basic lucidity. Above all there is the vital force that surges through his work and bursts out in a dominating rhythm. It is triumphant and unstoppable. He lived, one recalls, in an era when steam was a scientific miracle. As you listen to one of his galops or to one of those headlong choruses, you can glimpse the spectral figure of the man himself driving the orchestra with his merciless beat and dancing in a frenzy as he stabs out the rhythm and urges his sweating troops to play with the precision and energy of a steam engine. You seem to hear the raucous voice, heavy with its German accent, croaking: '*Chx! Chx! Plus fite! A la fapeur!*' He lives on in his music, glitter-eyed, compulsive, never still.

List of works by Offenbach

STAGE

1839   *Pascal et Chambord* (Anicet Bourgeois and Brisebarre), 1 act, 2 March, Palais-Royal

1847   *L'Alcôve* (De Forge–De Leuven), 1 act, 24 April, Théâtre de La Tour d'Auvergne

1853   *Le Trésor à Mathurin* (L. Battu), 1 act
       Pépito (J. Moinaux–L. Battu), 1 act, 28 Oct., Variétés

1855   *Oyayaie ou la Reine des Iles*, 1 act, 26 June, Folies Nouvelles
       Entrez, Messieurs, Mesdames (Méry-Servières), 5 July

       Les Deux Aveugles (J. Moinaux), 1 act, 5 July, Bouffes-Marigny
       Une nuit blanche (Plouvier), 1 act, 5 July, Bouffes-Marigny
       Arlequin Barbier, pantomime, 1 act, 5 July, Bouffes-Marigny
       Le Rêve d'une nuit d'été (Tréfeu), 1 act, 30 July, Bouffes-Marigny
       Pierrot clown (pantomime), 1 act, 30 July, Bouffes-Marigny
       Le Violoneux (Mestépès–Chevalet), 1 act, 3 Aug., Bouffes-Marigny
       Polichinelle dans le monde (pantomime), 1 act, 31 Aug., Bouffes-Marigny
       Madame Papillon (J. Servières), 1 act, 31 Aug., Bouffes-Marigny
       Paimpol et Périnette (De Lussan), 1 act, 29 Oct., Bouffes-Marigny
       Ba-ta-clan (L. Halévy), 1 act, 29 Dec., Bouffes-Choiseul

1856   *Élodie* ou *le Forfait nocturne* (Crémieux), 1 act, 19 Jan., Bouffes-Parisiens
       Le Postillon en gage (J. Adenis), 1 act, 9 Feb., Bouffe-Parisiens
       Trombalcazar (Dupeuty and Bourget), 1 act, 3 April, Bouffes-Parisiens

La Rose de Saint-Flour (M. Carré), 1 act, 12 June, Marigny
Les Dragées du baptême (Dupeuty and Bourget), 1 act, 12 June, Marigny
Les Bergers de Watteau, 1 act, 12 June, Marigny
Le '66' (De Forge and Laurencin), 1 act, 31 July, Marigny
Le Savetier et le Financier (H. Crémieux), 1 act, 31 July, Marigny
La Bonne d'enfants (Bercioux), 1 act, 23 Sept., Bouffes-Choiseul

1857   *Les Trois baisers du diable* (Mestépès), 1 act, Bouffes-Parisiens
Croquefer ou *le Dernier des paladins* (Jaime and Tréfeu), 1 act, 12 Feb., Bouffes-Parisiens
Dragonette (Mestépès and Jaime), 1 act, 30 April, Bouffes-Parisiens
Vent du soir, ou *l'Horrible festin* (P. Gille–Battu), 1 act, 16 May, Bouffes-Parisiens
Une Demoiselle en loterie (Jaime–Crémieux), 1 act, 27 July, Bouffes-Parisiens
Le Mariage aux lanternes (M. Carré–Battu), 1 act, 10 Oct., Bouffes-Parisiens
Les Deux pêcheurs (Dupeuty–Bourget), 1 act, 16 Nov., Bouffes-Parisiens

1858   *Mesdames de La Halle* (Lapointe), 1 act, 3 March, Bouffes-Parisiens
La Chatte métamorphosée (Scribe–Melesville), 1 act, Bouffes-Parisiens
Orphée aux enfers (Crémieux–Halévy), 2 acts, 21 Oct., Bouffes-Parisiens

1859   *Un mari à la porte* (Delacour–Morand), 1 act, June, Bouffes-Parisiens
Luce et Lucette, 1 act, Bouffes-Parisiens
Les Vivandières de la Grande Armée (Jaime–De Forge), 1 act, Bouffes-Parisiens
Geneviève de Brabant (Tréfeu), 2 acts, 19 Nov., Bouffes-Parisiens

1860   *Le Carnaval des revues* (Grangé–Gille–Halévy), 1 act, 6 Feb., Bouffes-Parisiens
Daphnis et Chloé (Clairville–Cordier), 1 act, 27 March, Bouffes-Parisiens

Le Papillon, ballet (Saint-Georges–Taglioni), 2 acts, 26 Nov., Opéra
Barkouf (Scribe–Boissaux), 3 acts, 24 Dec., Opéra-Comique

1861   *La Chanson de Fortunio* (Crémieux–Halévy), 1 act, 5 Jan., Bouffes-Parisiens
Les Musiciens de l'orchestre (Bourdois–De Forge), 1 act, Bouffes-Parisiens
Le Pont des soupirs (Crémieux–Halévy), 2 acts, 23 March, Bouffes-Parisiens
M. Choufleuri restera chez lui (Saint-Rémy–Crémieux–Halévy), 1 act, 14 Sept., Bouffes-Parisiens
Apothicaire et perruquier (Élie Frébault), 1 act, 17 Oct., Bouffes-Parisiens
Le Roman comique (Crémieux–Halévy), 3 acts, 10 Dec., Bouffes-Parisiens

1862   *M. et Mme Denis* (Laurencin–Delaporte), 1 act, 11 Jan., Bouffes-Parisiens
Bavard et Bavarde (C. Nuitter), 2 acts, 11 June, Ems
Le Voyage de MM Dunanan père et fils (Siraudin–Moinaux), 2 acts, 22 March, Bouffes-Parisiens
Jacqueline (Crémieux-Halévy–d'Arcy), 1 act, 14 October, Bouffes-Parisiens

1863   *Lieschen et Fritzchen* (P. Boisselot), 1 act, 5 Jan., Bouffes-Parisiens
L'Amour chanteur (Nuitter-L'Épine), 1 act, 5 January, Bouffes-Parisiens
Il Signor Fagotto (Nuitter–Tréfeu), 1 act, 13 Jan., Bouffes-Parisiens
Les Bavards (Nuitter), 2 acts, 20 Feb., Bouffes-Parisiens (enlarged from *Bavard et Bavarde*).

1864   *Rheinnixen* (Nuitter–Tréfeu), 3 acts, 4 Feb., Vienna
Les Géorgiennes (Moinaux), 3 acts, 16 March, Bouffes-Parisiens
La Belle Hélène (Meilhac–Halévy), 3 acts, 17 Dec., Variétés

1865   *Les Refrains des Bouffes*, 21 Sept., Bouffes-Parisiens
Jeanne qui pleure et Jean qui rit (Nuitter–Tréfeu), 1 act, 3 Nov., Bouffes-Parisiens
Les Bergers (Crémieux–Gille), 3 acts, 11 Dec., Bouffes-Parisiens

Coscoletto ou *le Lazzarone* (Nuitter–Tréfeu), 1 act, 24 July, Ems

1866   *Barbe-Bleue* (Meilhac–Halévy), 3 acts, 5 Feb., Variétés
La Vie parisienne (Meilhac–Halévy), 5 acts, 21 Oct., Palais-Royal

1867   *La Leçon de chant* (Bourget), 1 act, 17 June, Marigny
La Permission de 10 heures (Melesville–Carmouchet), 1 act, 4 Sept., Renaissance
La Grande-Duchesse de Gérolstein (Meilhac–Halévy), 3 acts, 12 April, Variétés
Robinson Crusoé (Cormon–Crémieux), 3 acts, 23 Nov., Opéra-Comique

1868   *Le Château à Toto* (Meilhac–Halévy), 3 acts, 6 May, Palais-Royal
L'Ile de Tulipatan (Chivot–Duru), 1 act, 30 Sept., Bouffes-Parisiens
Le Fifre enchanté (Nuitter–Tréfeu), 1 act, 30 Sept., Bouffes-Parisiens
La Périchole (Meilhac–Halévy), 2 acts, 6 Oct., Variétés

1869   *Vert-Vert* (Meilhac–Nuitter), 3 acts, 10 March, Opéra-Comique
La Diva (Meilhac–Halévy), 3 acts, 22 March, Bouffes-Parisiens
La Princesse de Trébizonde (Nuitter–Tréfeu), 3 acts, 7 Dec., Bouffes-Parisiens
Les Brigands (Meilhac–Halévy), 3 acts, 10 Dec., Variétés
La Romance de la Rose (Tréfeu–Prével), 1 act, 11 Dec., Bouffes-Parisiens

1871   *Boule de neige* (Nuitter–Tréfeu), 3 acts, 14 Dec., Bouffes-Parisiens

1872   *Le Roi Carotte* (Sardou), 3 acts, 15 Jan., Gaîté
Fantasio (Musset), 3 acts, 18 Jan., Opéra-Comique
Fleurette (Ascher), 1 act, Vienna
Le Corsaire noir (Offenbach), 3 acts, 21 Sept., Vienna

1873   *Les Braconniers* (Chivot–Duru), 3 acts, 20 Jan., Variétés
Pomme d'api (Halévy–Busnach), 1 act, 4 Sept., Renaissance

Madame l'Archiduc (A. Millaud–Halévy), 3 acts, 31 Oct., Bouffes-Parisiens
La Jolie Parfumeuse (Blum-Toché), 3 acts, 29 Nov., Renaissance

1874   *Bagatelle* (Crémieux–Blum), 1 act, 21 May, Bouffes-Parisiens
La Haine (Sardou), 5 acts, incidental music, 5 Dec., Gaîté

1875   *Whittington et son chat* (Nuitter–Tréfeu), 4 acts, 2 Jan., Alhambra, London
Les Hannetons (Grangé–Millaud), 22 April, Bouffes-Parisiens
La Boulangère a des écus (Meilhac–Halévy), 3 acts, 19 Oct., Variétés
Le Voyage dans la lune (Leterrier–Vanloo–Mortier), 4 acts, 26 Oct., Gaîté
La Créole (A. Millaud–Meilhac). 3 acts. 3 Nov., Bouffes-Parisiens
Tarte à la crème (A. Millaud), 1 act, 14 Dec., Bouffes-Parisiens

1876   *Pierrette et Jacquot* (Noriac–Gille), 1 act, 13 Oct., Bouffes-Parisiens
La Boîte au lait (Grangé–Noriac), 3 acts, 3 Nov., Bouffes-Parisiens

1877   *Le Docteur Ox* (Gille–Saint-Albin–Mortier), 3 acts, 26 Jan., Variétés
La Foire Saint-Laurent (Crémieux–Saint-Albin), 3 acts, 10 Feb., Folies Dramatiques

1878   *Maitre Péronilla* (Offenbach), 3 acts, 13 March, Bouffes-Parisiens
Madame Favart (Chivot–Duru), 3 acts, 28 Dec., Folies Dramatiques

1879   *La Marocaine* (Ferrier), 3 acts, 13 Jan., Bouffes-Parisiens
La Fille du Tambour-Major (Chivot–Duru), 3 acts, 13 Dec., Folies Dramatiques

1880   *Belle Lurette* (Blum–Blau–Toché), 3 acts, 30 Oct., Renaissance

1881   *Les Contes d'Hoffmann.* (Barbier–Carré), 4 acts, 10 Feb., Opéra-Comique
       Moucheron (Leterrier–Vanloo), 1 act, 10 May, Renaissance

FRENCH SONGS

1838   *Le Sylphe* (Léon Laube)
       Le Pauvre prisonnier (Léon Laube)
       Ronde tyrolienne (Charles Catelin)
1839   *Jalousie* (Aimé Gourdin)
       J'aime la rêverie (Gay de V . . .)
1840   *L'Attente*
1842   *L'Aveu du page* (Plouvier)
       Fables de La Fontaine:
          Le corbeau et le renard
          Le rat de ville et le rat des champs
          Le savetier et le financier
          Le loup et l'agneau
          La laitière et le pot au lait
          Le Berger et la Mer
1843   *A toi* (Numa Armand)
       L'Arabe à son coursier (Reboul)
       La Croix de ma mère (Numa Armand)
       Dors mon enfant (Numa Armand)
       Doux Ménestrel (C. Saudeur)
       Rends-moi mon âme (Reboul)
       Virginie au départ . . . (E. Plouvier)
1844   *Meunière et fermière* (E. Plouvier)
1846   *Le Moine bourru* ou *les Deux poltrons* (Plouvier)
       Le Sergent recrutateur (E. Plouvier)
       La Sortie de bal
       Sarah la blonde
       Le langage des fleurs (E. Plouvier)
          La branche d'oranger
          La rose
          Ne m'oubliez pas
          La marguerite
          L'églantine
          La pâquerette
1850   *Sérénade du torero* (Théophile Gautier)
1851   *Chanson de Valéria* (E. Lacroix and A. Maquet)
       Chanson de Fortunio (De Musset)
       L'Étoile (Émile Chevalet)
       Si j'étais petit oiseau (Jousselin)

1852   *Les Voix mystérieuses*
   L'Hiver (A. Barthet)
   Chanson de Fortunio (Musset)
   Les Saisons (Jules Barbier)
   Ma belle amie est morte (T. Gautier)
   La Rose foulée (Charles Poncy)
   Barcarolle (Théophile Gautier)
1854   *Sérénade* (E. Plouvier)
1857   *Valse des animaux (les Petits prodiges)*
1859   *La Chanson de ceux qui n'aiment plus*
1860   *La Cigale et la fourmi*
   Bibi Bambou (Bourget)
1862   *La demoiselle de Nanterre* (*Et digue digue don*)
1863   *Ronde du Brésilien* (Meilhac and Halévy)
1864   *Jeanne la rousse* (Arsène Houssaye)
1865   *La pêche* from *La Fille de l'air* (Coignard and Raymond)
1873   *Chanson béarnaise* (Gustave Mathieu)
   Ronde savoyarde (Noriac and Ph. Gille)
Le Tambour du collège (Edmond Leschevin)
La Fleur de Zirka
Ça ne s'est jamais vu . . . (A. Avocat)
Sur la grève . . .
Deux fleurs . . .

GERMAN SONGS

Das Vaterland (1848)
Bleib bei mir Vaterland lied (Rheinnixen)
Leb Wohl
Catherinen Was Willst du Mehr?
Was fliesset auf dem felde
Lied des deutschen knaben
Blein mir treu
Staendschen
In grunen mai . . .
Mein lieb bleicht dem Bächlein

CHORAL

Venise, (Van Hasselt)
Vive la Suisse
Der kleine Trommler (1863)

PATRIOTIC SONGS

Dieu sauve la France

WORKS FOR VIOLONCELLO

Divertimento über Schweizerlieder (op. 1)
Introduction et valse mélancolique (1839, op. 14)
Capriccio sur *le Cor des Alpes* de Proch (op. 15, 1841)
Prière et Boléro (op. 22)
Musette (air de ballet du dix-huitième siècle, op. 24, 1843)
Quatrième mazurka (op. 26)
Caprice sur la romance de *Joseph*, de Méhul (op. 27)
Les Chants du crépuscule (op. 29):
   Souvenir du bal
   Sérénade
   Ballade
   Le Retour
   L'Adieu
   Pas villageois
La Sylphe (op. 30)
Caprice sur *La Somnambula*, de Bellini (op. 32)
   I Puritani, de Bellini (op. 33)
Deux âmes au ciel (élégie, 1844)
Las Campanillas (1847)
Trois grands duos concertants (pour 2 violoncelles, op. 43)
Cours méthodique de duos (pour 2 violoncelles, 1847, op. 49, 50, 51, 52, 53, 54)
Trois duos dédiés aux amateurs
Trois difficiles
Trois très difficiles
Adagio et *Scherzo* (pour 4 violoncelles)
Rêverie au bord de la mer (1849)
La Course en traineau (1849)
Gaietés champêtres
Harmonie du soir (op. 68)
Fantaisie sur:
   Richard Coeur de Lion, de Grétry (op. 69)
   Jean de Paris, de Boieldieu (op. 70)
   le Barbier de Séville, de Rossini (op. 71)
   les Noces de Figaro, de Mozart (op. 72)
   Norma, de Bellini (op. 73)
Fantaisie facile et brillante (op. 74)
Tambourin, d'après Rameau (op. 75)

Chant des mariniers galants, de Rameau (op. 76, 1851)
Vingt petites études pour le violoncelle avec accompagnement de basse (op. 77)
Douze études pour violoncelle et basse (op. 78)
Marche chinoise
Harmonies des bois:
  Élégie *Le Soir*
  Les larmes de Jacqueline
Fantaisies caprices sur:
  Anne de Bolène (Donizetti)
  La Dame blanche (Boieldieu)
  Elisire d'Amore (Donizetti)
  Parisina (Donizetti)
  Béatrice di Tenda (Bellini)

WORKS FOR PIANO

Fleurs d'hiver (suite de valses, 1836)
Les Jeunes filles (suite de valses, 1836)
Brunes et blondes (suite de valses, 1837)
Les Trois Grâces (suite de valses, 1837)
Rébecca (suite de valses sur des motifs hébraîques du quinzième siècle, 1837)
Le Décameron dramatique (1854, dédiées aux artistes de la Comédie-Française):
  1° *Rachel*, grande valse
  2° *Émilie*, polka-mazurka
  3° *Madeleine*, polka villageoise
  4° *Delphine*, rédowa
  5° *Augustine*, scottish des clochettes
  6° *Louise*, grande valse
  7° *Maria*, polka-mazurka
  8° *Élisa*, polka trilby
  9° *Nathalie*, scottish du tambourin
  10° *Clarisse*, varsoviana
Herminie, valse
Berthe, suite de valses
The Times, grande valse
Les Feuilles du soir, valse (1864)
Jacqueline, suite de valses (1865)
Valse favorite
Les Roses du Bengale (six valses sentimentales)
Offenbach-valse (1876)
Le Fleuve d'or (1876)

Les Belles Américaines (1876)
Souvenir d'Aix-les-Bains, valse
Polka des singes
Polka du mendiant
Polka burlesque
Kissi-Kissi, polka
Sum-Sum, polka
Schuler polka
Toxopholite, polka-mazurka
Quatrième mazurka de salon
Postillon-galop
Cachucha
Parade militaire

WORKS FOR VIOLONCELLO BY OFFENBACH AND FLOTOW

Chants du soir
   Au bord de la mer
   Souvenir du bal
   Prière du soir
   La Retraite
   Ballade du pâtre
   Danse norvégienne
Rêveries
   La Harpe éolienne
   Scherzo
   Polka de salon
   Chanson d'autrefois
   Les larmes
   Redowa brillante

A detailed list of many youthful and/or unpublished works is to be found in Brindejont-Offenbach and in Anton Henseler (see bibliography).

Select Bibliography

UNPUBLISHED SOURCES:

Manuscripts, documents, photographs, portraits, etc. preserved in the Bibliothèque de l'Opéra, Paris. Here are kept the manuscript scores, some incomplete, of: *Les Contes d'Hoffmann*, *Orphée aux enfers*, *La Chanson de Fortunio*, *Croquefer*, *Les Deux Aveugles*, *Les Deux pêcheurs*, *Le Papillon*, *Trombalcazar*. The scores of *Ba-ta-clan*, *La bonne d'enfant* and *Lischen et Fritzchen* seem to have been written out by a copyist called 'J. Mauran'.

PUBLISHED SOURCES:

Adam, Adolphe, *Souvenirs d'un musicien*, Michel Lévy, 1857
Bekker, Paul, *Offenbach*, Verlag von Marquardt & Co., 1909
Brancour, René, *Offenbach*, Félix Alcan, 1929
Brindejont-Offenbach, Jacques, 'L'opérette' in *Cinquante ans de musique francaise de 1874 à 1925*, vol. II, ed. Rohozinsky, Librairie de France, 1925
Brindejont-Offenbach, Jacques, *Offenbach Mon grand-père*, Plon, 1940
Bruyas, Florian, *Histoire de l'opérette en France 1855-1965*, Emmanuel Vitte, Lyon, 1974
Clarétie, Jules, *La vie à Paris, 1908*, Charpentier, 1909
Decaux, Alain, *Offenbach*, Pierre Amiot, 1958, Perrin, 1966
Goncourt, Edmond and Jules de, *Journal*, vols I, II, and II, Fasquelle/Flammarion, 1956
Guichard, Léon, *La musique et les lettres au temps du Wagnérisme*, PUF, 1963
Henseler, Anton, *Jakob Offenbach*, Max Hesses Verlag, 1930
Hughes, Gervase, *Composers of Operetta*, Macmillan, 1962
Kracauer, S., *Offenbach and the Paris of His Time*, Constable, 1937
Kristeller, Hans, *Jakob Offenbach*, Adalbert Schutz Verlag, 1931
Lubbock, Mark, *The Complete Book of Light Opera*, Putnam, 1962
Lyon, Raymond, and Saguer, Louis, *Les Contes d'Hoffmann*, Mellottée, 1948
Martinet, André, *Offenbach*, Dentu, 1887

Mirecourt, Eugène de, *Les Contemporains: Auber, Offenbach*, Havard, 1869

Offenbach, Jacques, *Histoire d'une valse*, no publisher, c. 1872

Offenbach, Jacques, Preface to *Les soirées parisiennes par un monsieur de l'orchestre*, Arnold Mortier, Dentu, 1875

Offenbach, Jacques, *Offenbach en Amérique. Notes d'un musicien en voyage*, Calmann-Lévy, 1877

Offenbach, Jacques, [On Wagner], article in *Paris-Murcie*, 1879

[Renaud-Barrault], *Le siècle d'Offenbach*, Cahiers de la Compagnie Renaud-Barrault, Julliard, 1958

Rouff, Marcel, and Casewitz, Thérèse, *Hortense Schneider*, Tallandier, 1930

Schneider, Louis, *Offenbach*, Librairie Académique Perrin, 1923

Sitwell, Sir Sacheverell, *La Vie Parisienne*, Faber & Faber, 1937

Walsh, Tom, Second Empire Opera, Calder, 1980

Zola, Emile, *Nana*, Charpentier, 1880

INDEX

Index